MOBILITIES OF RETURN
PACIFIC PERSPECTIVES

MOBILITIES
OF RETURN
PACIFIC PERSPECTIVES

EDITED BY JOHN TAYLOR AND HELEN LEE

Australian
National
University

PRESS

PACIFIC SERIES

ANU PRESS

Published by ANU Press
The Australian National University
Acton ACT 2601, Australia
Email: anupress@anu.edu.au
This title is also available online at press.anu.edu.au

NATIONAL LIBRARY OF AUSTRALIA

A catalogue record for this book is available from the National Library of Australia

ISBN(s): 9781760461676 (print)
9781760461683 (eBook)

Cover design and layout by ANU Press. Cover photograph: John Taylor, c. 2006, MV *Brisk* arriving at Loltong Bay, North Pentecost, Vanuatu.

Contents

1

Beyond dead reckoning: Mobilities of return in the Pacific

John Taylor

Abstract

In recent decades, the term 'mobility' has emerged as a defining paradigm within the humanities. For scholars engaged in the multidisciplinary topics and perspectives now often embraced by the term Pacific Studies it has been a much more longstanding and persistent concern. Even so, specific questions regarding 'mobilities of return'—that is, the movement of people 'back' to places that are designated, however ambiguously or ambivalently, as 'home'—have tended to take a back seat within more recent discussions of mobility, transnationalism and migration. Situating *return* mobility as a starting point for social inquiry gives rise to important questions regarding the broader context and experience of human mobility, community and identity. This represents an important contribution to emerging perspectives that seek to move beyond binary optics of domestic or translocal versus international migration, local versus foreign identity, and indeed of stasis versus mobility itself. This introductory chapter foregrounds the ways in which the volume as a whole demonstrates the extent to which the prospect and practice of returning home, or of navigating returns between multiple homes, is a central rather than peripheral component of contemporary Pacific Islander mobilities and identities.

From wild 19th-century theorising around the origins of Pacific settlement (see Howe 2003), Malinowski's pioneering study of *kula* exchange circuits (Malinowski 1961) and Hauʻofaʼs seminal revisioning of 'our sea of islands' (Hauʻofa 1994), the reality of life lived reciprocally within and across wide Oceanic expanses has ensured that questions of human movement have remained central to Pacific scholarship. Even so, and while by no means rendered invisible or irrelevant, specific questions relating to what we here refer to as 'mobilities of return'—that is, the movement of people 'back' to places that are designated, however ambiguously or ambivalently, as 'home'—have tended to take a back seat within more recent discussions of mobility, transnationalism and migration. As this book demonstrates, situating *return* mobility as a starting point for social inquiry, rather than a middle or end point, postscript or afterthought, gives rise to important questions regarding the broader context and experience of human mobility, community and identity. This, we argue, represents an important contribution to emerging perspectives that seek to move beyond binary optics of domestic or translocal versus international migration, local versus foreign identity, and indeed of stasis versus mobility itself (Glick Schiller and Salazar 2013; and for an excellent overview of Pacific scholarship, see Keck and Scheider 2015). More importantly still, the chapters collected here demonstrate the extent to which in the current 'age of migration' (Castles and Miller 2009) the prospect and practice of returning home, or of navigating returns between multiple homes, is a central rather than peripheral component of contemporary Pacific Islander mobilities and identities.

Oral-historical, linguistic and archaeological evidence shows that the earliest colonisers of the Pacific not only expertly navigated their way across vast ocean expanses as they sought out new lands. From the very beginnings of human settlement to the region people were also travelling 'the other way'. Across the Pacific, aiding rather than hindering voyages of discovery, the prevailing south-easterly trade winds helped to ensure a fast and safe return in the event of landfall not being made (Irwin 1992). In this way, in possession of diverse strategies including what later European navigators called 'dead reckoning', by which navigators attempted to ascertain their present position based on direction and distance travelled from a fixed point of departure, the promise and safety net of 'return mobility' formed an epistemological as well as practical basis for island-to-island colonisation and dwelling. Inevitably, as social and affective as well as practical networks of trade and kinship obligation emerged over the course of such journeys, the notion of returning to departure points, homelands, bases of refuge or other familiar locations inevitably became tied up in the everyday habitus of Pacific Islander experience and existence.

Borrowing the nautical concept of dead reckoning here, taking account of the social, economic and political implications of dead reckoning has also been central to scholarship on human return migration and mobility in the Pacific region and beyond. Importantly, these terms and what they represent have also become increasingly important within aid and development policy and discourse within the 21st century. Even so, terminological distinctions are often vague and limited in usefulness, with migration and mobility often taken to refer solely to movements from one place of residence to another (migration), rather than including other forms of mobility, such as tourism or visits to friends and family, itinerant trading, travel for education or to access goods and services, or to perform unpaid domestic work (for an in-depth discussion of migration and mobility in international development policy, see Willis 2010). Where the Pacific is concerned, however, touted by a recent World Bank *Pacific Possible, Labour Mobility* report as 'the ten billion dollar prize' (Curtain et al. 2016), questions and issues around labour mobility are rapidly coming to the fore, especially in relation to seasonal labour schemes in New Zealand and Australia.

As discussed by Howard and Rensel, and Lee (both this volume), and reviewed by Gmelch (1980), scholarship up and into the 1980s tended to emphasise returns to homelands on simple binary terms both spatially and conceptually, especially in terms of reflecting either failure or success in meeting economic goals of migration. Reflecting and refracting these analytic trends, from the mid-1980s the highly influential MIRAB model likewise emphasised the central importance of migration (MI) and remittances (R) alongside foreign aid (A) and the bureaucratic public sectors (B) to the functioning of Pacific Island states (Bertram and Watters 1985; and for a more recent discussion Bertram 1999).

Highly structural, political-economic and governance-oriented perspectives such as these clearly failed to take into account the sociocultural, ideational or affective dimensions of migration. These aspects have come to the fore in more recent scholarship, particularly within anthropology, sociology, human geography and related disciplines (see especially Sheller and Urry 2006; Urry 2007; for the Pacific, Ward 1997; D'Arcy 2006; Lee and Francis 2009; Keck and Schieder 2015).

Cathy Small's groundbreaking book, *Voyages: From Tongan Villages to American Suburbs* (2011), presented an highly intimate description and subtle analysis of Tongan diasporic mobilities and connections traced through in-depth fieldwork over some 15 years. Leulu Felise Va'a's *Saili Matagi: Samoan Migrants in Australia* (2001) and Cluny Macpherson's pioneering work on Samoan migration, which has included asking important questions around the possibilities of homecoming within diasporic populations (1985, 1994, 1999, 2004), also represent important early contributions (and for a more recent important example focusing on American Samoa, see Van der Ryn 2012). Such issues have also been central points of concern within historical evaluations and re-evaluations around topics also defined by human mobility. This includes most notably the periods of early European exploration and cross-cultural encounter in the Pacific (e.g. Thomas 2009; Jolly et al. 2009), and more especially the contexts of Christian missionisation and the labour trade (Shineberg 1999; Sivasundaram 2005; Banivanua-Mar 2007). While rarely forming an explicit focus of interest, such works are replete with stories of Pacific Islander mobility, both across the Pacific and beyond, and often back again. In one particularly telling example, focusing on the theme of return across multiple generations, the documentary film *Sugar Slaves: The Secret History of Australia's Slave Trade* (Graham 1995) follows the story of Joe and Monica Leo, South Sea Islander descendants of Queensland plantation workers, recruited during the labour trade from Pentecost Island, Vanuatu (also see Taylor 2008). Undertaking a journey to recover a portion of their stolen past, the Leo's 'return' to Pentecost is fraught with the kind of emotionally unsettling ambivalence that also permeates many of the chapters in this volume.

Of particular importance to coming to grips with the profound complexities of return mobility have been studies focusing on the experience of children, adoption and the children of migrants (see Lee, this volume). As Yngvesson and Coutin (2006) have demonstrated in their comparison of US deportees to El Salvador and the 'roots trips' of Swedish transnational adoptees, for example, the return journeys of long-term migrants especially are often jarringly unsettling, if not dismantling of the mythologies of home and identity that configure them. Likewise, since Epeli Hau'ofa's cogent postcolonial critique of the hegemonic Western stereotypes that are so often bound up in models such as MIRAB (Hau'ofa 1994), scholars have struggled to take into account the high degree to which Pacific Islander diasporic practices also entail a profound disruption of easy notions of home and away, and with it the idea of 'return', even as these concepts retain vital practical and even embodied value. Just as Jolly (2001), inspired by Hauʻofaʻs vision, demonstrates the need to account for the copresence of values of 'roots' and 'routes', or stasis and mobility, in Pacific epistemologies and discourses, what is demonstrated time and again across these chapters is the necessity of understanding how meanings of values of home and away, as well as departure and return, are produced and transformed dialectically through context and time.

Dislodging the Western stereotypical location of Pacific 'Islander' homes—from static, tiny island to the fluid sea—Hauʻofa persuasively argued that Pacific Islanders have always been on the move, and in doing so have always made and remade homes in multiple locations. His broad vision took in a vast global circulation of people and material goods, including in 'seaports and airports throughout the central Pacific, where consignments of goods from homes abroad are unloaded as those of the homelands are loaded' (1994: 156). Similarly, refusing to accept stereotypes of 'home Islanders' gobbling up remittances 'like parasites on their relatives abroad' (1994: 157), Hauʻofa instead highlighted the ethos of reciprocity that lies 'at the core of all oceanic cultures' and, as he put it:

> the fact that for everything homeland relatives receive, they reciprocate with goods they themselves produce, by maintaining ancestral roots and lands for everyone, homes with warmed hearths for travelers to return to permanently or to strengthen their bonds, their souls, and their identities before they move on again (Hauʻofa 1994: 157).

Each of the chapters presented here focuses on the contemporary experiences that accompany such homecomings, as well as the shifting meanings and values of home that occur within the context of diaspora over time. While recognising and respecting that Hauʻofaʻs vision of the Pacific as a 'boundless sea of possibilities' (D'Arcy 2006: 7) presents an important ideological countermeasure to past and present colonial and neocolonial thinking, in this volume we are witness to a broad range of life predicaments, and personal and collective responses to these. Home, homecoming and relationships with homeland relatives are in some instances experienced positively as unproblematic and fundamentally life affirming, working to strengthen bonds of identity and community. More often, however, the individual contributions of this volume reveal the ambiguities and ambivalences that so often arise within the shifting contexts of human movement, migration and return mobility. Central to all analyses, however, is a strong sense of the individual and collective agency that is felt and exerted in such contexts. So too is the profoundly affective nature of experience relating to return migration and mobility, including the often unsettling mixtures of longing and anticipation, disappointment and danger, and happiness, hope and security that are all linked to the meanings and embodied practice of returning home.

The following chapter, by Wolfgang Kempf, explores 'diversification of return' as experienced by diasporic Banaba Islanders and their descendants. As Kempf outlines in nuanced detail, colonial and more recent histories of migration and mobility among Banabans is uniquely complex. The underpinnings of the present predicament began following the Second World War with the large-scale, involuntary collective resettlement of Banaba Islanders to Rabi, Fiji, and the subsequent carving out of Kiribati and Fiji as nation-states in the 1970s. As a result of these events, and while continuing to elevate the grounded identity of 'home island' over that of 'home nation', diasporic Banabans have not only developed an ambivalent and plural understanding of home and homeland, but also as a consequence of what (and where) it means to 'return' home. Presenting a cogent critique of methodological nationalism, Kempf provides a valuable terminological and analytic framework through which to conceptualise and understand the complex sequencing of displacement, resettlement, international migration and formation of transnational ties that may occur in diasporic settings everywhere. Kempf begins by noting the important distinction between 'return migration' on the one hand, and shorter 'return visits' on the other. From this basis, he offers three conceptual terms, all of which contribute to an overall understanding of the 'diversification of return': 'differentiation', 'reversal' and 'ramification'. First, and highlighting the distinction between homeland and nation-state, 'differentiation' acknowledges that assignations of home may differ significantly across contexts and through time. Secondly, noting the ways in which many Banabans have come to prioritise Rabi over Banaba as their home island and place of return, 'reversal' refers to the way in which directional reference points may shift along with the differentiation of homelands. Finally, recognising that the majority of those who *do* 'return' to Kiribati tend to resettle on the nation's main atoll of Tarawa, rather than Banaba itself, 'ramification' refers to the observation that this proliferation of homelands also entails directional perspectives on return mobility.

In addition to the fine-grained detail he provides with regards to Banaba Islanders, this framework is particularly valuable to analysing contextual shifts in engagement of migrants with homelands everywhere.

The third chapter, by Howard and Rensel, similarly focuses on the migratory context of a specific island population, many of whom have also resettled in Fiji, along with making new homes in other international locations. Their chapter deftly analyses qualitative and quantitative research data spaning over 50 years to examine the complexly networked rather than purely dyadic ties to place that are formed across diasporic settings. As they demonstrate, the case of Rotuma is somewhat unusual for the overwhelmingly positive image of home and appraisals of homecoming journeys that are held by Rotumans. Even so, in doing so they highlight a key theme across all the chapters, that of the emotional or affective importance of home within the context of return mobility. Here, the value and expectation for Rotumans abroad to 'keep their relationships warm' demonstrates how rights to land form an important factor in defining mobility and settlement patterns, and how the emotional physicality of place and community remain entangled despite the distances of migration.

Compared to the overwhelmingly positive Rotuman experience of return migration and home visits, the predicament of Tongan youth described by Helen Lee is much more mixed. Applying classic anthropological theories of 'rites of passage', Lee examines the fraught experiences of Tongan youth who are sent home to learn their culture, and in doing so become 'truly Tongan'. Reflecting Kempf's concept of 'reversal', many of the youth in Lee's study are in fact returning home for the first time, and as such have very little knowledge of the Tongan cultural context they are stepping into. Ambiguously if not contradictorily situated 'betwixt and between' the categories 'stranger' and 'at home', and often racially designated as *pālangi* (foreign/white) these young people often experience harsh physical punishment alongside elements of Tongan traditional culture (*anga fakatonga*), which are together incorporated by local leaders and family members into disciplinary practices aimed at 'straightening them out'. Importantly, given the sometimes criminal or antisocial backgrounds of the young returnees, in this way Lee's study underscores the need to seriously examine the perspectives and experiences of the broader society that receives returnees, including here for example the sense of burden and potential risks that may accompany their arrival and presence. Even so, in her analysis of what for many is a journey into identity and acceptance, Lee also emphasises the importance of recognising the more positive and redemptive elements of homecoming.

Also focusing on the predicaments of youth in migration, Rachana Agarwal's chapter examines the social negotiation of agency and selfhood among young Palauan returnees. Centring especially on young women, this example emphasises the importance of gender to analyse return mobility. As she argues, while the young returnees she describes generally hold a stable and positive perception of home, the social experience of 'homecoming' is rarely smooth or seamless. A key reason for this is the disjuncture that exists between the social contexts across which such homecoming journeys are taken. In Palau, young people are expected to assume subordinate positions, including in terms of situations of age, class and social rank. Yet, as Agarwal demonstrates, young educated returnees do not passively submit to these expectations, but rather actively strive to assert positions of autonomy while at the same time integrating into the broader social contexts of Palauan society. As demonstrated through several case studies, and reflecting the situation of liminality described by Lee (this volume), within this context of social 'cognitive dissonance' young Palauan returnees must constantly refashion their sense of selfhood through careful and strategic processes of balancing and asserting agency. Such process not only entail conscious acts of self-fashioning, but also see them uniquely positioned to bring about positive social change at a local level.

Kirsten McGavin, in her chapter on diasporic Pacific Islanders living in Australia, emphasises and examines the crucial vitality of meanings and feelings of *peles* (place) in relation to 'home' and identity. Juxtaposing three richly detailed oral testimonies, McGavin argues for the importance of distinguishing between different forms of return mobility. In this way, her analysis adds an important dimension of agency and intentionality to the typology presented by Kempf (this volume, and see above), especially around what he terms 'reversal'. As she also recognises, the question of whether not return mobilities are conceptualised and performed as 'homecomings' is often a matter of choice and personal perspective, and as such becomes tied up with broader ambiguities surrounding personal identity and social acceptance. As her ethnographic findings demonstrate, and running counter to stereotypically positive meanings and values associated with notions of 'home', island visits and excursions that are specifically *not* conceptualised as 'homecomings'—such as touristic or business-related visits—are more likely to be experienced in a more positive way than those that are explicitly or primarily about 'visiting family back home'. Even so, as she also contends, the distinction between 'homecoming' and 'non-homecoming' is often ambiguous or unclear, which may itself give rise to situations of competing expectations between visitors and their family 'hosts'. As she concludes, these deeply situational, affective and relational qualities of return mobility are fundamental to the individual experience of *peles* (place) for diasporic Islanders.

Butt, Munro and Numbery also critically examine the gendered dimensions of homecoming, in their case as experienced and negotiated by women diagnosed and living with HIV in Tanah Papua, Indonesia. As they note, despite the strong association between mobility and HIV, especially as coupled with narratives of 'risk' in the case of female mobility, there have been surprisingly few studies of the moral expectations and emotional experiences that occur as women with HIV return home in search of treatment and support. This chapter presents a vital intervention of research findings and analysis aimed at filling this gap, and thereby contributing to the formulation of positive public health interventions in the region and beyond. As the authors demonstrate and examine through three contrasting ethnographic case studies, where relatively high infection rates are accompanied by contexts of deep stigmatisation, many such returns are fraught with unmet expectations on both sides. Indeed, in a context where the gendered expectation is that women give rather than receive care, far from finding the support they require, many women living with HIV are forced to avoid ostracism or abuse through strategies of secrecy and deception. As the authors argue, taking account of these social insights should be considered of critical importance to future public health planning and response around HIV. This is especially so considering the extent to which dominant responses in contexts such as Tanah Papua have, to date, been motivated by standardised international intervention strategies. In particular, those interventions need to tackle the 'hard truths' that lie beyond the optic of individual treatment adherence. This includes, as they forcefully demonstrate, that existing social contexts and discourses may and often do exacerbate rather than positively affect the situation of HIV-positive women.

Demonstrating a somewhat ironic reversal of hegemonic discourses and values involving urban opportunity and rural backwardness, Kolshus examines the prospects, promises and perils associated with travel to and from the small island of Mota and Vanuatu's urban centres Port Vila and

Luganville. As he shows, for these islanders, choices around whether to leave or stay in either rural homeland or urban locations are informed by a complexly shifting combination of structural and ideational factors. With few educational or economic opportunities, and precariously positioned in terms of basic resources, the 'bright lights of town' have over the last several decades lured Mota islanders in search of new opportunities. As Kolshus demonstrates, however, faced with difficult and confronting situations of relative social alienation, increased economic hardship and the ontological uncertainties of sorcery, such excursions have continually been met with disappointment and peril. As a result, Mota islanders have come to cherish as a matter of pride and source of resilience the realisation that the world outside of their small island home has little to offer them. Even so, and despite this apparent reversal in orientation, the population continues to keep its options open, just as it has in the past. Indeed, as they recognise, the maintenance of footholds elsewhere is crucial given present and future ecological prospects associated with climate change.

The final chapter by Shu-Ling Yeh rounds out the examination of local agency in the context of return migration, in this case focusing on the homemaking practices of the indigenous Amis of Taiwan. As she explains, mobility among Austronesian-speaking indigenous populations in Taiwan are often described negatively at a national level, in terms of vagrancy, displacement or 'aimless drifting'. In stark contrast to these hegemonic descriptions, Yeh shows in great detail the high extent to which the members of one particular community constructed and imagine their village within the context of wider interactions with Taiwanese society. Here, the relationship between mobility and return mobility is a vital component to the generation and regeneration of community at a local level. Community activities such as church and house building, and annual or more sporadic ritual contexts are all dependent on the pooling of resources generated through dynamic exchanges within and across the local and translocal community. Underscoring the need to recognise the importance of home to contexts of migration and mobility seen otherwise in terms of negative precariousness or dependency, these relationships of exchange and development centred on home form an important source of pride, motivation for hard work and source of stability for those living outside of the village context.

The individual contributions to this volume each demonstrate the high methodological value of employing fine-grained ethnography to contexts of mobility, especially to understanding social relations, identity, and transforming meanings and values of home. While diverse in their core approaches, ranging from individual, life-story case studies, quantitative and survey-based approaches, and in-depth ethnographic description, each employs participant observation to reveal complexly shifting contexts, practices and experiences associated with return migration in and across the Pacific region. These range from largely domestic movements in which migrants are able to maintain relatively close ties with their homelands to wider scale international contexts of return mobility in which designations of home and away can become unsettlingly blurred, if not in some instances reversed. As such, the collection exemplifies the ongoing importance of ethnographic comparison to understanding processes of mobility in relation to home and return, and to showing how specific contexts of return mobility work to define individual and collective experience.

References

Banivanua-Mar, T 2007, *Violence and colonial dialogue: the Australian-Pacific indentured labor trade*, University of Hawai'i Press, Honolulu.

Bertram, G 1999, 'The MIRAB model twelve years on', *The Contemporary Pacific*, vol. 11, no. 1, pp. 105–138.

Bertram, G & Watters, RF 1985, 'The MIRAB economy in South Pacific microstates', *Pacific Viewpoint*, vol. 26, no. 3, pp. 497–519.

Castles, S & Miller, MJ 2009, *The age of migration: international population movements in the modern world*, Macmillan, Basingstoke.

Curtain, R, Dornan, M, Doyle, J & Howes, S 2016, *Pacific Possible, Labour mobility: the ten billion dollar prize*, World Bank Group and The Australian National University, Washington DC and Canberra.

D'Arcy, P 2006, *The people of the sea: environment, identity and history in Oceania*, University of Hawai'i Press, Honolulu.

Glick Schiller, N & Salazar, NB 2013, 'Regimes of mobility across the globe', *Journal of Ethnic and Migration Studies*, vol. 39, no. 2, pp. 183–200. doi.org/10.1080/1369183X.2013.723253

Gmelch, G 1980, 'Return migration', *Annual Review of Anthropology*, vol. 91, no. 1, pp. 135–159. doi.org/10.1146/annurev.an.09.100180. 001031

Graham, T 1995, *Sugar slaves: The secret history of Australia's slave trade*. Film Australia. Director/Co-Producer T. Graham. Producer P. Robbins.

Hau'ofa, E 1994, 'Our sea of islands', *The Contemporary Pacific*, vol. 6, no. 1, pp. 148–161.

Howe, KR 2003, *The quest for origins: who first discovered and settled New Zealand and the Pacific Islands?*, University of Hawai'i Press, Honolulu.

Irwin, G 1992, *The prehistoric exploration and colonization of the Pacific*, Cambridge University Press, Cambridge. doi.org/10.1017/CBO 9780511518225

Jolly, M 2001, 'On the edge? Deserts, oceans, islands', *The Contemporary Pacific*, vol. 13, no. 2, pp. 417–466. doi.org/10.1353/cp.2001.0055

Jolly, M, Tryon, D & Tcherkézoff, S 2009, *Oceanic encounters: exchange, desire, violence*, ANU E Press, Canberra.

Keck, V & Schieder, D 2015, 'Contradictions and complexities—current perspectives on Pacific Islander mobilities', *Anthropological Forum*, vol. 25, no. 2, pp. 115–130. doi.org/10.1080/00664677.2014.999644

Lee, H & Francis, ST (eds) 2009, *Migration and transnationalism: Pacific perspectives*, ANU E Press, Canberra.

Macpherson, C 1985, 'Public and private views of home: will Western Samoan migrants return?' *Pacific Viewpoint* vol. 26, no. 1, pp. 242–262.

Macpherson, C 1994, 'Changing patterns of commitment to island homelands: a case study of Western Samoa', *Pacific Studies*, vol. 17, no. 3, p. 83.

Macpherson, C 1999, 'Will the "real" Samoans please stand up? Issues in diasporic Samoan identity', *New Zealand Geographer*, vol. 55, no. 2, pp. 50–59. doi.org/10.1111/j.1745-7939.1999.tb00542.x

Macpherson, C 2004, 'From Pacific Islanders to Pacific people and beyond', in P Spoonley & DG Pearson (eds), *Tangata tangata: the changing ethnic contours of New Zealand*, Cengage Learning Australia, Sydney, pp. 135–155.

Malinowski, B 1961 [1922], *Argonauts of the Western Pacific: an account of native enterprise and adventure in the archipelagoes of Melanesian New Guinea*, E.P. Dutton, New York.

Sheller, M & Urry, J 2006, 'The new mobilities paradigm', *Environment and Planning A*, vol. 38, no. 2, pp. 207–226. doi.org/10.1068/a37268

Shineberg, D 1999, *The people trade: Pacific island laborers and New Caledonia, 1865–1930*, Pacific Islands Monograph Series no. 16, University of Hawai'i Press, Honolulu.

Sivasundaram, S 2005, *Nature and the godly empire: science and evangelical mission in the Pacific, 1795–1850*, Cambridge Social and Cultural Histories, vol. 7, Cambridge University Press, Cambridge.

Small, C 2011, *Voyages: from Tongan villages to American suburbs*, Cornell University Press, Ithaca.

Taylor, JP 2008, *The other side: ways of being and place in Vanuatu*, Pacific Islands Monograph Series, no. 22, University of Hawai'i Press, Honolulu. doi.org/10.21313/hawaii/9780824833022.001.0001

Thomas, N 2009, *Entangled objects: Exchange, material culture, and colonialism in the Pacific*. Harvard University Press, Cambridge, Massachusetts, and London, England.

Urry, J 2007, *Mobilities*, Polity Press, Cambridge.

Va'a, LF 2001, *Saili matagi: Samoan migrants in Australia*, Institute of Pacific Studies and Iunivesite Aoao o Samoa, Suva.

Van der Ryn, F 2012, 'Return migration to American Samoa', *Pacific Studies*, vol. 35, no. 1, pp. 252–279.

Ward, G 1997, 'Expanding worlds of Oceania: implications of migration', in K Sudo & S Yoshida (eds), *Population movement in the modern world I: contemporary migration in Oceania: diaspora and network*, JCAS Symposium Series 3, The Japan Center for Area Studies, National Museum of Ethnology, Osaka, pp. 179–196.

Willis, K 2010, 'Introduction: mobility, migration and development', *International Development Planning Review*, vol. 32, no. 3–4, pp. i–xiv. doi.org/10.3828/idpr.2010.15

Yngvesson, B & Coutin, SB 2006, 'Backed by papers: undoing persons, histories, and return', *American Ethnologist*, vol. 33, no. 2, pp. 177–190. doi.org/10.1525/ae.2006.33.2.177

2

The diversification of return: Banaban home islands and movements in historical perspective

Wolfgang Kempf

Abstract

The international return mobility of the Banaban community has been significantly influenced by post–Second World War collective resettlement and the resulting transnational space of multiple belongings. Thus, with their politics of translocal linking of original and new home islands, the first generation of Banabans prepared the way for cross-border movements between Fiji and Kiribati. The central issue here is a historical development that extends from the organised return of younger Fiji-Banabans—as part of the repossession politics of the island of origin, Banaba, during the 1970s—and the more recent migration of members of the second and third Banaban generations to the capital atoll Tarawa in Kiribati through to imaginings of return from Tarawa to Rabi Island in Fiji, should the atoll country be rendered uninhabitable following possible future climate changes and subsequent rising sea levels. Viewed over the course of time, the directions and places of return have proven multiple and mutable. This diversification of return mobility is the product of the historical practices of different generations of Banabans in the context of a networked world of Pacific islands and island states.

Introduction

In this paper, I shall examine the phenomenon of international return mobility among diasporic Banabans. The Banabans' original home was the island of Banaba (also known as Ocean Island), now part of the central Pacific state of Kiribati. Discovery and exploitation of phosphate reserves on the Banabans' island of origin led to the British colonial authorities deciding to relocate the whole community to distant Fiji. Involuntary collective resettlement is a form of (forced) migration that hardly features in the literature on international return migration. This is due primarily to the fact that large-scale displacements and relocation of individuals and communities, such as those caused by natural and technological disasters, but also by large infrastructure projects, almost always occur within a single national framework (see Cernea and McDowell 2000: 1; Oliver-Smith 2009a: 3–4; 2009b: 129–132). Furthermore, the prospect of those affected ever returning is slim indeed, especially in the case of development-forced displacement and resettlement, as a result of subsequent radical transformations to the zones of origin (see Oliver-Smith 2009a: 4). As opposed to research on resettlement, migration studies in the field of diaspora and transnationalism focus mainly on the individual members of households or families who emigrate in the hope of a better life, act within transnational networks and, at times, initiate return movements (see for example, Brettell 2015: 151–153; Cassarino 2004). The focus has also widened to include return mobilities exhibited by descendants of the first generation, the so-called 'next generations' (Conway and Potter 2009a, 2009b; cf. Potter et. al. 2005).

In the Banaban case, collective resettlement and transnational migration, two areas that are usually kept separate, tend to intermingle. Thus community resettlement has an international character and is associated with return mobility, whereas transnational ties by Banabans living in Fiji and Kiribati originated in forced and collective migration. The analytic relevance of this case has its rationale in the historical sequence of displacement, resettlement, international migration and transnational ties, but also in diverse forms and phases of return mobility. On the conceptual plane, I take my bearings from Russell King and Anastasia Christou (2014: 2, 8–9), who introduced 'return mobility' as a generalising concept, further refining it into two distinct segments. One is 'return migration', in the sense of a voluntary return by a migrant to his or her country of origin—it might be just for a limited period of time or it could be permanent. The second and wider notion of 'return' includes voluntary and forced return but also variants of return mobility that are imagined or temporary (for example, brief visits). What matters most, from my perspective, is to resolve how the displacement and resettlement of the first generation impacts on the international return mobility exhibited by second and third generations. In this connection, I argue that over the span of 70 years a process of diversification of return mobility can be observed, based on the concepts of differentiation, reversal and ramification.

The concept of differentiation highlights the distinction between homeland and nation-state. The point is to advance an alternative perspective to 'methodological nationalism' (Wimmer and Glick Schiller 2002; Glick Schiller and Salazar 2013). When Banabans talk of homeland and returning there, they are not thinking of nation-states, but of islands; that is, for them, homeland and home island are congruent. The historical background explains why: the Banabans were collectively relocated from what was then known as the Gilbert and Ellice Islands Colony to the then Crown Colony of Fiji, where they were resettled on Rabi Island. Out of this transcolonial movement the first generation grew a vision of Banaba, the island from which they had been removed, as their ancestral homeland, a place that had to be protected and preserved for future generations and eventual resettlement. To shore up this vision and also for more pragmatic reasons, the settlers on Rabi Island decided to transfer the identity-conferring structures of ancestral Banaba to the landscape of their new island, duplicating the number and names of villages. With the backing of the colonial administration, they built their new home island into a geographically, politically and culturally distinct enclave within Fiji (Kempf and Hermann 2005). When Fiji and Kiribati achieved independence in the 1970s, Rabi and Banaba now found themselves in two different sovereign states; however, this hardly changed the historically sanctioned practice of equating homeland with home island (see Figure 1).

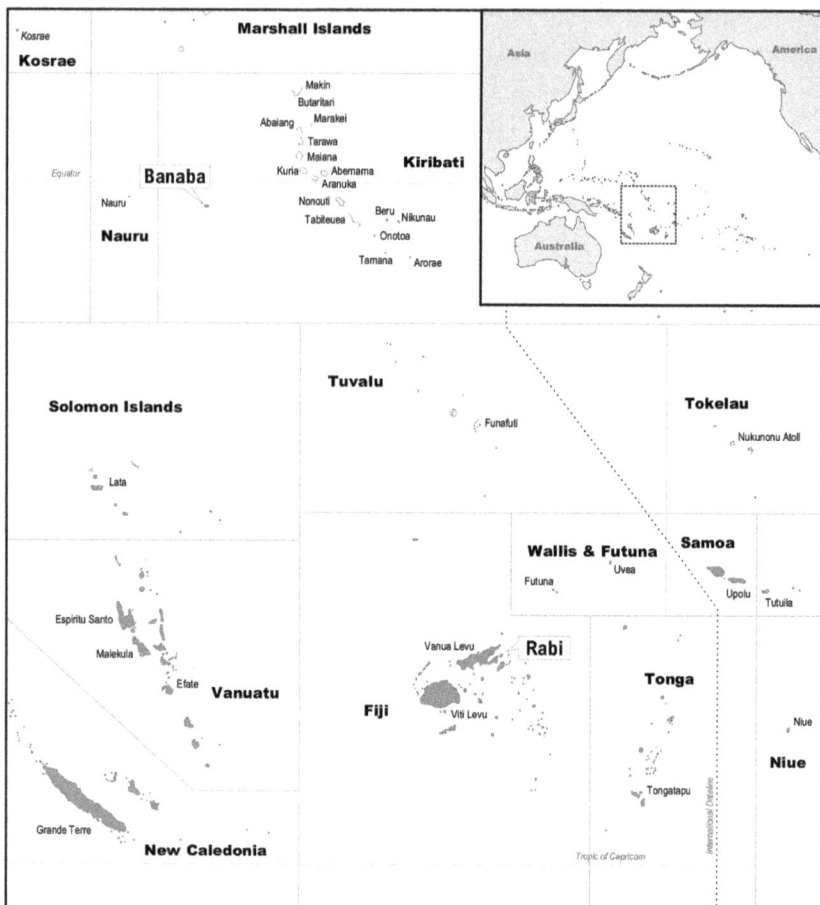

Figure 1: Section of map of Oceania showing the islands of Banaba (Kiribati) and Rabi (Fiji)
Source: Wolfgang Kempf.

Reversal is the name given to the direction of return. It signifies a development where the (at the time) newly acquired island of Rabi came to be prioritised as home island and place of return. In the early decades following resettlement, it was ancestral Banaba that stood at the heart of indigenous constructions of home and return. However, as a result of their determination to anchor in the collective memory of future generations the idea of two interconnected homelands—Banaba being the first (ancestral) and Rabi the second (acquired)—the pioneer generation simultaneously paved the way for new forms of identification. Thus the community came to see itself as a transnational ethnic minority, possessing not one but two home islands, each in a different sovereign state. In Fiji, the Banabans are known as an ethnic group inhabiting Rabi Island but also possessing an ancestral island in Kiribati, while being Banaban in Kiribati now implicates a second home island in faraway Fiji (Kempf 2012). This transnational terrain of multiple belonging enabled second- and third-generation Fijian-born Banabans to reverse their focus and primarily turn attention on Rabi Island in case of migration. Other studies of return migration interpret the reversal of homeland and return primarily through the perspective of transnational links between nation-states, with the second generation returning to their country of origin and maintaining links with their country of birth, now seen 'as a different kind of homeland' (King and Christou 2014: 6). Yet, when the idea of homeland and return, as in the Banaban case, is predominantly focused on islands within nation-states, as opposed to the nation-states themselves, a more nuanced approach will surely be needed.

To talk of ramification is to recognise the fact that Banabans not only live on their respective home islands, but frequently build island homes elsewhere in Fiji or Kiribati. Island homes are nodes of identification with Rabi and Banaba. When island homes lie outside the home islands, they are instrumental in altering the perspectives and directionality of return mobility. Ramification chiefly takes the form of migration into the urban centres of the two island nations—mainly Suva and Lautoka on Viti Levu in the case of Fiji, and Tarawa in that of Kiribati. For our analytic purpose, it is the international migration of second- and third-generation Banabans from Fiji to Kiribati that is of especial interest. The overwhelming majority of returnees do not settle on the home island of Banaba; rather, they have their sights set on Tarawa, the capital atoll. Were we to follow the postulate of congruence between home island and homeland, this would not seem to amount to a case of return mobility. In fact, Banabans only think of Banaba as homeland or motherland, not the main atoll of Tarawa and not the nation-state of Kiribati. On the other hand, Fiji-Banabans hold special rights, meaning that not only can they reside and work permanently in Kiribati, but they become citizens upon arrival. On top of that, many Banabans share intimate ties with Kiribati and its people, ranging from kinship ties (blood or marriage) to emotional ties of all kinds; nor should we overlook the many landholdings claimed by returnees (Hermann 2003). Such family, material and emotional references (cf. King and Christou 2014: 2) mean that when Fiji-Banabans migrate to Tarawa there is a real-world dimension to their return.[1] Residing on Tarawa for Fiji-Banabans also holds the possibility of a reversal of return, since many prioritise Rabi Island (not Banaba) as their home island.

The first generation of resettled Banabans, via a politics of forging translocal linkage between island of origin and island of relocation, could widen the range of options open to the second and third generation for international migration and return within the region. This historically oriented study will prioritise the specifically regional nature of resettlement, migration, transnationality, and return mobility between islands and island states. Contrary to the South–South perspective I am following here, the bulk of studies dealing with return migration usually target migration flows from the 'global South' to the 'metropolitan global North' (Conway and Potter 2009a: 2–3). In Oceania, more specifically, this includes movements away from the small island states of the Pacific into metropolitan states like Australia, New Zealand or the USA (see for example, Lee 2003, 2009). To be sure, Banabans do emigrate to all of the above destinations. But this should be seen as a more or less recent phenomenon— and yet to be fully researched. For that reason, further consideration of this more recent migration flow (and its possible contribution to a further diversification of return mobility) is omitted here.[2]

Therefore, I shall focus on three historical pathways of return mobility. I begin with the politically motivated return movement from Rabi in Fiji to Banaba in the central Pacific during the 1970s and early 1980s. At the time, the resettled Banabans were intensifying their anticolonial struggle for indemnification and national sovereignty. A central plank in this struggle was the organised return by young, for the most part unmarried, Fiji-Banabans of the second generation, as part of a politics of occupying and resettling ancestral Banaba. The second return migration to be considered here is that of Fiji-Banabans to Tarawa, an influx that began in the 1990s and continues to this day. Despite many of the newcomers returning to urban Kiribati for educational facilities, scholarships and

---

1   For second-generation returnees in the Caribbean, Tracey Reynolds (2014) has analysed comparable aspects of ramification, albeit on the level of island states. Her argument, namely that strict adherence to a 'bi-polar origin-destination framework' does not always do justice to the realities of a region-wide return (Reynolds 2014: 86), shows structural similarities to the perspective developed here of a ramification of Banaban return mobility.

2   Of the metropolitan nations New Zealand probably now has the largest Banaban diaspora (cf. Teaiwa 2014). However, no exact figures are available on first-generation emigration and return mobility.

job opportunities, this particular motivation shall not detain me here. Instead, I shall concentrate on the case of Fiji-Banabans seeking to reclaim family property on Tarawa. Return in such cases often resulted in disputes over land, a scarce resource on Tarawa. My third and last area of investigation is the return mobility exhibited by Banaban migrants living on Tarawa. Rabi Island is usually their preferred destination of return, whether for permanent relocation in advanced age, for short family visits or for imagined ones on the plane of contingency planning. Why the last one? Fiji-Banabans have, over recent years, been increasingly confronted with contemporary discourses on the considerable risks facing Kiribati—an atoll state—from climate change and rising sea levels. Against this background, Fiji-Banabans on Tarawa are more mindful than ever that Rabi, a volcanic island, could one day offer a suitable place of refuge from the projected risks of environmental change—if only in the distant future.

Banaba, Tarawa, Rabi—all three destinations have, over time, drawn in members of the Banaban diaspora, indicating just how multiple and protean are the directions and places of return. The diversification of return combined with the constitutings of home island and island home are relational products of the historical agency manifested by various generations of Banabans, unfolding within a context of colonial and postcolonial structures in a networked world of Pacific islands and island nations.

Relocation and the vision of return

Following discovery of lucrative phosphate deposits on Banaba in 1900, Banaban islanders were confronted by unprecedented radical change. First came the British annexation of their island in 1901; then, some 15 years later, Banaba was included in the Gilbert and Ellice Islands Colony (GEIC). Powerless to stop this colonisation of their home island, the Banaban Islanders soon found themselves facing epidemics, land expropriations, resource destruction and racial segregation, not to mention the unstoppable expansion of an industrial and administrative infrastructure. The extraction of the island's high-grade phosphate reserves—first by the Pacific Phosphate Company, then, after 1920, by the

British Phosphate Commissioners (BPC)[3]—set in motion a veritable machinery of destruction, stripping the local population progressively and irreversibly of its land.

Soon it was clear that if mining continued much of Banaba would be rendered uninhabitable. Therefore, beginning in 1909, the colonial administration and phosphate company repeatedly floated scenarios that, in their final form, envisaged resettling the islanders elsewhere (see Williams and MacDonald 1985: 89, 148, 257). For many years the Banabans remained utterly and vehemently opposed to any such plans. But so massive was the scale of the forced expropriations, so progressive the inroads on their land, that eventually they integrated the idea of purchasing another island for the sake of future generations into their anticolonial discourse (see Maude 1946: 10–11). By the early 1940s, the Banabans were expressing the wish to purchase an island in Fiji, also a British colony. Finally, in March 1942, the Western Pacific High Commission in Fiji acquired the plantation island of Rabi on their behalf, using for that purpose money from the 'Banaban Provident Fund', which was administered by the commission. Rabi Island, belonging at the time to Lever's Pacific Plantations Pty Ltd., was purchased for 25,000 Australian pounds (see Kempf 2011: 19–20; Maude 1946: 11–12).

Shortly thereafter, with the coming of the Second World War to the Pacific in August 1942, Banaba was occupied by the Japanese army. Logistic shortfalls led to the Japanese occupiers deporting the Banabans to the islands of Tarawa, Nauru and Kosrae (Maude 1946; Ellis 1946; cf. Hermann 2003; Kempf 2004). In the immediate aftermath of war, the British colonial administration seized the opportunity presented by the Banabans being scattered and displaced. Officials gathered the survivors—much weakened by disease and undernourishment—using Tarawa as a temporary collection point. Insisting that a return to Banaba was simply not possible due to war-related destruction, the administration proposed that the Banabans might like to make a fresh start on Fiji's Rabi Island. Finally, on December 15, 1945, some 703 Banabans and 300 Gilbert Islanders (who had been taken into the Banaban community) landed on their new island in Fiji (see Maude 1946: 12–13; Silverman 1971: 147–148). Despite major difficulties in the early years, chiefly due to the unaccustomed climate, the strange new

---

3   The governments of Great Britain, Australia and New Zealand decided in 1919 to jointly exploit the phosphate reserves. Each country had its own representative on the Board of Commissioners (Ellis 1935: 178–181; Macdonald 1982: 103).

environment, and the bewilderment and deep-seated uncertainty afflicting the migrants, the majority of the Banabans decided, in a secret ballot held in May 1947, to make Rabi their future home. This decision, to which over 80 per cent of the Banabans gave their backing, was codified by the colonial administration in a 'Statement of Intentions', which was subsequently signed by the community's political representatives (see Silverman 1971: 167).

After a phase of spatial and social consolidation on Rabi Island, the Banabans intensified their political struggle, from the mid-1960s on, against what they saw as continued discrimination, exploitation and dispossession by the British colonial power and the BPC, the body responsible for the phosphate mining (see 'Banabans seek better phosphate deal' 1965; cf. Macdonald 1982; Silverman 1971). The chief negotiators for the Banabans attempted, via political channels, to manoeuvre the British government into a series of concessions. One of their core demands—political independence for Banaba in association with Rabi Island in Fiji—aimed at winning back control over land and phosphate, including a fair share of the profits in the form of royalties. They also pressed for the complete rehabilitation of terrain laid waste in the course of decades of high-intensity mining operations, so that they might, one day, be able to return to Banaba (or Ocean Island). In a memorandum to a petition the Banabans submitted to the United Nations in 1968, the community stated: 'We are deeply attached to Ocean Island because it is our homeland—the land on which God originally planted us … We are, therefore, naturally anxious to return to our homeland and thereby preserve our national, racial and cultural identity' (National Archives of Fiji (NAF) High Court of Justice 1968: 7). A few pages later, they had this to say about their demand for independence:

> [The Banaban people] seek political independence for Ocean Island as their homeland and the Rabi Island Council as the elected representatives of the Banaban people wishes to secure the agreement of the United Kingdom Government to the immediate granting of independence to Ocean Island and the re-establishment of our people there. The right of our people to independence on Ocean Island rests on the United Nations Declaration on the granting of independence to Colonial Countries and people … The Banaban people intend to return to Ocean Island and, in terms of Resolution 1514 (xv), they 'have the right to self-determination, so that by virtue of that right they freely determine their political status and freely pursue their economic, social and cultural development' (National Archives of Fiji (NAF) High Court of Justice 1968: 13).

The petition to the United Nations in June 1968 lent additional weight to their demands for sovereign status, financial compensation, terrain rehabilitation and the belated restoration of justice. Although the petition was formally directed at the UN, the real addressee was the British government of the day. A few months later, in October 1968, Banabans taking part in the Ocean Island phosphates discussions in London distributed a comprehensive demand catalogue, which was, however, rejected by Lord Shepherd, representing the government (see Foreign and Commonwealth Office 1968). The Banabans appealed the decision in 1970, but this was dismissed (see Posnett 1977: 5).

Tauan Banaba—the politics of return

Repeatedly rebuffed by the British government, the political leadership of the Banaban community finally resorted to legal action, lodging an appeal with the British High Court in London (see Binder 1977: 146–167; Macdonald 1982: 268–269). One principal issue negotiated was compensation for the damage done to Banaba, another was rehabilitation of the island by the phosphate company. In parallel with legal action, Banaban leaders returned to an earlier demand that Banaba should be detached from the GEIC and awarded sovereign status. Accordingly, in 1974, they submitted a petition to this effect to the British government and the United Nations. The background to this move was the ongoing negotiations about, and the preparations for, granting independence to both the Gilbert Islands (later Kiribati) and Ellice Islands (later Tuvalu) (see Macdonald 1982: 263–275; Posnett 1977: 5).

In the course of the 1970s, with a view to underscoring these demands, the Banabans branched out into a politics of return. This historical phase is anchored in the community's collective memory as *Tauan Banaba* (literally 'Keep Banaba'), that is, physical occupation of the home island in order to forestall possible appropriation by other parties, especially Gilbertese Islanders (later I-Kiribati). Organised return was designed to signal the community's determination to uphold their ownership rights to their home island (cf. Hermann 2004:198). This, however was not the first time that members of the Banaban community in Fiji had returned to the land of their ancestors. As early as 1947, only a few years after their original relocation, the BPC had briefly brought a sizeable group of islanders back to do boundary marking (*te tautia*) so the remaining land could then be mined for phosphate (see Silverman 1971: 170–171). Twenty years later, a delegation of Banabans again set foot on the island. Shocked at the extent of its despoliation, they complained about what they saw as blatant infringements by the mining company against existing agreements, one particularly egregious case being the destruction of the Banabans' graveyard.[4] Other Banabans also arrived on Ocean Island, having found work with the BPC (see for example, Posnett 1977: 10). Then, in March 1975, around 60 men—mainly young and unmarried— as well as four women left Rabi Island on the *Ai Sokula*, a vessel bound for Banaba. This was a political action, designed to garner publicity. In an article headlined 'Banabans set sail for their island home' *The Fiji Times* explained the rationale: 'They say their move back to their old homeland is their way of telling the British—and the GEIC: "This island is ours".' ('Banabans set sail for their island home' 1975). Tom Teai, at the time Rabi administrator, publicity officer and co-organiser of the *Tauan Banaba* initiative, later recalled these events with the hindsight of 20 years:

> I belonged to an age where fighting was the mood. You know. We were more aggressive back then. We had our objective—we had very definite objectives about Banaba. That concerned Banaban identity and Banaban separation and [the] political future of Banaba. You know … They [the Banabans who went to Banaba] were just told [by the Banaban leaders]: 'Go there, take the place—while we go and fight our case. You physically take the place. We'll go and try and take it politically'. (Interview recorded 16 July 1998)[5]

Docking at Banaba, the islanders had to wait before disembarking. The GEIC had declared Banaba a restricted area. This meant that the new arrivals could only visit their old home after being issued with special permits. In addition, a second vessel carrying tents for the returnees was delayed, so that they initially had to overnight on the *Ai Sokula*. Only later could they set up camp on dry land ('Ocean Island welcomes 60 from Fiji: Rabi settler group stays' 1975). Two years later, an official of the British government visited the island briefly; among other things, he reported on how the new settlers were faring. His impression of what he estimated to be 50 Banabans was of a largely marginalised and 'aimless' community, occupying huts partly constructed from the remnants of old, torn-down BPC buildings (Posnett 1977: 10–11).

---

4   See NAF 1968, Documents 46/1968.
5   All interviews cited in this chapter were conducted by the author.

In the spring of 1979, Rabi's Council of Leaders again sent some 100 Fiji-Banabans across to Banaba to build upon their earlier foothold there (see 'Petrol bombs on Banaba' 1979: 22). The signs pointed to confrontation. The long and costly appeal to the High Court in London had not brought the desired success (see Macdonald 1982: 268–269). Worse, the Banaban leadership had ultimately failed in all its attempts to detach Banaba from the newly created state of Kiribati. Now installed on Banaba, the returnees organised a protest march and, later on, attempted to destroy machinery and other installations of the mining company, using improvised petrol bombs (see 'Petrol bombs on Banaba' 1979: 22). The radicalisation of the Banabans led to arrests, injuries and increased conflict pitting Gilbertese against Banabans, further deepening already existing rifts between the two groups. Integration of the island of Banaba into the new state of Kiribati in July 1979 could not be prevented by the Banabans, for all their many initiatives.

In that same year the phosphate mine on Banaba ceased operations. The last of the BPC workforce departed in January 1980 (Williams and MacDonald 1985: 522). One of the Fiji-Banabans, a man who in younger years had returned to occupy Banaba, reflected on this turning point, coinciding as it did with the closing of the mine. Here, then, is a passage from our conversation, which I reproduce at length because it gives a good account of his experiences as a returnee:

> So I stayed there until BPC left. And it was very interesting thing to me, because we've been with [all the people], you know. The island was very, very noisy. [Later] the atmosphere was very different ... And it's a sad story, because at one time you were staying with lots and lots of people. Then all of a sudden they were all gone ... And then we—well, this is what I experienced. Before the boat left—the Europeans were leaving, so the boat came to pick them up. This was the last lot. I was watching them and along with my Banaban friends we stayed behind. We watched them, we said goodbye to them ... Now there was nobody else on the island except the police and the Gilbertese administrative people ... And then the Government of Kiribati tried to operate the lighting plant [on Banaba] ... But they couldn't afford it! [laughs] So that was that. That's when we experienced darkness. Like we were there with our great-great-grandfathers. And we were really happy. We lived happily on the island. Because here, on this island, we don't even have a power plant in our villages ... But we didn't mind. We didn't mind at all. And we said: 'Okay, we are back to square one. The phosphate company has abandoned this island. Abandoned us too. Without any water. Without any means of

transport. So here we are—anyway—we're back to square one.' … And that's what our experience has been. Life after BPC. And then the Kiribati Government, one way or another, tried to punish us—the Banabans. So it cut off communication with us. When the radio—the radio telephones on the island broke down, nobody from Kiribati came [to fix them] … Even the food!

WK: So how did you survive then? I mean you had no food supply.

K: We are Banabans! We get by—we only eat fish. We eat fish only … (Interview recorded July 24 1998)

The end of phosphate mining and the departure of the Europeans had, as these remarks by a second-generation returnee indicate, fundamentally transformed life on Banaba. Silence, darkness, isolation, deprivation and bare subsistence had become the new normal, marking a caesura in the island's fortunes. 'Life after BPC' generally exhibited aspects of liberation and a new beginning, but perhaps the main thing associated with it was the positive experience of returning to one's roots. This historical experience of consolidating ethnic awareness and cultural belonging went hand in hand with a newly achieved spatial control over the island. These factors, in combination, strengthened the hand of second-generation Banabans when it came to dealing with the small numbers of I-Kiribati living on their ancestral island as outsiders.

Now, this return to Banaba movement would have been unthinkable without close coordination from the political leadership and families back on Rabi Island in Fiji. This transnational terrain was a key prerequisite of what later followed: the reversal of return. Not all Fiji-Banabans of the second generation who returned to Banaba wanted to settle there permanently. So Rabi Island, the second home island, became a focus as a place of return. A woman of the second generation, who had grown up on Rabi but been sent to Banaba in 1979 by her politically active mother, recalled after 30 years the period following the BPC's departure:

By that time we had all gone our separate ways. Some of us were travelling back to Fiji and some staying behind … I don't know, my heart just told me to stay behind. I really wanted to stay on Ocean Island. And—but that's another thing—my mum said: 'If you accept what I think, please stay there forever. You can come back. Save your money, if you want to come and see me.' … So I stayed there during those years. That's when I became pregnant with my second daughter … I wanted my daughter to be a citizen. A Fijian citizen. So I tried to save up and go back to Fiji to my mum, so I could have my baby there. That was in 1982 … I really wanted to go back and have my baby there, because I knew that if you have your baby on Ocean Island, it will be very hard for them to go to school or back to Fiji, later on in the future … I wanted my daughter to go to school in Fiji. Because I know the difference … The difference is like this—in school it is very hard for people here [in Kiribati] to learn to speak English … That's why I wanted my daughter to grow up and learn English in Fiji. (Interview recorded 3 October 2013)

This woman, too, had obeyed the call by the political leadership for a return to Banaba, culminating in the demonstrative reoccupation of their ancestral home. Yet their stay-at-home relatives on Rabi Island continued to loom large as a vital source of support and care. Especially for young parents with small children, the economic downturn and the hardships in a period of time after the mine had closed, not to say the differences in living standards and educational facilities between Kiribati and Fiji, were important reasons for retaining access to these social resources. Returning to Fiji and taking out Fijian citizenship was, in the opinion of many, a prudent move, bearing in mind the future prospects of their own children and the considerable difference it might make.

Banaban migration to Tarawa

Today the Banabans find themselves in the position of having two separate 'home islands' that are more than 2,000 kilometres apart and belong to two different Pacific island states. Rabi Island with a population of approximately 3,000 constitutes something of a political, social and cultural node for the Banaban diaspora. The great majority of second- and third-generation Banabans, whose common denominator is having been born and grown up on Rabi, look on this Fijian island as their primary home (see Hermann and Kokoria 2005: 129). Yet Banaba in distant Kiribati resonates across the generational divide as the identity-conferring place of origin, to which Banabans everywhere feel bound by ancestry, traditions and land ownership, as well as collective narratives of exploitation, displacement and resettlement (see Kempf 2004; Hermann 2004; Kempf and Hermann 2005).

Ever since Kiribati won independence and all phosphate mining ceased, the task of administering and policing Banaba has been jointly handled by Kiribati officials on the one hand and the Rabi Council of Leaders, based in

Fiji, on the other. Today the island is a largely marginalised place, bearing the traces of a defunct phosphate industry, including much dilapidated infrastructure. Official census data put the number of those living there at just over 300 (Secretariat of the Pacific Community 2007: 104). Aside from some I-Kiribati working on behalf of the government, most of the present population are Banabans and their families,[6] employed by the Rabi Council of Leaders to work as stewards of the island. The State of Kiribati has granted the Banaban community special rights, now codified in the Constitution (see especially Chapter IX). These include extensive decision-making powers over Banaba, a seat in Kiribati's parliament and the provision of civil liberties within Kiribati (see Hermann 2006: Chap. 7; cf. Dagmar 1989: 206; Teaiwa 1997: 138). A core consideration here is that all Banabans upon entering Kiribati automatically acquire citizenship, and so enjoy an unrestricted right of abode.

When Fiji-Banabans travel to Kiribati they are 'going back' to a country in which their original homeland is now situated. However, in a development that goes back to the end of the 1990s, only rarely today does ancestral Banaba feature as the destination of return mobility; far more frequently the returnees have their sights set on Tarawa, at once Kiribati's capital and the largest atoll. According to my calculations, at least 600–700 Banabans from Fiji were living on Tarawa in 2013. Most had moved there for economic reasons. An important consideration was the highly restricted job market on Rabi Island and the low pay. The matter has been further complicated over the last three decades by the declining economic fortunes of the Rabi Council of Leaders (a body that is, along with the Fijian government, a principal source of jobs on Rabi) plus the often difficult economic situation that has overtaken Fiji generally, due not least to the coups and the resultant political instability.

When it comes to education, scholarships or simply finding work in Fiji, Banabans see themselves as frequently losing out to both Fijians and Indo-Fijians. Natan[7] from Rabi, a Banaban man in his late 60s, explained the advantages he saw from living in Kiribati. He had held an administrative

---

6   Today a small core of permanently resident Banaban-born migrants of the first generation (that is, children of the second-generation returnees) are keen to distance themselves from the Fijian-born next generations.

7   All personal names of interview partners cited in this article are pseudonyms, except for Tom Teai.

post on Banaba from the first half of the 1990s and well into the new millennium; at the time of our interview, he had been living for almost a decade on Tarawa, where three of his children had found good jobs:

> N: I think one thing [my children] prefer here is that there's more advancement than on Rabi. More advancement. Yeah, you got a lot of chances here! Because the Kiribati government is in touch with the outside world. But Fiji is difficult! Because the Fijians are always there. The Indians are always there. And they're the ones who always stop Banabans. I mean they want all the jobs.
>
> WK: Does that mean if you come here you have an advantage?
>
> N: Well, more than in Fiji!
>
> WK: Is that so?
>
> N: Yes! I'm telling the truth. Take my children. Now, the Kiribati government knew they were my children. They were not brought up here, they were brought up in Fiji. But because they are part and parcel of Kiribati—they are Gilbertese too and they have a very good [general] understanding. So [the Kiribati government] didn't block their way. They gave them a chance. (Interview recorded 30 September 2013)

Migration from Rabi Island to Tarawa is, fundamentally, a cross-border movement of people exchanging rural for town life. As the seat of government—in that respect quite unlike the relative backwater that is Rabi—Tarawa offers an urban milieu with multiple links to the world beyond Kiribati. It is, moreover, a place with job openings and other entrepreneurial opportunities for Banabans. For the younger members of Banaban migrant families, there is the additional prospect of a scholarship to higher educational institutions, which could, in turn, lead to an early return migration, as most of these institutions are located in Fiji. Where Banaban migrants hold a singular advantage is that they not only arrive already fluent in the local vernacular, but also, owing to their long diasporic existence in Fiji, with a rather better command of spoken English than most of the I-Kiribati.

Especially important, in this connection, is that a sizeable number of Fiji-Banabans possess landholdings on Tarawa deriving from their close kinship ties with other I-Kiribati. The fact that such genealogical anchorings of place and identity provide a basis for Banaban migrants to search out land on Tarawa suffices, in my view, to talk of a 'mobility of return' in this connection. For Fiji-Banabans able to mobilise pre-existing social ties with Tarawa, land usually plays a significant economic role. Land, after all, is a scarce resource on this large, urbanised atoll; accordingly, its monetary value is high. By way of contrast, owning land on ancestral Banaba, an island still scarred from phosphate mining and marginalised within Kiribati, is of secondary importance in today's economic realities. Back on Rabi, land is allocated to resident Banabans for private use and cannot be alienated; it is held de jure as the collective possession of all Banabans, as represented by the Rabi Council of Leaders. Land on Tarawa, to the contrary, can be used in a variety of ways, ranging from residential and business premises for an extended family to a source of added income from leasing and sale (see Namai 1987: 31–32; Paterson and Itibita 2013: 94–95, 97).

The status of land on Tarawa, at once scarce and controversial, makes returning there anything but an easy choice for Fiji-Banabans. Natan, the second-generation Banaban from Rabi quoted above, points to a problem his fellow Rabians sometimes face on this urban atoll. Although his family does not hold land on Tarawa itself, but on one of Kiribati's larger outer islands, he enunciates a widespread Banaban sentiment of ambivalence regarding the legal and ownership status of at least some land in this context:

> Some already came [over] and [wanted to] find their home—I mean their land. Because many people on Rabi own land on Tarawa. And some came back and then died, you know. Because they were destroyed by *te wawi* [sorcery] … Because [the owners from Rabi had] been away quite a long time. And these [local] people they told the land department that: 'No, they have [all] died.' And all of a sudden, they [that is, the Banaban owners from Rabi] came. The right people. But the land was already sold to somebody else. Very interesting. Very interesting. This is how the land on Tarawa is—very upside down. (Interview recorded 30 September 2013)

The charges of sorcery which many Fiji-Banabans level against I-Kiribati point to social tensions, confrontations and fault lines elicited by the claims of returning landowners. In isolated instances, Banaban returnees try to avoid conflicts of this kind. Tera, a third-generation Fiji-Banaban who grew up on Rabi but had emigrated with her (now divorced) husband 10 years earlier to Tarawa, decided not to enforce her land claims. The reason was she feared being targeted by her opponents for sorcery:

> We got the land. But we don't want to go and stay [there]. Because here are so many magicians [laughing]. Witchcraft! … Like so many people from Rabi came over for the land and they died here … [T]hat's why we were afraid. We just leave [them] our land, because we can survive [without it]. That's why we never bothered about the land. If we were not qualified and had come over—[say] we couldn't make a living, find a way to live or [get] a job, then we would seek to get our land back. But since we are here and are qualified, we have a job and can live, that's why we never bothered. We just leave it as it is. (Interview recorded 9 July 2014)

Although this woman has clearly bought time by opting not to fight for her land rights, it hasn't solved the problem. It remains to be seen how her brothers and sisters, or even her own children in the next generation, will fare. For the opponents of the returnees, for those who do not welcome their relatives from Fiji, the unresolved issue of the legality of existing landholdings continues to resonate.

Fiji-Banabans wishing to reclaim land on Tarawa return to an urban atoll where half of Kiribati's entire population now lives. Here they find themselves competing with a steadily growing local population for land that is often insufficiently documented or under-registered. A consequence of this uncertain status has been an upturn in litigation (see Lodge 1987: 76; Namai 1987: 34, 38–39; Paterson and Itibita 2013: 103–104).[8] Return mobility to Tarawa by landowners from Rabi is probably contributing to this development. This is well illustrated by the case of an elderly Fiji-Banaban born on Tarawa in 1945, not long before the Banaban community was resettled on Rabi. This man told me how, some years earlier, he had travelled with his wife from Rabi to Tarawa to clarify the status of land inherited through his father's line. As well as having several parcels certified to his name, at the time of our interview he was still embroiled in no less than four legal actions over separate land issues. He stated the following:

> My father is a Banaban. Half Banaban, half Gilbertese. So I have to come and search for his land. My father's land. That's why I am staying here now for seven years. I take it to the court. Because we came here and my land was taken by fraud. Was just taken. We don't know how they took it. So we have to take it to the court. We are still in court now … [And] I've

---

8   Complicating matters somewhat is the fact that the land register for South Tarawa, which is the most densely populated part of the entire island state, went missing in 1987 in a manner that has never been explained (Paterson and Itibita 2013: 98).

got more cases. Yes. There are about four. Now I am waiting for the High Court. And more, plenty more to come [laughing]. Yes, because my father had a lot of land here. (Interview recorded 25 July 2014)

In this concrete case, the length of the couple's stay on Tarawa derived less from a desire to settle there permanently than from the time-consuming nature of the endless court battles over land. This impression is backed by the fact that the man's grown-up children had opted, without exception, to remain on Rabi. Moreover, according to both parents, their children regularly urged them to return to Fiji, instead of concerning themselves with endless land squabbles.

Other family groups on Rabi organise the return of members to Tarawa. In such cases, the aim is not simply to get land claims certified, but to take possession of the land and put it to good use. Over the last 10 to 15 years, return mobility has led to Fiji-Banabans of the second and especially the third generation settling on Tarawa. This trend is illustrated by the story of a Fiji-Banaban woman in her mid-30s. Gina is a third-generation Rabi-Banaban. Her father was chosen by his extended family in the 1990s to migrate with his wife to Tarawa. The aim of relocation was twofold: to manage the family's landholdings on Tarawa and to remit rents from parcels of land that had been leased out to family members on Rabi. The children, Gina among them, remained on Rabi with relatives, and only after finishing their schooling did they follow their parents. Today Gina lives on Tarawa where she has a good job with a secure future. Asked whether she felt 'at home' there, she stated:

G: Yeah. Like now I can feel that Kiribati is my home …

WK: What about Rabi then?

G: I don't know. Probably [laughing] we can call it home too because that's where we were brought up. Yeah, but like—right now, all I want to do is visit Rabi … like for a short term, something like that … Now I feel that Kiribati is my home. Since we do have a home—our own home—here. We have a house of our own here. (Interview recorded 23 July 2014)

Land ownership, jobs, education—or a combination of all three—have led to a situation where Fiji-Banabans of the third generation acquire island homes on Tarawa. They work, look after their elderly parents (invariably Fiji-Banabans of the second generation), get married (not infrequently to I-Kiribati partners), have a family, help to expand their family networks in Kiribati, and, by return visits to Fiji, maintain contact with relatives there.

Such island homes, beyond the home islands of Banaba and Rabi, could in the long run broaden the concept of homeland, especially for future generations of Banabans.

Turning again? Fiji-Banabans and discourses on climate change in Kiribati

But what do long-term Banaban residents on Tarawa think of return mobility? In fact, a number of Fiji-Banaban migrants to Kiribati view it in a positive light. The motives behind this desire to return are often closely dependent on age and the degree of personal attachment to Rabi. This is well illustrated by the case of 67-year-old Natan. He was adamant that he wanted to leave soon for Rabi Island, where he planned to spend his last years. Already, during 2012 and 2013, he had visited his son on Rabi, spending several months on that island; but he had not stayed, returning to Tarawa and his other children. Asked in September 2013 about his future plans, he told me that it was up to his children and their families to decide where, if anywhere, they wanted to migrate to in future, but for him the matter was clear:

> N: [I] will go back to Rabi. So much for me. I've never changed my mind about this. I'll just stay in my home. I want to be buried next to my father and my mother—on Rabi.
>
> WK: But didn't you ever think of Banaba?
>
> N: Well, no … Because I wasn't brought up there. I was born on Rabi and was brought up on Rabi. (Interview recorded 28 September 2013)

Like many other Banabans, he viewed his kinship ties with Kiribati—in this case, his ancestors on the Kiribati atoll of Tabiteuea—as central to his personal identity. Therefore, in the context of musing about a return to Rabi, he also entertained thoughts about what the future held for his relatives in Kiribati. The background can be found in official discourses about the possible consequences of climate change and sea-level rise for Kiribati. Though long in circulation and nothing new, such discourses have in recent years weighed increasingly heavily on the population of what is, after all, an atoll state:

I am thinking of my Kiribati relatives who could then come to Rabi …
[Some are] on Tabiteuea. Some on Tarawa. Some of them are here [Ambo,
WK], and some on Eita … And I worry about them. If there is climate
change, where are they going to run to? Where will they run? They have
to go [back] to Tabiteuea. [But] Tabiteuea will be just the same. One way
or another, [they] will be affected … Now, there is nothing against them
coming to Rabi. (Interview recorded 28 September 2013)

The government of Kiribati, under President Anote Tong, has for many
years pursued an active policy of adjustment to the impact of climate
change and higher seas. Among the central planks of this policy was,
first, the implementation (over the short and medium term) of adaptive
measures within the framework of the Kiribati Adaptation Program
(KAP), with the primary goal of reducing Kiribati's vulnerability. Despite
it being premature to talk of an acute danger from climate change and sea-
level rise—despite the alarmist reports circulating in the global media and
disseminated by more than a few NGOs—if we take the longer perspective,
existential risk to this atoll state cannot be excluded.[9] The second plank
has been neatly encapsulated by President Tong in the motto: 'Migration
with Dignity'. Thus, he sought to initiate a long-term process of planned
labour migration, designed to prevent uncontrolled migrant flows where
émigrés end up in camps, marginalised and impoverished for decades
to come.

Fiji-Banabans living on Tarawa are, to be sure, aware of such discourses,
countermeasures, developments and scenarios. Yet it is a fact that for many
the hazards of global warming are primarily a problem for tomorrow.
Gina, the Fiji-Banaban lady of the third generation, who now feels
completely at home on Tarawa, saw no immediate threat on the horizon:

Yeah, we have been hearing all about that from other people. Like they
were planning to move out, something like that. But to me it's like—it's
God's plan [laughing] … It is not really threatening us. And people—
when we were in Fiji—they were always saying that before too many years
Kiribati would be under[water], something of that. But so far Kiribati is
still developing, [laughing] you know, building more buildings. (Interview
recorded 23 July 2014)

---

9   In any event, recent studies point out that 'atoll islands are robust rather than fragile systems'
(McLean and Kench 2015: 456). According to these authors, sea-level rise does not necessarily mean
that all atoll islands in the central and western Pacific will be engulfed by the end of the 21st century.
On the other hand, the impact of climate change on Pacific islands and their inhabitants is more
complex and cannot be limited solely to sea-level rise (see Lazrus 2012: 288–289).

As a result, she saw no immediate need to think of emigrating. At the same time, most Banabans living in Kiribati derive comfort from the thought that returning to Rabi or Fiji (or in rare cases, Banaba) will always be there on the table as the safe option, should ever the perils of climate change arrive. Here it may be noted that Fiji-Banabans on Tarawa primarily associate climate change with sea-level rise and the ensuing flooding of low lying atolls. Any risk to their own home islands of Rabi and Banaba—volcanic and raised coral islands, respectively,[10] and therefore significantly higher—is therefore discounted by most Banabans. Ethnic difference from the I-Kiribati, which Banabans often justified by citing the geographic differences separating Banaba and Rabi from the islands of Kiribati, was only confirmed anew by this discourse of the variable effects of climate change. For these Banabans it was clear that they, unlike the I-Kiribati, would always possess a secure place of refuge, should the worst-case scenario eventuate. Here the Fiji-Banabans on Tarawa chiefly had Rabi Island in mind. Tera, the Fiji-Banaban woman of the third generation who had come to Kiribati more than 10 years earlier, said this:

> But when it comes to global warming, to the climate warming up, why then, for us Rabians [or Rabi-Banabans]—we are not too worried, because we have another land in Fiji. That's the main thing, so we never worry about anything. If the time for evacuation ever comes, we just go to our land … That's how it is with us Rabians, we're never bothered because we've got land of our own. By the time the water rises, [when] the government has to do something and says: 'Okay, it's time to leave Kiribati'. well, we know we have another place to go. We don't know about the Gilbertese. (Interview recorded 9 July 2014)

To take another example, according to a second-generation Banaban, who some 10 years earlier had migrated with his family from Rabi to Kiribati and now lived with two of his sisters and their families (also émigrés from Rabi) on family-owned land on Tarawa:

> When I go to bed at night, sometimes I find myself thinking about the sea level. I don't know when my time will come. But when it does, what will happen to my kids? What will they do? So I think we'd better think now

---

10   Rabi Island in Fiji measures all of 68 square kilometres; it is a high volcanic island with the highest peak, *Maungani Banaba*, rising more than 460 metres above the waves. Banaba or Ocean Island with an area of 16 square kilometres is somewhat smaller. It is the only raised coral island found in Kiribati with high ground in the order of 80 metres, making it the highest island in this atoll state. By comparison, all of Kiribati's other atolls and reef islands rise by no more than 2 to 3 metres above the ocean.

about how to protect them … And yet, we are not so worried after all, we have a homeland, you know, and we have mountains! Just like that, eh?! We do have a homeland! That's why we don't worry or really care about the sea level rising here. Because we have our island Rabi, you know. (Interview recorded 5 September 2009)

In the further course of our conversation, this man emphasised that returning to Rabi was always on the table, it could be done any time, and because this was so, it stripped from an uncertain future some of its power to terrify. He also pointed out that returning was far from the only possible option for him as a Banaban living in Kiribati:

The time is coming close. More people talk about it now because the time is not far off. I've no doubt that the government will do something for the people. That's the government's job. It will do something for the people, and I was telling [my wife], 'Rabi is very close for us, but first we'll listen to the government, where they wanna migrate to.' … So like if they [government officials] say 'Australia or New Zealand', I will certainly be among them. Right?! That's gonna be important, because this land [knocks the ground] is our mother's land. She's got land here and we are part of the I-Kiribati too. (Interview recorded 5 September 2009)

Owning land on Tarawa allows Banaban migrants to justify their Kiribati identity. They then build on this by affirming their right as citizens to be included in whatever international migration programs the government may one day put in place. For this head of an extended Banaban family living on Tarawa, there is, therefore, no doubt that the government of Kiribati would bear primary responsibility for the population's fate should catastrophe ever strike. While returning to Rabi Island is certainly uppermost in this man's future imaginings, he is careful, on the other hand, not to rule out the chance of migrating to one or other of the metropolitan states in the region, especially if this was promoted by Kiribati's government or organised by those states.

Not all of Tarawa's Banabans find it easy to come to terms with returning to Rabi Island in Fiji, should it come to that. A middle-aged married woman who had grown up on Rabi Island but had lived for many years on Tarawa with her husband, a pastor of the Kiribati Protestant Church, and the children from their union, explained what she thought about returning to Fiji in the following words:

> As for climate change—yeah, we thought about it [return migration]. But being married cuts two ways [laughing]. So we thought about it and we thought, maybe when we retire we can go back to Fiji. But then I thought, my kids are here [in Kiribati] … If my children are here, they can't go back to Fiji, because they are not Fiji-born. [My husband] is Fiji-born, I am Fiji-born and our eldest son is Fiji-born. So we can go back with one of them. But not with the other two and their children … It is very hard for me to imagine that I should go back to Fiji because of sea-level rise, when my kids are here. So I might as well let them migrate, do whatever they want. I'll be the last one to leave the ship [laughing]. (Interview recorded 8 October 2013)

The possibility of returning to Fiji (Rabi Island is not explicitly mentioned here) occupies an important place in this woman's speculations about what to do in the future, should climate change and sea-level rise ever seriously imperil her present country of residence, Kiribati. Her view shows that return is a problematic issue, considering the family's differences in citizenship. She will therefore make her final decision contingent on the future abode of her children and grandchildren. In this connection, she hints that migration by family members to another country is likely, indeed probable, over the medium to long term. But only when she knows her own family would be safe, so her thinking goes, could she decide where to go herself.

These Banaban discourses envisioning a future of international return migration from Tarawa to Rabi, or, more generally, to Fiji, afford insights into variable motives and multiple scenarios. Two basic positions are evident in this connection. On the one hand, Rabi is affirmed as a place of belonging, as home island, as somewhere to retire to and a peaceful haven in old age. On the other hand, within the context of discourses on the future consequences of climate change and sea-level rise, Banaban migrants on Tarawa see Rabi Island or Fiji as a potential place of refuge for themselves and their I-Kiribati relatives. Even so, they do not exclude the option of international migration to the metropolitan states of the region.

Conclusion

From a historical perspective, return mobility for the resettled Banabans is a multidirectional phenomenon with multiple destinations. When community leadership was locked in an anticolonial struggle for financial compensation, rehabilitation of all areas affected by mining, and national sovereignty, return to Banaba loomed large. The first generation was able to mobilise the then still-young second generation for their political aims of collective return and organised occupation of their ancestral home. Since that time, the community's claim to Banaba is primarily upheld by the routines of return of employees of the Rabi Council of Leaders in Fiji, while, at the same time, Kiribati exercises state control through its own on-site representatives.

Banaba continues to function for the Banaban diaspora as an important point of historical and political reference for ethnic identification and cultural belonging. That said, the home island is *not* a primary destination for return migration by the next generations. True, the pioneer generation, with its politics of transcolonial linkage between Rabi and Banaba, was determined to anchor the latter in the community's collective memory; yet, in achieving this goal, they inadvertently paved the way for a diversification of return by the second and third generations. Without actually questioning the congruence between home island and homeland, the second and third generations are, in fact, able to tap into the enlarged spectrum of opportunities resulting from the transnational belonging to Fiji *and* Kiribati. Reversal and ramification are important principles in this process.

Recent migration by Fiji-Banabans to Kiribati is an exemplary case of what I mean by ramification of return. Thus the returnees from Fiji, when choosing where to build their island home, usually look now beyond the home island of Banaba to the capital atoll of Tarawa. This is chiefly prompted by a desire for improved access to social, cultural and economic resources in a transparent urban environment. Having island homes on Tarawa may one day serve to redefine what homeland means to future generations of Banabans born in Kiribati. Being based there may, in individual cases, even serve as a springboard for further migration, this time to the ambient metropolitan states of the Pacific region. At present, though, a lot of these Banaban island homes point toward a reversal of return mobility. Hence, for the majority of second- and third-generation Fiji-Banabans living on Tarawa, Rabi Island remains the primary home island and preferred place of return. Whether it takes the form of brief visits, longer stays, concrete plans to return or an imagined safe haven, a place of refuge, in the event of future fallout from climate change and sea-level rise, return to Rabi Island resonates strongly with Banabans dwelling on Tarawa. By contrast, Banaba has slipped increasingly into the background, albeit without losing its elemental function as ancestral homeland.

The historical sequence of displacement, collective resettlement, translocal linkages, international migration and transnational relations has given rise to a specific genealogy of return. The strategic duality of belonging, which the first generation of resettled Banabans bequeathed to the next generations, constitutes a fundamental ordering principle. At the same time, it is the motor driving diversification of return. Of especial note is that the continued reticulation of home islands fosters (reverse) transnationalism, which lets the second and third generations extend belonging to a larger field of island homes. Thus the analysis of Banaban return mobility indicates the seminal importance of seeing homelands and movements from a historical perspective, the better to locate (and understand) diversification of return in a shifting terrain of colonial and postcolonial structures.

Acknowledgements

I am particularly indebted to the members of Banaban community on Tarawa in Kiribati who shared with me their stories, experiences and views in connection with return mobility. My special thanks to Steffen Herrmann for preparing the map. For their reading of and valuable suggestions to an earlier version of my paper I wish to thank Leslie Butt, Jenny Munro, Helen Lee and Jack Taylor. To Elfriede Hermann my particular thanks for her insightful critiques and support. Responsibility for the views in this article is, of course, mine alone.

References

'Banabans seek better phosphate deal' 1965, *Pacific Islands Monthly*, November, p. 17.

'Banabans set sail for their island home' 1975, *The Fiji Times*, March 10.

Binder, P 1977, *Treasure islands: the trials of the Ocean Islanders*, Blond and Briggs, London.

Brettell, CB 2015, 'Theorizing migration in anthropology', in CB Brettell & J Hollifield (eds), *Migration theory: talking across disciplines*, 3rd edition, Routledge, New York and London, pp. 148–197.

Cassarino, J-P 2004, 'Theorising return migration: the conceptual approach to return migrants revisited', *International Journal on Multicultural Societies*, vol. 6, no. 2, pp. 253–279.

Cernea, MM & McDowell, C (eds) 2000, *Risks and reconstruction: experiences of resettlers and refugees*, The World Bank, Washington DC doi.org/10.1596/0-8213-4444-7

Conway, D & Potter, RB 2009a, 'Return of the next generations: transnational migration and development in the 21st century', in D Conway & RB Potter (eds), *Return migration of the next generations: 21st century transnational mobility*, Ashgate, Farnham, England and Burlington, VT, pp. 1–18.

Conway, D & Potter, RB 2009b, 'Return of the next generations: transnational mobilities, family demographics and experiences, multi-local spaces', in D Conway & RB Potter (eds), *Return migration of the next generations: 21st century transnational mobility*, Ashgate, Farnham, England and Burlington, VT, pp. 223–242.

Dagmar, H 1989, 'Banabans in Fiji: ethnicity, change, and development', in M Howard (ed.), *Ethnicity and nation-building in the Pacific*, The United Nations University, Tokyo, pp. 198–217.

Ellis, AF 1935, *Ocean Island and Nauru: their story*, Angus and Robertson Ltd, Sydney.

Ellis, AF 1946, *Mid-Pacific outposts*, Brown and Stewart Ltd, Auckland.

Foreign and Commonwealth Office 1968, *The Ocean Island Phosphates Discussions, October 1968*, Foreign and Commonwealth Office, London.

Glick Schiller, N & Salazar, NB 2013, 'Regimes of mobility across the globe', *Journal of Ethnic and Migration Studies*, vol. 39, no. 2, pp. 183–200. doi.org/10.1080/1369183X.2013.723253

Hermann, E 2003, 'Manifold identifications within differentiations: shapings of self among the relocated Banabans of Fiji', *Focaal*, vol. 42, pp. 77–88.

Hermann, E 2004, 'Emotions, agency and the dis/placed self of the Banabans in Fiji', in T van Meijl & J Miedema (eds), *Shifting images of identity in the Pacific*, KITLV Press, Leiden, pp. 191–217.

Hermann, E 2006, 'Korrelationen von Verschiedensein und Gleichsein als Ko-Differenz: Selbst und Ethnie bei den Banabans in Fiji', University of Göttingen: Habilitation Thesis.

Hermann, E & Kokoria, TT 2005, 'Feelings of connectedness - the Banabans and their home islands', in J Shennan & MC Tekenimatang (eds), *One and a half Pacific Islands: stories the Banaban people tell of themselves*, Victoria University Press, Wellington, pp. 128–129.

Kempf, W 2004, 'The drama of death as narrative of survival: dance theatre, travelling and thirdspace among the Banabans of Fiji', in T van Meijl & J Miedema (eds), *Shifting images of identity in the Pacific*, KITLV Press, Leiden, pp. 159–189.

Kempf, W 2011, *Translocal entwinements: towards a history of Rabi as a plantation island in colonial Fiji*. GOEDOC, Dokumenten- und Publikationsserver der Georg-August-Universität.

Kempf, W 2012, 'A promised land in the diaspora: Christian religion, social memory, and identity among Banabans in Fiji', *Pacific Studies*, vol. 35, no. 1/2, pp. 90–118.

Kempf, W & Hermann, E 2005, 'Reconfigurations of place and ethnicity: positionings, performances and politics of relocated Banabans in Fiji', *Oceania*, vol. 75, no. 4, pp. 368–386. doi.org/10.1002/j.1834-4461.2005.tb02897.x

King, R & Christou, A 2014, 'Of counter-diaspora and reverse transnationalism: return mobilities to and from the ancestral homeland', in R King, A Christou & P Levitt (eds), *Links to the diasporic homeland: second generation and ancestral 'return' mobilities*, Routledge, London and New York, pp. 1–16.

Lazrus, H 2012, 'Sea change: island communities and climate change', *Annual Review of Anthropology*, vol. 41, pp. 285–301. doi.org/10.1146/annurev-anthro-092611-145730

Lee, H 2003, *Tongans overseas: between two shores*, University of Hawai'i Press, Honolulu.

Lee, H 2009, 'The ambivalence of return: second-generation Tongan returnees', in D Conway & RB Potter (eds), *Return migration of the next generations: 21st century transnational mobility*, Ashgate, Farnham, England, Burlington, VT, pp. 41–58.

Lodge, M 1987, 'Land law and procedure', in R Crocombe (ed.), *Land tenure in the atolls: Cook Islands, Kiribati, Marshall Islands, Tokelau, Tuvalu*, University of the South Pacific, Suva, pp. 73–107.

Macdonald, BK 1982, *Cinderellas of the empire: towards a history of Kiribati and Tuvalu*, Australian National University Press, Canberra.

Maude, HE 1946, *Memorandum on the future of the Banaban population of Ocean Island: with special relation to their lands and funds*, Western Pacific High Commission, Suva.

McLean, R & Kench, P 2015, 'Destruction or persistence of coral atoll islands in the face of 20th and 21st century sea-level rise?', *WIREs Climate Change*, vol. 6, September/October, pp. 445–463. doi.org/10.1002/wcc.350

Namai, B 1987, 'The evolution of Kiribati tenures', in R Crocombe (ed.), *Land tenure in the atolls: Cook Islands, Kiribati, Marshall Islands, Tokelau, Tuvalu*, University of the South Pacific, Suva, pp. 30–39.

National Archives of Fiji (NAF) High Court of Justice 1968, Documents 46/1968. *Memorandum on Petition of the Banaban People Presented to the United Nations Committee of Twenty-Four* (5 June 1968).

'Ocean Island welcomes 60 from Fiji: Rabi settler group stays' 1975, *The Fiji Times*, March 24.

Oliver-Smith, A 2009a, 'Introduction. Development-forced displacement and resettlement: a global human rights crisis', in A Oliver-Smith (ed.), *Development and dispossession: the crisis of forced displacement and resettlement*, School for Advanced Research Press, Santa Fe, pp. 3–23.

Oliver-Smith, A 2009b, 'Climate change and population displacement: disasters and diasporas in the twenty-first century', in S Crate & M Nuttall (eds), *Anthropology and climate change: from encounters to actions*, Left Coast Press, Walnut Creek, pp. 116–136.

Paterson, D & Itibita, B 2013, 'Kiribati', in D Paterson & S Farran (eds), *South Pacific land systems*, USP Press, Suva, pp. 93–105.

'Petrol bombs on Banaba' 1979, *Pacific Islands Monthly*, April, p. 22.

Posnett, RN 1977, 'Ocean Island and the Banabans: a report to the Minister of State for Foreign and Commonwealth Affairs', London, Manuscript.

Potter, RB, Conway, D & Phillips, J (eds) 2005, *The experience of return migration: Caribbean perspectives*, Ashgate, London.

Reynolds, T 2014, 'Caribbean second-generation return migration: transnational family relationships with "left-behind" kin in Britain', in R King, A Christou & P Levitt (eds), *Links to the diasporic homeland: second generation and ancestral 'return' mobilities*, Routledge, London and New York, pp. 85–101.

Secretariat of the Pacific Community 2007, 'Kiribati 2005 Census. Volume 2: Analytical Report', Statistics and Demography Programme and Kiribati Statistics Office, Noumea, New Caledonia.

Silverman, MG 1971, *Disconcerting issue: meaning and struggle in a resettled Pacific community*, The University of Chicago Press, Chicago and London.

Teaiwa, KM 2014, *Consuming Ocean Island: stories of people and phosphate from Banaba*, Indiana University Press, Bloomington and Indianapolis.

Teaiwa, TK 1997, 'Rabi and Kioa: peripheral minority communities in Fiji', in BV Lal & TR Vakatora (eds), *Fiji in transition*, Research Papers of the Fiji Constitution Review Commission, vol. 1, The University of the South Pacific, Suva, pp. 130–152.

Williams, M & MacDonald, B 1985, *The Phosphateers: a history of the British Phosphate Commissioners and the Christmas Island Phosphate Commission*, Melbourne University Press, Carlton.

Wimmer, A & Glick Schiller, N 2002, 'Methodological nationalism and beyond: nation-state building, migration and the social sciences', *Global Networks*, vol. 2, no. 4, pp. 301–334. doi.org/10.1111/1471-0374.00043

3

The Rotuman experience with reverse migration

Alan Howard and Jan Rensel

Abstract

This paper examines responses to a questionnaire concerning migration experiences and attitudes administered to 90 individuals on the island of Rotuma in 2012 by high school students under our supervision. The results are divided into four sections: (1) perceptions of Rotuma; (2) the migration experience abroad; (3) getting resettled following return; and (4) readaptation to life on the island. The predominant reported reason for returning to Rotuma was to look after parents, grandparents or other close kin, followed by other family considerations. Responses concerning resettlement reflected highly positive images of the island and its culture, and satisfaction with the return experience. We conclude that networks of kinship ties that transcend the island's boundaries facilitate both movement away and return. This has resulted in a situation in which the frequently used definition of migration and reverse migration—that migrants go with the intent to remain—is problematic for many, if not most, of the Rotumans who travel or return from abroad. Most appear to keep their options open, with ties to kin providing opportunities for visiting and resettlement in multiple venues.

Introduction

This paper is the product of over 50 years of research concerning the flow of population from and to the island of Rotuma, which has been politically part of the Republic of Fiji since cession to Great Britain in 1881. In 1960, during Alan's first period of ethnographic fieldwork on Rotuma, he conducted a census of the island that included residential histories of all adults, and in 1989 Jan organised a similar census during her dissertation research.[1] The latest of our 12 visits to the island since 1987, in 2012, provided us with an opportunity to supervise students at Rotuma High School interviewing return migrants using a questionnaire of our design. Along with historical documentation, these data provide a long-term perspective on the patterns of mobility that have characterised the Rotuman population over the years.

The overall picture that emerges from our research both on the island and among Rotumans abroad is of a people who manifest exceptionally high rates of out-migration; at present approximately 85 per cent of Rotumans and part-Rotumans live abroad, mostly in Fiji, but also scattered around Pacific Rim countries and in Europe. They have been extraordinarily successful educationally and occupationally, with little evidence of the social problems that have afflicted many other Pacific populations. This has led to a very positive cultural identity that is reinforced by an idealised image of Rotuma as a kind of paradise, which encourages both short- and long-term visits to the home island. Both our ethnographic observations and our latest survey data make it clear that return visits to the island, whether for a few weeks or long-term, rarely disappoint, in contrast to other studies we know of among Pacific populations.

---

1   In 1960, two Rotuman assistants (Amai Sakimi and Rejieli Mejieli) interviewed adults from each household on the island, under Alan's supervision. In 1989, after a full-day training workshop, 14 teachers from Rotuma's primary and secondary schools interviewed households in assigned areas. Unfortunately, the individuals enlisted to survey the district of Pepjei and part of the district of Noa'tau were unable to complete their assignments. However, by December 1989, the remaining teachers had completed surveys of 85 per cent (415) of Rotuma's households.

Theoretical perspectives on reverse migration

As George Gmelch noted in his review of return migration literature in 1980, most of the literature up to that time dealt with persons who originally migrated to urban-industrialised countries or regions, notably in northern Europe and north-eastern North America. The typologies that resulted from those studies were heavily weighted toward economic considerations. The neoclassical economics approach, for example, viewed return migration as the result of miscalculating the costs of migration while not reaping the benefits of higher earnings; in other words, returning to one's homeland was seen primarily as a failed migration experience in economic terms. The counterpoint to this approach was the New Economics of Labour Migration (NELM) perspective, which viewed return migration as the successful culmination of calculated economic goals (Cassarino 2004: 255).

In reaction to these economic models, the structural approach to return migration contends that returning to one's homeland is a social as well as a personal issue, although financial and economic factors have been heavily, though not exclusively, privileged in studies relying on this perspective (Cerase 1974). The structuralist approach has also been criticised for its assumption that little information or material exchange takes place between migrants and their home communities (Murphy 2002), an assertion particularly inappropriate for most Pacific Islands populations and certainly for the Rotuman case. More appropriate for Pacific populations are the transnational and social network approaches to return migration, both of which assume that migrants maintain strong linkages with their homelands while abroad. While most studies from these perspectives also tend to emphasise the mobilisation of resources, social network theory makes room for social capital as a valued resource. Even though some studies of return migration have allowed for a range of considerations affecting the phenomenon, our reading of the literature suggests a strong rationalistic bias—of calculating actors primarily interested in economic advantage—that is not as appropriate for the Pacific region as it may be elsewhere. Helen Lee and her associates deserve much credit for providing a Pacific perspective to the issues involved (Lee and Francis 2009). This paper attempts to build on their insights with the goal of formulating some propositions that may help to account for the nature of reverse population flows from diasporic destinations to Pacific Island homelands.

A historical overview of the Rotuman diaspora

Like many other Pacific Islanders, Rotumans began emigrating from their home island as soon as the opportunity presented itself. Voyaging was an integral part of their cultural tradition prior to European intrusion, but European vessels provided a wider range of opportunities to visit, and settle, in distant lands. Commenting in 1867 on the extent of emigration, Reverend William Fletcher, the first European Methodist missionary to be stationed on Rotuma, wrote that upwards of 700 young men were known to have left the island in recent memory (Fletcher 1870).

Labour recruiters came to Rotuma from all over the Pacific, and Rotumans were employed in such places as the Sandwich Islands (now Hawai'i) and Samoa, but in 1881, when Rotuma was ceded to Great Britain, the island was closed as a port of entry and labour recruiters ceased to call there. All traffic between Rotuma and the outside world was diverted through the Colony of Fiji, from which Rotuma was governed. However, during this early period the basic pattern was for emigrants to return to Rotuma after a few years, and therefore the flow of population back to the island nearly balanced the outward flow.

While most of the men who left the island—either as sailors or as workers abroad (for example, pearl diving in the Torres Strait)—returned home after some time away, a significant number did not. They left the ships in Australia, New Zealand, England or elsewhere and took employment, married local women and settled into a new life. Rotuma's isolation made it difficult for emigrants to keep in contact with their home island, and most of them disappeared as far as their homebound relatives were concerned. For whatever reasons—limited literacy curtailing letter writing; transportation into the Pacific being too complicated, sporadic and unpredictable; Rotumans being extraordinarily adaptive to and successful in new environments; or a combination of such factors—communication was extremely limited at best.

As members of the Fiji polity since cession, Rotumans have been able to move freely about the archipelago and have taken advantage of the possibilities this has offered. The flow of this migration path accelerated markedly during the last half of the 20th century as young Rotumans moved to Fiji's urban centres to pursue education and employment opportunities. Also stimulating out-migration was a rapid increase in the population of Rotumans resulting from a dramatic decrease in the death rate following the Second World War while the birth rate remained high, which strained the island's carrying capacity. Thus, whereas the 1956 Fiji census found 68 per cent of Rotumans in the country living on their home island, by 2007 the figure had dropped to 19 per cent. The overall number of Rotumans in Fiji as a whole (including Rotuma) increased during this time span from 4,422 to 10,137.

Furthermore, Fiji has been a way station for many Rotumans who have emigrated elsewhere, including Australia and New Zealand, where substantial identifiable communities have developed, often around Rotuman-oriented churches. Rotuman communities of lesser size and varying cohesion have developed elsewhere, including Hawai'i, the San Francisco Bay Area, Vancouver in British Columbia and Fort McMurray in Alberta, Canada. In addition, a substantial number of Rotumans emigrated to England, where they are widely scattered, making organisation impractical. A few families with Rotuman members settled in other places, including Sweden and Norway, for example. While no figures are available for Rotumans outside of Fiji, we estimate their numbers to be around 2,000–3,000.

Improved transportation and telephone services following the Second World War helped to relieve Rotuma's isolation, resulting in a substantial increase in the volume of visits to and from the home island and telephone contact with kin in far-flung lands. However, such contact remained episodic until the last decades of the 20th century, when an airstrip was built on the island and a modern telephone system installed. And although it continues to be erratic, shipping services to the island from Fiji have improved from colonial times when government vessels made only four visits a year.

As the Rotuman population grew in Fiji and transportation between Rotuma and Fiji significantly improved, the flow of population between Rotuma and Fiji took on the quality of a two-way traffic, with people moving back and forth with regularity. The flow to Fiji from Rotuma was characterised by short-term visits for special events such as weddings, funerals and births; for specialised medical treatment; for workshops or training programs; to participate in sporting events; to visit relatives; or just for fun. Such sojourns have become increasingly routine, as shown in Figure 1.

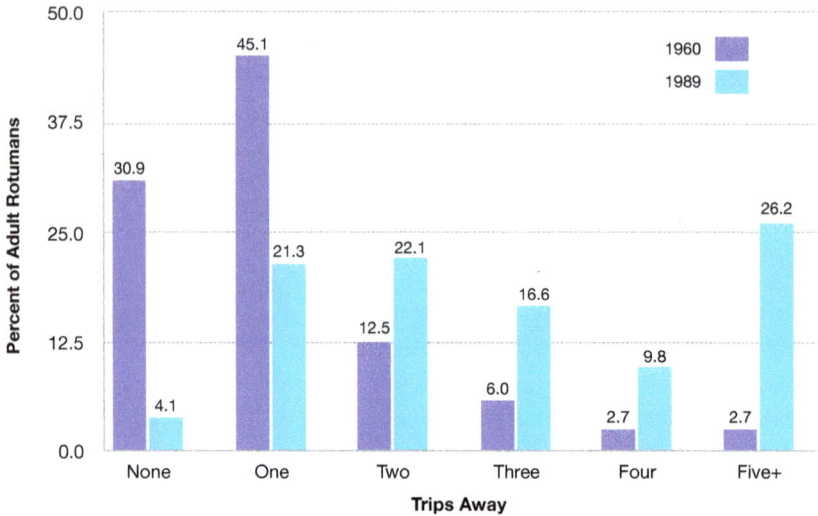

Figure 1: Per cent of Rotumans by trips away, 1960 and 1989

Source: 1960 survey conducted by A. Howard; 1989 survey conducted by A. Howard and J. Rensel.

According to Alan's initial survey in 1960, 76 per cent of the adults surveyed had been off-island only once or not at all, but in 1989 this was true of only 25.4 per cent. And while only 11.4 per cent of the 1960 group reported three or more trips abroad, 52.6 per cent of the 1989 sample had made at least three trips. Fifty-seven individuals in the 1989 group reported making 10 or more trips, and a few reported as many as 40. Indeed, we were aware of a number of people who travel back and forth several times a year.

In the years that we have made return visits to Rotuma, beginning in 1987 (12 times in all), we have seen manifestations of this circulating population in the form of newly constructed houses, while others have been abandoned; men returning to the island to take chiefly titles, then leaving again after a period of time; and skilled workers returning for the duration of development projects. Teachers and health personnel come and go, as do other government workers whose assignments may shift between Rotuma and other parts of Fiji. In many cases it would be difficult to define people who were born on Rotuma and left for extended periods of time, then came back, as 'return migrants',[2] because the contingencies that govern their movements are often unpredictable—a condition that is prevalent in many Pacific societies characterised by circular migration, or as we would prefer to phrase it, by the fluid movement of population streams among multiple locations.

Some Rotumans of our acquaintance maintain what amounts to dual residence in both Fiji and Rotuma. They travel back and forth quite frequently, often with their families, sometimes alone. They are well-off financially and enjoy prestigious positions in Fiji, but they travel back to the island in order to spend time with relatives, participate in policy decisions, or simply to enjoy activities such as fishing and gardening that have special appeal for them. In most instances they own homes in Fiji and stay in houses jointly owned by relatives on Rotuma.

Attachment to the physical beauty and culture of the island, with its ethos of sharing and caring, are lures for people who spent their childhood on the island and maintain idealistic, nostalgic memories of their time there. Indeed, in contrast to some other Pacific societies, for example, Samoa (Gerber 1975) and Tonga (Morton 1996), childhood in Rotuma is a particularly benign period (see Howard 1970). This helps account for the strong impulse of diasporic Rotumans to return for holidays, particularly during the Christmas period, which extends for six weeks or so and is a time for picnics, beach parties, feasting, dancing and general socialising. Emigrants from a particular village or district may organise reunions during this period, sometimes in conjunction with donations of valued items such as generators, transport vehicles, or building materials for common purposes.

Households and social networks

Among the more significant changes associated with the expansion of the Rotuman population abroad have been modifications to household composition and the nature of social networks. These changes need to be understood in light of the number of Rotumans who now reside abroad

---

2 · Gmelch (1980: 136) defined return migration as 'the movement of emigrants back to their homeland to resettle'. This makes the definition dependent on motivation, which is difficult, if not impossible to determine with authority. In our experience, Pacific Islanders are especially responsive to changes within generally extensive social networks that may affect their proclivities toward migratory moves, so that 'settlement' may in most cases be highly provisional.

and a significant drop in population on the island of Rotuma. Whereas the 1966 census showed a total of 3,235 persons on Rotuma, by the 2007 census the figure had dropped to 2,002 and has since dropped below 2,000.[3] Correspondingly, average household size declined from a high of 7.4 in 1956 to 5.8 in 1986. The change is reflected in our own survey data. In 1960 Alan recorded 417 households on Rotuma with a total of 2,892 persons, or 6.9 persons per household, whereas the survey Jan organised in 1989 revealed an average of 5.3 persons per household. This drop in average household size can be accounted for mainly by a dramatic increase in small households, those with three or fewer persons, and to a lesser extent by a decrease in large households, those with seven or more persons. In part, this reflects the loss of individuals from existing households through out-migration.

But that is not the whole story. There has been a substantial increase in the total number of households as well, from 417 in 1960 to 493 in 1996. To some extent, the increase in small households represents return migration by individuals who have opted to establish their own households rather than join existing ones. It also reflects investments in maintaining an active link to the island by Rotumans abroad. By building a home and having it occupied by close kin, out-migrants ensure that they and/or their immediate family will have a place to return to in Rotuma. Where whole families have migrated, it may be especially important to leave at least one person behind to ensure continuance of rights in *kainaga* (kin group) land. A number of houses on Rotuma are in fact occupied on a caretaking basis for relatives who have sent remittances to have houses built and improved. In other words, the occupants of many small households are in the position of protecting the resettlement rights of their close kin abroad.

A comparison of findings from the 1989 survey with that from 1960 gives additional insights into changes in household structure. The major change was a substantial increase in households composed of single persons or married couples (27 in 1989 compared to only six in 1960). This difference, and a smaller proportion of 'expanded' households, accounts for most of the variation between the two surveys. Considering the fact that single individuals are not viable production units for subsistence

---

3   Since 1986, Fiji censuses have not distinguished Rotumans by ethnicity, placing them in the category of 'other', so the 1996 and 2007 figures for the island of Rotuma include Fijian and Indo-Fijians who are employed there, as well as non-Rotumans married to Rotumans.

purposes, the data on household structure would appear to support the interpretation offered above—that an increased number of households are occupied by caretakers for kin abroad.[4]

The 1989 survey included three questions concerning household membership: (1) Who are members of this household and are currently here? (2) Who are members of this household and are currently away? and (3) Is there anyone staying here now who is not a member of this household? The first question generated a list of 2,199 individuals, the second question 1,265, and the third question 20 individuals. Of the household members away, 208 were staying in other households on the island, but 1,057 (or nearly one-third of those people considered to be household members) were away from the island.[5] Nearly 70 per cent of the households surveyed listed at least one absentee household member; most of those were close relatives, such as children (59 per cent) or siblings (19 per cent) of the household head and his/her spouse. Many of these individuals provided periodic or regular support for their households through remittances and gifts of household goods, building materials and other costly items. We asked when absent household members departed and we were able to obtain approximate dates for 874 of the 1,057 leavers. Of these, 36 (4.1 per cent) had been away for 30 or more years, 130 (14.9 per cent) for 20–30 years, 217 for 10–20 years (24.8 per cent), 351 for 1–10 years (40.2 per cent), and 140 (16 per cent) for less than one year. Given the accelerating rate of out-migration during this period, it appears that the length of time people had been away did not have a significant effect on their membership in a household.

The overall impact of this extension of household members beyond the island's perimeter has been to shift the centre of gravity of social networks toward family members abroad and away from local sources such as neighbours, village-mates and more distant kin on the island. In the past, people on the island were much more dependent on one another for

---

4   The question can be raised as to whether smaller household size is at least in part the product of a growing preference for nuclear family households resulting from experience abroad. We don't think that's the case. Rather, we think it is mostly the result of increased reliance on support from abroad, mostly in the form of remittances, which reduces reliance on household labour resources, making it more a matter of practicalities than ideology.

5   The vast majority of these were listed as living in Fiji (861), with Australia (52), New Zealand (22), other Pacific Islands (18), the United States (13), Europe (10) and Canada (7) accounting for most of the rest. Ten individuals were listed as sailing, and nine others as serving in the army in the Middle East at the time.

labour in such projects as building houses,[6] for sharing limited resources and for other kinds of economic support when needed. Now, for many households, the main source of economic security comes in the form of remittances and material goods gifted by kin abroad.

According to the 1989 study, just under half (49 per cent) of Rotuman households reported receiving remittances; the number of individuals listed as contributing financial resources to a given household ranged from none to seven. Reported amounts ranged from F$10 to F$4,000 at a time, with a median amount of F$100. Cash was sent primarily for general support, that is, to be spent on food and other household needs. Other remittances came as monetary gifts for special occasions—Mother's Day or Father's Day, birthdays, Christmas, funerals—or periodic needs such as school fees. Larger amounts were sent (often in response to a request) for church fund-raisers or for house construction or improvement projects. Dependence on remittances and tangible resources has no doubt increased in subsequent years.

This increased reliance on family members abroad has resulted in a diminishing of the formerly strong ethos of sharing and caring that pervaded the island in the past and a greater emphasis on payment for labour and the commercialisation of exchange of food and other products (see Rensel 1994). We do not mean to imply that sharing and caring is disappearing from the local scene—people still are likely to be comparatively generous and helpful when their compatriots are in need, or when they wish to affirm relationships with other island residents— but less resource dependence on one another has freed those relationships of the necessity that interdependence promotes.

Rotumans abroad are expected to 'keep their relationships warm' *(mahmahan)* with those on the island if they want to assure their rights to land on Rotuma, which is a major concern for many, if not most, Rotumans away. Land rights on Rotuma are distributed bilineally, with multiple parties having rights in ancestral lands. Stewardship of land in which multiple parties have rights is left in the hands of someone on the island who is designated as *pure* (overseer); it is he, or she, who decides who can rightfully have access to the land under his or her control.

---

6   See Rensel (1997) for an analysis of the social implications of the change from thatched houses, which were built with freely available materials by exchange labour, to houses that are made mostly of imported materials and paid labour.

Out-migrants who have maintained an active relationship with relatives who oversee family lands are much more likely to gain access to land for building a house and/or for planting crops. Out-migrants who fail to maintain active relationships (through visits, remittances, gifts etc.) are more likely to find their claims disputed.

On the other side of the equation, material goods flowing from Rotumans on the island to those in Fiji have also increased in volume over the intervening years. In large measure this is the result of the increased size of the Rotuman community in Fiji, which continues to value products from the island. These items include Rotuman handicrafts, especially fine white mats (vital for presentation on ceremonial occasions such as weddings and funerals); livestock such as pigs and goats; island produce such as taro, yams, coconuts and oranges; and prepared Rotuman delicacies, frequently sent by plane with a passenger. Any of these items may be sent to relatives for special occasions, to accompany a visiting family member or just as *te fakhanisi* (a gift), helping to express and maintain ties. Improvements in transportation between Rotuma and Fiji have facilitated the flow in both directions.

Although the circulation of resources throughout family networks is undoubtedly of major importance, it would be a mistake to overemphasise the role that it plays in reverse migration. Family networks are valued by Rotumans for much more than the material advantages they offer. We would argue that they are also valued in and of themselves as a source of identity and a sense of self-worth. One reason access to land is so important to Rotumans, as it is to most other Pacific Islanders, is because association with particular parcels of land is central to identity, and land rights are deeply embedded in the social networks of descendants from ancestors who held rights in those parcels. Likewise, ancestral figures play a major role in people's sense of self-worth, and being embedded in the family network of common descendants solidifies one's association with desirable ascendants. Indeed, we know of many instances in which individuals have sacrificed materially in order to maintain, strengthen or expand social ties, particularly within extended families, as our data on return migration will illustrate.

A survey of return migrants

In August 2012, we were honoured guests at a Founder's Day celebration at Rotuma High School.[7] We were hosted by the principal, Perry Gabriel, and his wife, Siteri, with whom we stayed for two weeks. Principal Gabriel asked us to hold workshops for both teachers and students regarding how to conduct research, and we were more than glad to oblige. The main reason for the request was that doing a research project is now a graduation requirement, but neither the faculty nor the students have had much experience in this regard.

After we discussed potential research topics with Principal Perry and informed him of our special interest in return migrants, he suggested that we work with the advanced students in Forms 3, 4, 5 and 6 on the topic.[8] We had already constructed a questionnaire for interviewing returnees, and we adapted it for survey purposes. We held a pre-interview workshop with the students, going over the questionnaire in detail to explain its purpose and to answer any questions they might have. They were instructed to select an interviewee who had been away from the island for several years before returning. Several teachers volunteered to be interviewed if a student could not find someone suitable. The students ended up turning in a total of 90 usable protocols.

We must emphasise that this was an availability sample only, for which we do not claim statistical validity. The fact of the matter is that a significant portion of the adults on the island can be considered returnees. Almost all of the teachers, only a few of whom were interviewed, had been away for a number of years for tertiary education. Likewise, virtually all other government employees—medical personnel, agricultural officers, technicians, etc.—had spent years abroad. Most of these personnel had been posted to Rotuma, some by choice, some not. In addition, as our earlier survey data indicate, a good many other adults had spent

---

7   For information about the 2012 event (in honour of Wilson Inia, the school's founder), see the Rotuma High School section of the Rotuma website: www.rotuma.net/rhs/.

8   Each form at the high school was divided into an advanced group and a normal group. We had the normal group do a separate project on household economies. There were 105 students in the advanced group, of whom 94 turned in a protocol. One of these contained too little information to be useful, and in three instances two students interviewed the same returnee, leaving 90 usable protocols.

significant time abroad. However, we do think the results of the survey by the high school students provide a valuable insight into many, if not most, returnees' experiences.

Of the 90 usable protocols, 60 were from male interviewees, 30 from females. Ages ranged from 19 to 83, with the majority (55.6 per cent) in the 30–49 bracket, 28.9 per cent in the 50–69 bracket, and 20 per cent in the 60 or over bracket. Only three interviewees were under the age of 30. Responses came from all seven districts on the island, with Itu'ti'u, the largest district, contributing 36.7 per cent; Malhaha and Juju 12.2 per cent each; Noa'tau 11.1 per cent; Oinafa 10 per cent; and the two smallest districts, Pepjei and Itu'muta, contributing 6.7 per cent and 5.6 per cent respectively (see Tables 1 and 2 and Figure 2).[9]

Table 1: Age and gender of interviewees

	10–19	20–29	30–39	40–49	50–58	60+	Total
Males	1	3	11	20	15	10	60
Females	0	0	11	8	3	8	30
Total	1	3	22	28	18	18	90

Table 2: Location of interviewees by district

Itu'ti'u	Malhaha	Juju	Noa'tau	Oinafa	Pepjei	Itu'muta
33	11	11	10	9	6	5

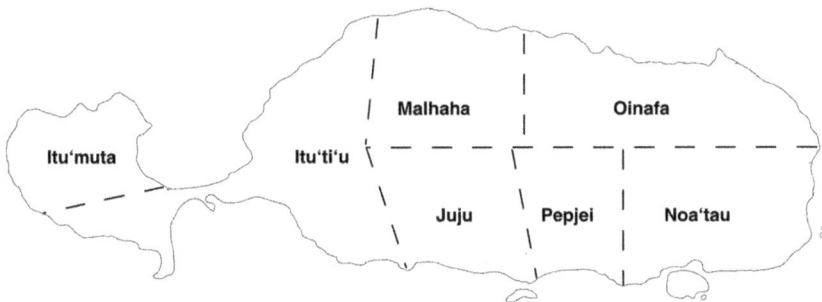

Figure 2: Districts of Rotuma
Source: Drawing by A. Howard.

---

9   All tables reflect authors' summaries of research results.

Results

The results of the survey reported below are divided into four sections: (1) perceptions of Rotuma; (2) the migration experience abroad; (3) getting resettled following return; and (4) readaptation to life on the island.

Perceptions of Rotuma

Perceptions of Rotuma are important for several reasons—as a symbolic focus for cultural identity among diasporic Rotumans, as a stimulus for visits to the island and as an inducement to returning to the island to live after spending years abroad. Generally speaking, the image of Rotuma bandied about by diasporic Rotumans is idealised to a considerable degree. Rapturous postings on social media are common, with the term 'paradise' used frequently. A posting on the Rotuma Website Forum by Henry Enasio in 2004, then living in Australia, poetically illustrates this mindset:

> Thoughts about Rotuma
> Rotuma Hanua Aier 'Ontou [Rotuma, my true land]
> As I reflect and reminisce about those vivid moments growing up in Rotuma, it reminds me of the good old days, of the kinship and life of peace and tranquility I have sorely missed.
> From a distance I see the holistic beauty of Rotuma:
> an island in the sun, given to me by my father's hands
> with its emerald green and lush rain forest, cupped in leafy hands
> its white sandy beaches, soft as maidens hands
> with its sky blue crystal waters, bound by reefy hands
> abundant in fish, like an exotic dancer's twinkling hands
> that calls to me by the most seductive sunset I have ever seen
> from Ahau through Maka Bay to Uea.
> From a distance I feel the soothing effect of Rotuma:
> that calls me all the days of my life
> from Lagi te Maurea with its cool and enchanting effect
> to the tranquility that captivates my senses
> with the security that I can sleep at night with my doors and windows open
> with no worries of being robbed or mugged,
>
> From a distance I smell the fragrance of Rotuma:
> the Tieri and Ragkari that graces the maidens heads
> to the Sea and Kori that also anoints their heads
> the fragrances that permeate, I have longed for in my head
> From a distance I hear the call of Rotuma:

carried to me by the wind of my imagination
with laughter of women and joy of children
free of worries
that begs me home

With these in mind, I know for certain the meaning of Rotuma Hanua Aier 'Ontou. For wherever I go, I will always long for and miss Rotuma all the days of my life.

It is there that I promise that I will one day return to retire and live for the rest of my life. To rekindle the kinship and repay Rotuma for what I owe it, and to be buried with the rest of my loved ones.[10]

Many of these themes are reflected in the childhood memories of the returnees in the survey, who were asked, 'What do you remember most about Rotuma in the time before you left?'

Twenty-one respondents (23.3 per cent) mentioned the physical environment, either as a distinctive memory or in comparison with the state of the environment today. Examples of the former were beautiful sandy beaches, sea breezes, moonlight and lush greenery. Examples of the latter were that the island was unspoiled or there was less rubbish; there were not many cars and bikes; the roads were white and sandy and shady with a lot of huge trees, but now there are few; fishing was easy because fish were large and plentiful, but now it's harder to fish because there are fewer; there were mostly thatched houses, but now there are more cement and concrete structures.

Twenty respondents (22.2 per cent) made general reference to aspects of the lifestyle they remembered, often in very positive terms, such as how peaceful and carefree life was then; how life was simple but good; that people felt safe and secure; that Rotuma seemed like a paradise. Some more specific responses in this category referred to activities such as drinking orange wine, going fishing with village women, and weaving mats in the community hall with village women; the fact that men then did not drink so much 'grog' (kava); or how life on the island contrasted with that abroad, where road accidents or robberies were frequent and people have to work for money to support themselves.

---

10   Ahau, Maka Bay and Uea are Rotuman place-names; *lagi te maurea* refers to a cool breeze; *tieri*, *ragkari*, *sea* and *kori* are names of flowers. This topic of the Rotuma Forum is posted at www.rotuma. net/os/Forum/Forum27.html.

Sixteen respondents (17.8 per cent) referred to peoples' attitudes, always in positive terms, and often with the implication that nowadays they are no longer as idyllic. Examples: people were very friendly and hardworking; people were kind and cared for one another, sharing food with neighbours; kinship was very important; help was given freely; people were peace-loving and there was a strong feeling of togetherness.

Fifteen people (16.7 per cent) referred to categories of people or other social units from the earlier time, including grandparents and other elderly people, who were valued for their wisdom (and who have since died), parents, other relatives, friends and schoolmates, and lots of children in the villages.

Twelve interviewees (13.3 per cent) focused on how the island was less modernised before, with no electricity in the villages, less government support and development, fewer vehicles and the boat only came every three or four months.

Nine respondents (10 per cent) made reference to traditional customs; for example, customary values were more observed and respected, children still had respect for customs and traditions and were well behaved, people were obedient to chiefs and traditional ceremonies were valued highly.

Eight individuals (8.9 per cent) mentioned economic concerns, noting that prices for food and other goods were quite cheap compared to now; most people earned a living from copra and did not have to buy food; and the Rotuma Cooperative Association was the main business on Rotuma.

Seven respondents (7.8 per cent) mentioned food as a significant component in their memories, recalling that eating was simple and very cheap. People relied less on the shops for processed food and instead consumed 'natural' (homegrown) Rotuman food, which was available in abundance, including lots of *dalo* (Fijian for taro = Rotuman *'a'ana*) and fresh fish.

Overall, the majority of these responses reflect a very positive remembrance of the island and its culture during the period before people emigrated, with a degree of nostalgia and a lamenting of how things have changed. This suggests that such memories played a role in motivating emigrants to return later in life.

Answers to a question concerning the biggest changes they'd noticed upon their return to the island were nearly evenly divided by those focusing on physical (including environmental) changes (47 responses, 52.2 per cent) and those focusing on cultural and lifestyle changes (44 responses, 48.9 per cent). The main physical changes referred to included various aspects of development (electrification, water supply, mobile phones and more vehicles—20 responses, 22.2 per cent). Housing changes (from traditional thatch to cement structures) were mentioned by 13 persons (14.4 per cent), while five respondents (5.6 per cent) mentioned pollution or erosion.

Answers concerning cultural and lifestyle changes were more varied. Dietary changes were mentioned by eight respondents (8.9 per cent); seven (7.8 per cent) referred to an improvement in the standard of living; six (6.7 per cent) cited a loss of culture and/or a lack of respect for chiefs and elders; six (6.7 per cent) spoke to an increase in individualism; five (5.6 per cent) observed a more materialistic outlook and concern for money; four (4.4 per cent) mentioned changes in dress codes; and two (2.2 per cent) referred to an increase in kava consumption. Twelve persons acknowledged changes in lifestyle without noting specifics. An additional five (5.6 per cent) individuals reported seeing no significant changes since their return, even though two of them had been away for 10 or more years. (As someone who spent a year on the island in 1960 and did not return till 1987, and last visited in 2012, Alan has seen all of the changes referred to above, but continuities are equally apparent. Thus the emphasis given by each respondent can be seen as a personally selective perception.)

These responses reflect an ambivalence concerning the changes taking place, with some returnees emphasising the positive aspects of developments since their childhood, while others portrayed the changes in more negative terms. As we shall see from their responses to other questions, discussed below, perceived changes have had little effect on the satisfaction that returnees express concerning their current life circumstances.

The migration experience

Rotuma is an isolated island that, until 2008, was closed as a port of entry, requiring all traffic to and from the island to go through Fiji. With no significant industries other than copra production, employment has been extremely limited. In the 1989 survey, 148 persons on the island reported being gainfully employed. Of those, 68 worked for either the Rotuma Cooperative Association or the Raho Cooperative, mostly in low-paying jobs. Within a few years both cooperatives failed and the jobs were eliminated. That left the schools (34 positions), the government station (22 positions) and the hospital (13 positions) as the main employers on the island. Almost all of these positions were filled by personnel from abroad, leaving few employment opportunities for people who had not been abroad. Over the years, copra production has accounted for the lion's share of income for local labour, and, as many Islanders have related to us, cutting copra is hard work that is poorly compensated.

Likewise, educational opportunities on the island have been limited. The high school was not established until 1958, with Form 4 as the highest grade. It wasn't until many years later that Forms 5 and 6 were added, and Form 7 was just initiated in 2013. That means that students used to have to go abroad to complete their secondary education and become eligible for higher education. Since Rotumans generally place a high value on education, the motivation to send children to Fiji and beyond for further education has been very strong.

It is not surprising, therefore, that the overwhelming reasons given for leaving Rotuma were education (53 responses, 58.9 per cent) and employment opportunities (24 responses, 26.7 per cent), with nine individuals (10 per cent) mentioning both. In a few cases it was the respondent's parent who moved to Fiji to take a job. Among the other responses were that the family migrated to Fiji, a divorce or family problems, a birth or death, for medical attention or for a better life.

The great majority of respondents (79, 87.8 per cent) had lived in Fiji when abroad, and only six of them (6.7 per cent) mentioned other countries of residence (mainly Australia and New Zealand). Of those who reported living in Fiji, 53 of them (58.9 per cent) lived in Suva; most of the rest stayed in other urban centres like Lautoka, Nadi or Levuka. While it is true that the great majority of off-island Rotumans are in Fiji, it is also true that substantial numbers of emigrants now live in Australia, New Zealand, England, Canada and the United States. But among returnees, those coming back from Fiji are clearly overrepresented. We suggest that two variables may account for this: (1) it is easier for people in Fiji to travel back and forth to Rotuma, and therefore to maintain close ties with family members and close relatives there, and (2) the great majority of Rotumans in other countries have achieved a standard of living and lifestyle that they are reluctant to give up. No matter how much money people have, limitations in the availability of goods, services, recreational facilities, etc. on Rotuma may be a serious deterrent to returning for those who have adapted well to living in first-world countries.

The importance of kinship networks for the migration experience shows up in response to a question regarding with whom one lived while abroad. The most frequent answer to this question was aunts and/or uncles (35, 38.9 per cent), with brothers and/or sisters (20, 22.2 per cent) next. Fifteen (16.7 per cent) had moved abroad with their parents, and in four cases (4.4 per cent) the returnees had established households abroad with spouse and children. Six interviewees (6.7 per cent) simply stated that they stayed with 'relatives'. Grandmother, cousins and daughter were named once each as hosts. Only two respondents said they went directly to boarding schools.

Sixty-three of the 90 respondents (70 per cent) reported schooling abroad, almost all of it in Fiji. Of those, 37 (41.1 per cent) reported attending secondary schools, and 24 (26.7 per cent) had received some form of tertiary education beyond high school. Two persons attended a maritime academy. This suggests that the motivation to leave Rotuma for additional education was fulfilled in the great majority of cases.

Rotumans, in general, are overrepresented in the higher occupational categories in Fiji, and this showed up in the returnees' responses to a question regarding employment abroad. Seventeen (18.9 per cent) had been skilled workers (carpenters, plumbers, electricians, welders, mechanics, foremen, gold miners, etc.); 10 (11.1 per cent) had been teachers (five were currently teaching in Rotuma, and the other five were retired); 10 (11.1 per cent) had been white-collar workers (receptionists, cashiers, office clerks, bank officers, etc.). Of the remainder, most had been in positions of responsibility as secretaries, police officers, in the Fiji military, etc. Only seven of the interviewees (7.8 per cent) reported working at positions requiring lower skill levels (labourers, waitresses, drivers, etc.), and five others (5.6 per cent) had been sailors.

Responses to a question regarding how long interviewees had been away before returning to Rotuma ranged from six months to 56 years, as shown in Table 3.

Table 3: Years abroad before returning to Rotuma

Less than 10	10–19	20–29	30–39	40+
26 (28.9%)	29 (32.2%)	17 (18.9%)	9 (10%)	7 (7.8%)

* Two questionnaires did not include an answer to this question.

Resettlement following return

The predominant reported reason for returning to Rotuma was to look after parents, grandparents or other close kin (32 instances, 35.6 per cent), followed by other family considerations (for example, to look after land, build a family home, help run a family business—19 instances, 21.1 per cent); lifestyle considerations (for example, peace and tranquillity, cheaper to live, a good place for retirement, to be with own people—18 instances, 20 per cent); employment transfer (five instances, 5.6 per cent); to be of service (five instances, 5.6 per cent); and to learn the language and/or culture (three instances, 3.3 per cent). Only four persons (4.4 per cent) reported returning to Rotuma because of push factors abroad (for example, lack of employment, visa expired). Five responses (5.6 per cent) were idiosyncratic or unintelligible. These results demonstrate quite clearly the overwhelming significance of kinship ties and obligations in motivating return mobility.

By subtracting reported age when returning from reported current age we were able to calculate how long interviewees had been away, resulting in Table 4.

Table 4: How long since returning (in years)

Years ago	No. of respondents
0–4	33 (36.7%)
5–9	15 (16.7%)
10–14	14 (15.6%)
15–19	6 (6.7%)
20–24	6 (6.7%)
25–29	6 (6.7%)
30+	10 (11.1%)

Thus slightly more than half of the respondents (53.4 per cent) reported returning to the island within the past decade.

When asked, 'How did you decide where to settle [following your return to Rotuma]?' the great majority of those providing answers (51 of 66 respondents, 77.3 per cent) replied that they went to a home occupied by close kin or to a home or plot of land to which their family had rights. The remaining 15 respondents (22.7 per cent) occupied government, school or mission quarters; asked relatives where they should stay; or stated that they chose a place that was attractive because of its location. Twenty-four of the interviewees did not answer the question.

Altogether, 13 individuals (14.4 per cent) reported problems with kin or neighbours following their return to Rotuma. Seven of them (7.8 per cent) reported having problems with relatives following their return. In three instances (3.3 per cent) land rights were at issue; in four instances (4.4 per cent) some form of family problems were involved: 'they would like to be my boss', 'staying with my uncle (not real father); they treat me different from their children', 'financial difficulties', or simply 'family problems'. Six interviewees (6.7 per cent) reported having problems with their neighbours: gossiping, jealousy and in one instance, a land dispute.

Our sense is that land disputes are more frequent than reflected in the questionnaire data. In addition to the likelihood that people on Rotuma are reluctant to talk about disputes, we know of several instances of people who intended to return to the island but were put off by disputes over land claims, as well as people who had returned and as a result of such disputes decided to leave again. Mute testimony to such circumstances can be seen in the considerable number of partially built and abandoned homes.

Readaptation to life on the island

Economic life on Rotuma for most families involves both access to plantation land and money. In the past, the main source of money was from copra, but that has been superseded in recent years by remittances, or in some instances by pensions or the sale of agricultural produce. In order to determine the sources that returnees relied on for their livelihood, we included questions about food production and sources of income.

The majority of the interviewees (66, or 73.3 per cent) reported maintaining a garden or plantation on which they grew food crops for their household. Almost all of them (59, or 65.6 per cent) planted the basic root crops of taro, yams, sweet potatoes and/or cassava. Other crops included tree crops such as bananas, papaya, breadfruit, oranges (28 respondents, or 31.1 per cent); pineapples and/or watermelons (nine respondents, or 10 per cent); and sugarcane (nine respondents, or 10 per cent). Ten persons (11.1 per cent) planted kava, and eight of these (8.9 per cent) reported selling it for income. It is interesting to note how many returnees who planted non-starchy vegetables such as cabbage, eggplant, beans and cucumbers (43, or 47.8 per cent). This is a marked change from past patterns when almost none of these foods were regularly cultivated. It suggests that having lived overseas and been exposed to more varied, 'healthy' diets, many returnees are in the process of altering traditional dietary patterns.

With regard to income, 25 individuals (27.8 per cent) reported getting a 'regular income from abroad such as a pension'. If so, they were asked if it was enough to care for all their needs; all but four persons responded that it was. Other sources of income were salaries from government jobs, including teaching (14, 15.6 per cent); remittances from relatives abroad (11, 12.2 per cent); cutting and selling copra (11, 12.2 per cent); selling produce and/or fish on the island (eight, 8.9 per cent); and other sources such as savings accounts, running a shop, building houses (five, 5.6 per cent). Twenty-four interviewees (26.7 per cent) reported no regular source of income at all. We assume that most of these individuals were in a dependent relationship with others who provided them with money when needed.

One important measure of the reintegration of returnees into the social life of the island is the degree to which they participate in community activities. The data we collected lend strong support for the success of returnees in this regard. Seventy-five of the 90 respondents (83.3 per cent) reported participating in community activities at various levels: village (27, or 30 per cent); district (19, or 21.1 per cent); church (34, or 37.8 per cent); school (seven, or 7.8 per cent); and voluntary associations such as women's clubs (seven, or 7.8 per cent). Participation in fundraising activities was mentioned by 14 respondents (15.6 per cent). Twelve of the interviewees (13.3 per cent) were in positions of responsibility or leadership such as district representative to the Rotuma Island Council or village headman. When asked, 'Are you able to use skills that you learned abroad here in Rotuma?' 67 persons interviewed (74.4 per cent) answered yes. The ways they described using what they had learned varied considerably but were heavily weighted toward teaching relevant skills, advising and counselling.

Of prime importance in assessing the successfulness of returnees' reintegration are their attitudes toward life on the island. We began by asking about the biggest changes they noticed since they left, and followed this up by asking them to assess the best and worst thing about living in Rotuma, whether they felt a need to leave Rotuma from time to time, whether they had any regrets about returning, and how they compared themselves with their compatriots who had not lived abroad. Finally, we asked them to assess their overall satisfaction with their experience since returning to Rotuma.

Concerning the biggest changes they'd noticed upon their return to the island, answers were nearly evenly divided by those focusing on physical (including environmental) changes (47, 52.2 per cent) and those focusing on cultural and lifestyle changes (44, 48.9 per cent). The main physical changes referred to included various aspects of development, such as electrification, water supply, mobile phones and more vehicles (20 responses, 22.2 per cent). Housing changes (from traditional thatch to cement structures) were mentioned by 13 persons (14.4 per cent), while five respondents (5.6 per cent) mentioned pollution or erosion.

Answers concerning cultural and lifestyle changes were more varied. Dietary changes were mentioned by eight respondents (8.9 per cent); seven (7.8 per cent) referred to an improvement in standard of living; six (6.7 per cent) cited a loss of culture and/or a lack of respect for chiefs and elders; six (6.7 per cent) spoke to an increase in individualism; five (5.6 per cent) observed a more materialistic outlook and concern for money; four (4.4 per cent) mentioned changes in dress codes; and two (2.2 per cent) referred to an increase in kava consumption. Twelve persons (13.3 per cent) acknowledged changes in lifestyle without noting specifics. An additional five individuals (5.6 per cent) reported seeing no significant changes since their return, even though two of them (2.2 per cent) had been away for 10 or more years.

These responses suggest that many returnees were not uncritical about the changes they observed, in part, perhaps, because they were comparing them to a somewhat idealised conception of earlier times. Criticisms were more vividly described when the interviewees were asked what they considered the worst thing about living in Rotuma.

At the time of the survey, a supply ship from Fiji had not come to Rotuma for about six weeks, resulting in a severe shortage of fuel, groceries and other valued commodities. The shortage led to a rationing of tap water (three hours a day), electricity (early morning and evenings), and transportation. This has been a recurring problem on Rotuma for many years, so it is no wonder that irregular transportation and resultant shortages headed the list of complaints, with 42 interviewees (46.7 per cent) mentioning it. This was followed by complaints about economic conditions (not enough jobs, expensiveness of imported goods, hard work to survive—13 responses, 14.4 per cent); environmental problems (flies and mosquitoes, hot weather, pollution—13 responses, 14.4 per cent); social problems (gossip, conflict over land, disrespect for authority—12 responses, 13.3 per cent); and the lackadaisical attitude of people on the island (six responses, 6.7 per cent).

However, when asked about the best things about living on Rotuma, the idyllic image re-emerged. We divided responses into five categories: (1) an emphasis on peacefulness, safety, the simple stress-free life (45 responses, 50 per cent); (2) the economic advantages of living in Rotuma, including free rent, abundant food resources, low cost of living (45 responses, 50 per cent); (3) a clean, unpolluted, and beautiful environment (19 responses, 21.1 per cent); (4) social benefits such as being with kin, harmonious relations, friendly people (15 responses, 16.7 per cent); and (5) the freedom to be your own boss, to move about freely, to work or not (12 responses, 13.3 per cent). Most people gave more than one response, hence the high overall count.

The discrepancy between the somewhat critical views expressed above and the rather idyllic views expressed in response to the latter question is to a large extent inherent in the nature of the questions asked, but it also is the product of the comparisons being made. In the first instance, criticisms are being reflected against a vision of a glorified past; in the second instance, praise emerges when returnees compare the advantages of contemporary life on Rotuma with their view of life abroad.

When asked if they felt a need to leave Rotuma from time to time, 48 of the respondents (53.3 per cent) said no. Of those who said yes, 25 (27.8 per cent) mentioned visiting family (mostly children and grandchildren); nine (10 per cent) wanted to pursue opportunities for employment or education; and six (6.7 per cent) offered idiosyncratic responses or no specifics.

Only three interviewees (3.3 per cent) expressed any regrets about returning to Rotuma. One said he missed 'the fast track life'; another rued the setback to his studies; and the third person complained that people on the island 'talk too much'. Eighty-five (94.4 per cent) said they had no regrets and two (2.2 per cent) gave no response.

In order to gain a sense of how returnees saw themselves in comparison with age-mates who had remained in Rotuma, we asked them, 'In what ways do you think your life as a returnee is different from other people your age who have lived most of their adult lives on Rotuma?' Answers were varied but fell into six basic categories: (1) an emphasis on the returnee's enhanced skills and experience (32 responses, 35.6 per cent); (2) an emphasis on the returnee's superior financial circumstances (eight responses, 8.9 per cent); (3) an emphasis on the returnee's superior health and/or younger appearance (five responses, 5.6 per cent); (4) general comments about differences in outlook, attitude, behaviour (24 responses, 26.7 per cent); (5) an emphasis on the superior skills of non-returnees for adapting to the local environment (nine responses, 10 per cent); and (6) no or negligible difference (seven responses, 7.8 per cent).

Finally, we asked interviewees to rate their experience since returning to Rotuma on a four-point scale: very satisfying, somewhat satisfying, not very satisfying, and not satisfying at all. The results are as shown in Table 5.

Table 5: Degree of satisfaction with return experience

very satisfying	somewhat satisfying	not very satisfying	not at all satisfying
61 (68.5%)	19 (21.4%)	7 (7.9%)	2 (2.2%)

The fact that nearly 90 per cent of the respondents rated their experience positively is testimony to the relative ease of reintegration of returnees to Rotuma. Neither gender nor length of time since return affected satisfaction significantly, and surprisingly, neither involvement in disputes nor problems with relatives or neighbours led to harsher assessments. In fact, of the 13 individuals who acknowledged such involvement, eight answered very satisfying, three somewhat satisfying, one not very satisfying, and one not at all satisfying, suggesting that there were sufficient advantages to offset such distressing encounters for most individuals.

Reflections on the data

The data we have presented are suggestive of several factors that encourage emigrants to return and to successfully reintegrate into Rotuman society. To begin with, it is apparent that networks of kinship ties that transcend the island's boundaries facilitate both movement away and return. This has resulted in a situation in which the frequently used definition of migration and reverse migration—that migrants go with the intent to remain—is problematic for many, if not most, of the Rotumans who travel or return from abroad. Most appear to keep their options open, with ties to kin providing opportunities for visiting and resettlement in multiple venues.

The circumstances of Rotuman mobility differ from most of the cases discussed in the migration literature insofar as the primary destination for emigration is Fiji, which, though socially and culturally distinct, is nevertheless within country. Only a small proportion of those who emigrate to Fiji go on to migrate transnationally. Also, the population of Rotuma has declined over the past quarter century. Thus, while slightly fewer than 2,000 Rotumans are now on their home island, over 8,000 reside in Fiji, and an estimated 2,000–3,000 are out of the country. It is not surprising, therefore, that only six of the 90 respondents in the student survey had lived outside of Fiji (New Zealand and Australia). This suggests that people are far more likely to return from Fiji than from transnational locations. We think there may be two main reasons to account for this discrepancy. First, transportation and communication are easier and less expensive between Rotuma and Fiji than between Rotuma and foreign countries. This facilitates more frequent contact via visits back and forth as well as communication via telephone calls, making it easier to keep relationships 'warm', and thus being able to count on the support of relatives when returning. Second, Rotumans who have emigrated from Fiji have, on the whole, been extraordinarily successful. The vast majority, many of whom have married someone who is native to their new home, enjoy a high standard of living by any measure. And although a good many of them cherish their Rotuman identity and are motivated to visit Rotuma on occasion, they would be giving up too much to move back to Rotuma. The same is less true of Rotumans in Fiji, where the discrepancies in lifestyle and living standards are less dramatic.

Another factor leading to reverse migration is the overwhelmingly positive image of Rotuma in the eyes of Rotumans everywhere. Not only is the beauty and bounty of the island idealised, but the great success of Rotumans overseas has lent strength to Rotuman identity, the core of which focuses on imagery of the island itself. Childhood memories elicited by the questionnaire were overwhelmingly positive, and the comments on the best things about living in Rotuma greatly outnumbered those about the worst things.

We attribute the overall success of returnees' reintegration in large measure to something we have observed consistently over the years: Rotumans—even those who were born and raised elsewhere—have demonstrated a remarkable social sensitivity and ability to adjust their behaviour to conform with cultural expectations. It is also our impression, both from our ethnographic experiences and the survey data, that communities on the island are receptive to returnees and appreciate their contributions.[11] The only exceptions we are aware of involve a small number of returnees who may be seen as displaying an air of superiority or arrogance.

Acknowledgements

We would like to express our sincere gratitude to Principal Perry Gabriel and his wife Siteri for hosting us during our August 2012 visit to Rotuma; to Principal Perry and the other teachers of Rotuma High School for their commitment to continually improving secondary education on the island; and to the following high school students who assisted with the interviews reported in this paper: Tausie Afasio, Moiro Hereta Afrete, Cynclaire Agatha, Henrietta Aisake, Lebron Aisake, Willy Aisake, Sariah Albert, Gabriel Antonio, Mere Antonio, Georeen Antrea, Lorane Atalifo, Jedidah Atalifo, Vilisoni Atalifo, Catherine Dominiko, Peni Drala, Jeanette Eliesa, Arthur Fesaitu, Kevin Fesaitu, Patricia Fonmoa, Margaret Gabriel, Chester Godfrey, Thomas Godfrey, Lesina Grace, Mani Inoke, Tabitha Inoke, Aron Jeremiah, Francis Kafoa, Vafo'ou Fonmoa, Anthony Collin Kaitu'u, Tausie Kamea, Ross Kunau, Linda Lia,

---

11   Although the survey results may well have been biased by the fact that the interviewers were high school students, leading interviewees to be reluctant to mention difficulties they experienced after returning to Rotuma, which they might have elaborated on during an in-depth interview with an adult, they are entirely consistent with our observations and interview materials compiled over a combined 83 years of research among Rotumans. We therefore are inclined to accept them at face value.

Adi Tuicakau Lilicama, Aqela Lilicama, Berutida Lorosio, Faith Marieta
Lorosio, Pherlaine Luenna, Ashley Managreve, Opteia Manava, Silomeci
Marama, Theresa Mateo, Esther Mausio, Samuela Marshon Mekatoa,
Hanisemao Morsio, Danielle Mose, Leysina Muaror, Caritas Nafaere,
Thomas Nafaere, Monalisa Nakaora, Waqa Naitini, Firomena Nawai,
Maria Olson, Natalie Onisimo, Daphne Ostonu, Olovia Paka, Peter Paka,
Vincent Panata, Samantha Petero, Kevin Pau'u, Emmanuel Pene, Lois
Penjueli, Philorina Raturaobe, Antonio Ravai, Flavia Ravai, Rigamoto
Isimeli Ravai, Emolina Rigamoto, Mika'yla Savea, Rahine Semesi, Dennis
Serenino, Stephen Solvalu, Joshua Sopapelu, Kristel Suliana, Shane
Tanumafili, Faretenoa Taukave, Makereta Tausea, Louisa Tifere, Naomi
Veisoi Tikomailepanoni, Bernadene Tomoniko, Crezelda Tonumafili,
Sam Jioje Tuvalu, Chris Ufamarata, Tipo Vaurasi, Kimberly Vernass,
Aaron Viliame, Poira Viliame, Ana Vitau, Jacqueln Vitori, Domonique
Vollmer, Nathan Vollmer, and Cameron Whippy.

References

Cassarino, J-P 2004, 'Theorising return migration: the conceptual
approach to return migrants revisited', *International Journal on
Multicultural Societies*, vol. 6, no. 2, pp. 253–279.

Cerase, F 1974, 'Migration and social change: expectations and reality:
a case study of return migration from United States to southern Italy',
International Migration Review, vol. 8, no. 2, pp. 245–262. doi.org/
10.2307/3002783

Fletcher, W 1870, *The Wesleyan missionary notices*, no. 13, vol. 3, Australian
Wesleyan Methodist Conference, Sydney.

Gerber, E 1975, 'The cultural patterning of emotions in Samoa',
PhD thesis, University of California, San Diego.

Gmelch, G 1980, 'Return migration', *Annual Review of Anthropology*,
vol. 9, pp. 135–159. doi.org/10.1146/annurev.an.09.100180.001031

Howard, A 1970, *Learning to be Rotuman*, Teachers College Press,
Columbia University, New York.

Lee, H & Francis, ST (eds) 2009, *Migration and transnationalism:
Pacific perspectives*, ANU E Press, Canberra.

Morton, H 1996, *Becoming Tongan: an ethnography of childhood*, University of Hawai'i Press, Honolulu.

Murphy, R 2002, *How migrant labor is changing rural China*, Cambridge University Press, Cambridge.

Rensel, J 1994, 'For love or money? Interhousehold exchange and the economy of Rotuma', PhD thesis, University of Hawai'i, Mānoa.

Rensel, J 1997, 'From thatch to cement: social implications of housing change on Rotuma', in J Rensel & M Rodman (eds), *Home in the islands: housing and social change in the Pacific*, University of Hawai'i Press, Honolulu, pp. 27–54.

4

Overseas-born youth in Tongan high schools: Learning the hard life

Helen Lee

Abstract

As the Tongan diaspora continues to grow it is increasingly common for the overseas-born children of migrants to attend high school in Tonga for one or more school terms. Sometimes the children themselves initiate the move and are keen to experience Tonga for themselves and 'understand the culture'. However, other young people have no say in this decision and many perceive their move to Tonga as a form of punishment. My paper explores the discourse around this form of mobility, focusing on ideas around risk, redemption and rite of passage. Tongans have divergent opinions about the value of this 'return' to the parents' homeland and there can be markedly different outcomes for the young people involved. Some Tongans point to the difficulties experienced by overseas-born youth, who are separated from their immediate family, friends and familiar environment and find themselves in a cultural context that can be extremely challenging. However, others see youth sent to Tonga as 'the lucky ones' who benefit from their exposure to Tongan culture and language. The young people who overcome the challenges of 'the hard life' in Tonga often value the experience as a way to become truly Tongan.

Introduction

Return migration has often been depicted as a fraught and challenging form of mobility. Whether it is adult migrants returning after a long sojourn away from home, or their adult children's 'roots migration', or younger children going to their parents' homeland, the literature is replete with descriptions of feelings of alienation, marginalisation and identity confusion. This paper focuses on the overseas-born children of Tongan migrants who 'return' to Tonga in their youth to attend high school. Although in many ways they, too, can find this a difficult and even distressing experience, it is also important to recognise the more positive aspects of their time in their parents' homeland. The discourse surrounding this movement of youth from the diaspora to the homeland has a strong theme of risk and danger yet it can also be about redemption: the value of the time spent in Tonga to overcome problems experienced overseas and undergo a process of self-transformation. This discourse can even encompass that of a rite of passage, as youth from the diaspora travel to Tonga to experience 'the hard life' and 'learn the culture' in order to become 'truly' Tongan.

Overseas-born youth spend time in Tongan high schools for a range of reasons. The most common reason is that they are sent, often against their will, because of their family's concerns about their behaviour or the risk of negative influences overseas. Others choose to go and learn more about their Tongan heritage or to experience the life in Tonga they have heard about from older family members. Other reasons include being sent to the care of relatives after the death of a parent, or going to live with grandparents who want to spend time with them and cannot travel overseas themselves. In some cases, one or both parents go to Tonga with them for some or all of their stay; or parents may be returning to Tonga temporarily or attempting to resettle permanently after years overseas (Maron and Connell 2008); or one or both parents may even have been deported for overstaying their visas or because of a conviction for criminal activities (Lee 2009). There are also young people who, after being raised overseas by relatives, go to Tonga during their high school years to live with their biological parent/s for a period of time.

The diverse circumstances of young people's temporary migration to Tonga means that some are living with close family members while others are left in the care of relatives such as grandparents or aunts and uncles, who they may not have met before going to Tonga. Their family situation, and whether they attend high school as day students or boarders, as well as the other characteristics of the school they attend, have a significant influence on their experiences in Tonga. Their experiences are also shaped by their prior knowledge of Tonga and its culture. Although the language of 'return' is often used to describe this movement from the diaspora to Tonga, in reality many of the youth who arrive to attend school are visiting the country for the first time. They may not speak the language or have any depth of knowledge of the intricacies of *anga fakatonga*, the Tongan way. The many factors influencing each young person's time in Tonga makes it difficult to generalise but examining the discourse used by and about 'returned' youth reveals some common themes that offer starkly contrasting views of the value of this experience.

Return migration through the generations

The literature on return migration and transnationalism has paid scant attention to young people such as the Tongan adolescents that are the focus of this paper and has been more concerned with adult migrants and adult members of the second generation. Adults returning to the country in which they were born and raised can have problems readjusting and they may be regarded as 'outsiders' and no longer feel 'at home' (Gmelch 1980; Arowolo 2000; but cf. Howard and Rensel, this volume). This was the case for Tongan return migrants in a 2001 study (Maron and Connell 2008), who faced difficulties including being regarded as *pālangi* (white) and therefore not fully accepted.

In recent years the emerging literature on the 'return' of the adult children of migrants reveals that they find adjustment even more difficult than their parents. Susanne Wessendorf reports that Italians born and raised in Switzerland who move to Italy in what she calls 'roots migration' often find it difficult and feel 'trapped in a place which they once hoped would be their home, but in which they feel like strangers' (2007: 1097). Similar experiences are reported for the adult children of migrants from Greece (Christou and King 2006; Panagakos 2004), the Caribbean (Conway and Potter 2007: 20; Potter and Phillips 2006a, 2006b) and the Pacific (Connell 1990; and see Agarwal, this volume). Two edited volumes on this topic of 'return' migration of adult second and later generations (Conway and Potter 2009; Tsuda 2009) provide a range of other case studies that also describe the difficulties this movement can involve. Given that these studies all involve adults moving voluntarily, it seems highly likely that for adolescents, particularly those moving against their will, these problems will be even more acute.

As Madeleine Hatfield argues, the field of migration studies has not paid enough attention to either return migration or to children, and as a result children who return with their families to their 'home' country are 'doubly invisible migrants' (2010: 243). Even less attention has been paid to children who move alone to their parents' home country. However, in many migrant populations, including Tongans, young children are sent to the homeland to be cared for in order to enable their parents to work and avoid formal childcare, because parents are worried about their children's undocumented status, or due to concerns about social problems in the host country or their own children's behaviour. Yvonne Bohr and Connie Tse discuss 'satellite babies' who are sent by Chinese migrant parents in Canada to live with kin in China, so the parents can work and the children can be exposed to the language and culture of their homeland (2009). Their findings support other research that shows 'immigrant children who have been separated from their parents are more prone to depression as well as self-esteem and behavioral problems' (Bohr and Tse 2009: 269).[1]

Some research has acknowledged that overseas-born children spending time in their parents' homeland does not always have such damaging outcomes. In his study of migration from Mali to the Republic of Congo, Bruce Whitehouse (2009) shows that many parents send young children to Mali to be raised by kin, or send their children for school holidays. He suggests that because child fostering is so common in West Africa the separation of children from parents does not have some of the negative impacts reported in other cultural contexts. Similarly, Ernestina Tetteh (2008) claims fosterage is common and valued in Ghana, including the practice of 'posted children': babies and young children who are sent to Ghana by migrant parents so the parents can work and avoid the cost

---

1   Some of the issues raised in the work on sending children 'home' recur in research into other ways children are separated from their immediate family through migration. This includes being left behind with relatives when parents migrate, or children moving alone, for example to find work or to attend school overseas. Most importantly, these children are reported to experience the emotional stress of separation, deterioration of relationships with parents, difficulties at school, and behavioural problems (e.g. Dreby 2007; Matthei and Smith 1998; Moran-Taylor 2008; Parrenas 2001; Zhou 1998). As Dreby found in Mexico (2007) these experiences can be particularly acute for adolescents.

of formal childcare.[2] Tetteh found that young children sent to live with relatives in Ghana while their parents worked accepted this 'as a lifetime opportunity for them to make it in future' (2008: 5).

Positive perceptions of fostering may make it easier for such children to adjust to separation from migrant parents. Children's acceptance of their situation can also be influenced by the reasons for the separation. When sending children to the homeland is motivated by their parents' desire to achieve social and economic mobility for the family, children may perceive the short-term pain of separation as being worth the long-term gains. As Suarez-Orozco, Todorova and Louie have argued:

> of critical importance to the adjustment process is how the child makes meaning of the situation of separation from parents and other loved ones. If the child is well prepared for the separation, and if the separation is framed as temporary and necessary, undertaken for the good of the family, the separation will be much more manageable than if the child feels abandoned (2002: 640).

When children are sent to the parents' homeland because of concerns about their behaviour the focus is primarily on the outcome for them as individuals rather than the benefit to other family members. This may be even more difficult to cope with than a sense of abandonment, since the child is likely to perceive the separation as his or her own fault and the move as a form of punishment. Even those who choose to spend time in the homeland are pursuing an individual identity journey rather than seeking to benefit their family, so they may feel less able to ask for support during their adjustment to the unfamiliar environment.

Studies of migrants' children going to the parents' homeland consistently show that older children and adolescents find the experience more difficult than younger children, especially those sent against their will. Young children sent to Ghana by migrant parents may accept their situation in the context of a common pattern of fosterage but older children have more negative attitudes, especially those whose parents send them for bad behaviour (Tetteh 2008). Tetteh reports they often live with relatives they barely know and are 'angry, bitter and unhappy about the whole arrangements to come to spend time in Ghana' (Tetteh 2008: 106; see also

---

2   I have described the 'brown paper parcel babies' in the Tongan case; infants sent from the diaspora to be cared for in Tonga (Lee 2003: 58). No detailed study has been done of these children although Kerry James has described them as 'a bond of love and living confirmations of kinship' while also expressing concern about the strain on families in Tonga (1991).

Coe 2008: 234). These children have grown up overseas so Ghana is unfamiliar and they experience difficulties adjusting to their new schools. They also worry about 'missing out on a lot of things taking place back home and the fact their friends will be way ahead of them in everything and that fitting back into the system will be difficult' (Tetteh 2008: 108).

These children may be moving within a transnational social space and a network of kin, yet from their own perspective their movement is from familiar to unfamiliar social spaces.

Little research has been conducted into overseas-born youth returning 'home' to attend high school in Tonga or other Pacific countries. In the 1980s Cluny Macpherson briefly observed for Samoans in New Zealand that it was common for parents to send or take children to Samoa for periods of time, and that 'many adolescents reported a sense of alienation that surprised and hurt them' (1985: 250). My own earlier research includes a small study in Tonga in 2006, in which a group of 15 boys boarding at a Wesleyan college expressed similar feelings of alienation but tried to make the best of their situation (Lee 2009). They focused on the benefits of getting to know their relatives and Tongan culture while also acknowledging the hardships they were enduring in their new environment.

Diasporic youth in Tongan high schools

To explore in more depth the experiences of overseas-born youth in Tongan high schools, research was conducted in Tonga in 2013. Two Tongan researchers, Rebecca Tauali'i and Ebonie Fifita, worked in six high schools on Tongatapu for the project. This involved working with small groups of overseas-born students (hereafter 'the students') at each school, holding weekly, two-hour '*talanoa* sessions' with them for four weeks.[3] The *talanoa* methodology has been described by Timote Vaioleti as 'a personal encounter where people story their issues, their realities and aspirations' with no rigid framework for the discussion (2006: 21). This kind of 'storying' approach has been widely used in Pacific research

---

3   In addition to the *talanoa* sessions, a total of 144 detailed questionnaires were completed by students from one class in each of five schools. Interviews also were conducted for the project with Tongan adults in Australia, New Zealand and Tonga by the author, Rebecca Tauali'i and Hainoame Fulivai. Hainoame also set up, with Meliame Fifita, two Facebook sites for the project.

and is particularly effective for working with youth. The students were guided through unstructured discussions of their experiences in Tonga by Rebecca and Ebonie, who had general themes for each week but allowed the students to direct the conversation to issues that concerned them, as well as engaging in a lot of joking and chat that helped them feel at ease.[4] In the final week they created colourful posters (see Figure 1) on which they were invited to make statements they wanted to get across to their families, teachers and schoolmates about their experiences.[5]

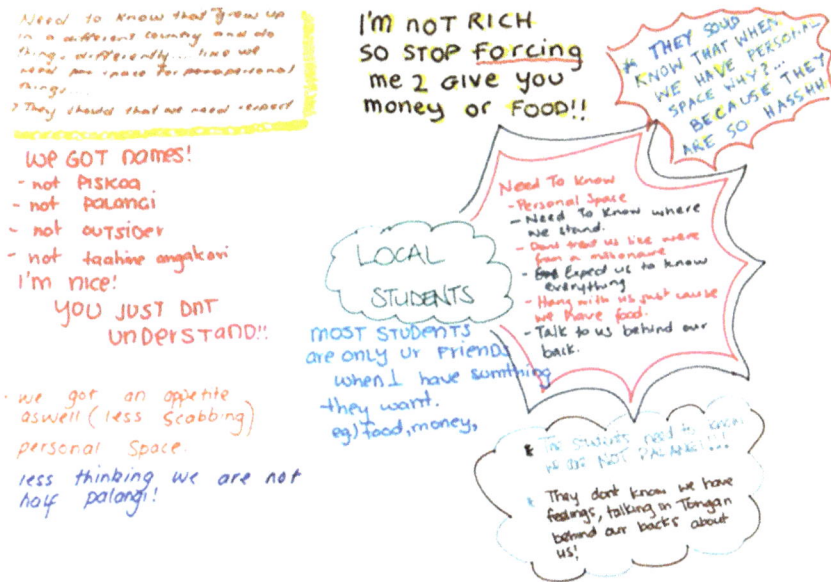

Figure 1: An example of the posters made by students

Source: Photographed by author.

The 28 students ranged in age from 11 to 19 but most were 15 to 17 and were from Australia, New Zealand, the US, Samoa and Fiji. There were 18 females and 10 males involved in the *talanoa* sessions, with the gender imbalance due to girls being more willing to volunteer to participate in

4   The students were also given cameras and invited to take photographs to capture their daily lives and things they cared about. Each week they discussed their photos with the researchers. They kept the cameras after the project concluded and were given USB sticks with copies of all their photographs.

5   The posters and the discussion sessions were used in a report on the research findings, '"The lucky ones"? Overseas born Tongan youth in Tongan high schools'. It was presented in June 2015 to the Tongan Government, participating high schools and other key stakeholders involved with Tongan youth issues.

the project. Anecdotal evidence suggests more males than females are sent to Tonga, however, no statistics are kept on overseas student numbers either by schools or the Ministry of Education and Training. Most of the students spoke little or no Tongan when they arrived in Tonga and only five said they already spoke Tongan very well. While one student had visited Tonga every year from an early age and another had been every two years, most had only visited once or twice and eight had never been to Tonga before arriving to attend school.

The schools they attend are very diverse. One is government-run and the others are Wesleyan, Mormon and Seventh-day Adventist. They are a mix of day and boarding schools, single sex and co-educational; located in the capital, Nuku'alofa, and out in the villages on the main island, Tongatapu. They differ significantly in other respects, such as the amount of English spoken in class and the quality of the buildings and student resources. For example, Liahona, the Mormon high school, is a day school, the classes are taught in English, and there are ample learning resources and support, including counsellors to deal with any problems. In contrast, the Wesleyan boarding school for boys, Tupou College, known as Toloa, holds most classes in Tongan, the boys are expected to do hard physical labour in the school gardens, the dormitories are dilapidated and crowded, and problems are often dealt with through harsh physical punishment rather than counselling.[6]

'Potential trouble': The discourse of risk

Tongan parents who send their older children to Tonga tend to frame their decision around a desire to give them the opportunity to spend time with kin and become familiar with the home language and culture, but they also are often intent on addressing what they perceive as bad behaviour. This can range from poor grades to rebellion to involvement with drugs and criminal activities. Sometimes it is a pre-emptive strike, to remove their child from negative influences before it is too late. In any case, their motives are interrelated—to ensure their children learn *anga fakatonga* as a way to 'straighten them out'.

---

6   When I revisited the school in 2015 a new principal was discouraging physical punishment of the boys, having new dormitories built and developing positive connections with other schools to address the problem of violent inter-school rivalry.

However, the idea that sending 'youth at risk' to Tonga will improve their behaviour and remove them from dangerous influences (Schoone 2008, 2010) contradicts the view held by some Tongans that this practice is itself putting them at risk. Both in Tonga and in the diaspora some believe sending troubled youth to Tonga is the only way to deal with their behavioural problems while others are equally adamant that it can psychologically damage children and create readjustment problems for them when they return overseas (Lee 2003: 86–89). In addition, the practice is seen as creating a risk for the country of Tonga and the families that are given the responsibility of caring for these young people.

Risks for the 'returned' youth

The main focus of concern for the wellbeing of overseas-born youth in Tonga is those sent because of perceived behavioural problems. Sending, or threatening to send, youth to the parents' homeland has been described for some other migrant groups as 'transnational disciplining' (Orellana et al. 2001). The sparse literature on this practice, which includes migrant parents from the Caribbean (Barrow 2010; Guarnizo 1997), Guatemala (Menjivar 2002), Belize (Matthei and Smith 1998), and Ghana (Tetteh 2008), shows behavioural and emotional problems are common as a result of being sent away from home and exacerbated when the young person feels abandoned by their parents (Suarez-Orozco et al. 2002).

Most of this research focuses on migrants in the US. Cecilia Menjivar (2002) found that Guatemalan immigrants in Los Angeles send their children 'home' when concerned about their involvement with gangs and crime. She reports that the children saw their move as 'punishment' and were unhappy, had difficulty communicating and did not understand cultural expectations of them. They were placed in a 'vastly different milieu living with people they could hardly recognise as family' (Menjivar 2002: 545). The impact on such young people's education is also of concern; for example, in Mexico some 'returned' students benefit from exposure to the language and culture of their parents' homeland while others remain 'between cultures' and their education suffers (Zúñiga and Hamann 2009). Research with Central American, Mexican and Yemeni migrants (Orellana et al. 2001) shows children sent to the parents' home country had difficulties with schooling after being used to all-English classes in the US.

The idea of the homeland as a space of discipline and enforced 'culture' is interesting in the Tongan context because Tongan homes, while usually spaces of love and laughter, are also typically spaces of discipline, with expectations that Tongan culture will be enacted. Sending youth from the diaspora to Tonga because of their behaviour is effectively an admission there has been a failure in the home to properly discipline a child and he or she is therefore 'at risk'. It is seen as an attempt to ensure proper discipline and cultural learning occurs in a space—that is, Tonga itself and in the homes of kin in Tonga—perceived as relatively safe from the risk of the external influences that undermine Tongan culture in the diaspora.

There is a tendency in Tonga for older, more conservative church and community leaders, who have limited direct contact with diasporic youth, to claim mostly positive outcomes for youth sent to Tonga. A leading figure in the Free Wesleyan Church claimed that 'more than 80 per cent' of cases of youth who are sent to Tonga are 'good stories'. However, those who have on-the-ground experience with these young people are typically more negative in their assessments. In fact, a representative of a prominent civil society organisation working with youth in Tonga said it was 'rare' that sending youth to Tonga actually helped them. People who work with youth in Tonga described a whole range of behavioural and emotional problems young people coming from overseas can experience and were concerned that most are not being given much support, if any. For example, in 2013 only two high schools had professional counsellors, and overseas-born youth are not acknowledged in most of the work being done around youth issues, such as the Tonga National Youth Strategy (Ministry of Training, Employment, Youth and Sports 2007). Even those who were positive about diasporic youth going to Tonga admitted that some of them do not cope well with the experience and have to return overseas.

In addition to the emotional problems associated with an unfamiliar and often challenging environment and separation from their immediate family, youth sent because of behavioural concerns face the danger of over-zealous relatives and others such as teachers and prefects harming them in their attempts to discipline them.[7] Even youth who have chosen to go to Tonga may experience violence in various contexts, in

---

7   In 2007 the Attorney General of Tonga at that time, Mrs 'Alisi Taumoepeau, told me of two cases of teenagers who had been sent to Tonga and had died at the hands of relatives who were attempting to 'straighten them out' using physical punishment.

the form of punishment from those of higher status and aggression from peers. Boys often get caught up in the intense inter-school rivalries that frequently erupt into violence including large-scale brawls in the streets. One of the boys in the discussion groups described being trapped on a bus with boys from a rival school who hit him repeatedly with a piece of wood; he had to have plastic surgery to repair his face. Some Tongans regard such experiences of violence as an inevitable part of adjusting to Tongan life. An older, high ranking man in Tonga told me that overseas-born youth should learn to fit in or they could expect 'to end up in hospital'.

Adults who grew up overseas and spent time in Tonga as adolescents draw on the discourse of risk in reflecting on their own experiences. Sela, a woman now in her 30s, had a particularly difficult experience. She grew up in New Zealand and went to Tonga at the age of 11 for what she thought was a family holiday but was left in Tonga with her grandparents because her younger brother had chosen to stay. She enjoyed being in Tonga while it was a holiday, 'But as soon as I was told I would remain there, Tonga just became my worst nightmare—literally'. She hated being a boarding student at Queen Sālote College, where she struggled with the language, the hard physical work expected of the students, and the regular physical punishment she witnessed and experienced. She described her stay as like being 'lost in the wilderness' or 'stuck in a female prison in a foreign country'. Although she stayed for eight months she never liked being in Tonga and was constantly homesick.

Sela eventually became ill from refusing to eat, developed eczema that led to bad skin infections, and suffered anxiety. The final straw was when her teacher hit all the students in her class for failing a test and Sela went back to her grandparents' house in distress, with bruises and welts on her hands and up her arms. Her grandfather took her out of the school immediately and soon sent her back to New Zealand. Sela's case is an extreme example but it is not uncommon for the young people who go to Tonga to find the experience so difficult they are sent back overseas. One of the boys who participated in the school discussion sessions was so unhappy at his school he was deliberately getting into trouble, hoping he would be 'deported back to NZ'.

Risk for Tongan society

Sending children 'home' from the diaspora can have negative consequences for the home country, as has been shown in a range of studies of the 'return' of migrants' children. For example, youth sent 'under punishment' to Belize in the 1990s had 'transnationalised' the Los Angeles gangs they belonged to and were negatively influencing young people raised in Belize, particularly those with absentee migrant parents (Matthei and Smith 1998: 284). It can also place strain on schools when students have poor language skills and are used to a different education system (Zúñiga and Hamann 2009: online). Luis Guarnizo reports that for Dominican migrants the decision to send children 'home' is 'often against the child's will' (1997: 301) and there are usually negative consequences, including the impact of family separation and the increased economic burden of sending money to support the children. There is also strain on ties with kin in the homeland: 'Fewer and fewer relatives have been willing to accept the considerable burden of caring for returned children and adolescents because of their difficult behavior' (Guarnizo 1997: 301).

The burden on families in Tonga and the difficulties posed for schools are certainly of concern in Tonga, however, the major risk these young people are perceived to bring is their 'bad influence'. Overseas-born youth living in Tonga are often regarded as much the same as the deportees who are increasingly being sent to Tonga by overseas governments, particularly from the US. Many of the deportees are young men who have been convicted of crimes and they are regarded with considerable hostility by most Tongans (Esser 2011; Lee 2009: 43; Pereira 2011). Just as deportees are blamed for rising rates of crime and violence in Tonga, youth from the diaspora, particularly those sent for bad behaviour, are accused of bringing social problems such as substance abuse and are blamed for the increasingly violent clashes between rival 'gangs' and between some of the high schools. One older male from a civil society organisation claimed the diasporic youth bring 'skills to do harm' and expressed the common view that they are a negative influence on the youth of Tonga.

A senior member of the Ministry of Education and Training confirmed the overseas-born youth and deportees tend to be seen as one category: 'potential trouble'. She said Tongans see the youth as 'bad' and admitted they tend to be 'blamed for anything bad that happens'. Another senior ministry representative confirmed that these youth are often blamed for instigating any trouble, particularly boys in relation to the inter-school fighting, which seems to be escalating and involving more use of weapons, which some claim have been brought from overseas by the youth. Rather than seeing them as victims of this violence they are depicted as instigators. More generally, overseas-born youth, both males and females, are often labelled as '*fie kovi*' (literally: wanting to be bad) or *anga kovi* (bad by nature) as well as various versions of *pālangi* (white), which have negative connotations of bringing dangerous and unwanted influences.

The students were well aware of and strongly resented these negative labels. One of the posters they created has the exclamation: 'We're all the same, we are Tongans, so don't treat us like foreigners'. At another school, a girl wrote on her group's poster: 'We got names!—not piskoa [Peace Corps]—not pālangi—not outsider—not ta'ahine angakovi [bad girl]. I'm nice! You just don't understand!'

'The lost children': The discourse of redemption

The term redemption, with its biblical connotations, seems appropriate to capture another common theme in discussions of diasporic youth going to Tonga, which is that of being saved from real or potential problems. As the corollary of 'risk' it encompasses ideas of rescue and rehabilitation. It also captures the motives of their families in removing them from the perceived risks that exist overseas and placing them in the Tongan context of culture and discipline.

This discourse focuses on the time in Tonga as a way to overcome behavioural problems and get on the right path—or be 'straightened out'. It is about a process of transformation where the individual returns overseas reformed and more properly 'Tongan'. The focus of this discourse tends not to be explicitly on the role of 'culture' in the transformation but on the positive impact of hard work and discipline, and the benefits of youth spending time with members of their extended kinship group. The focus is on changes in attitude and behaviour and often an association is made with the young person learning to appreciate the life they have overseas. By experiencing the 'hard life' in Tonga they realise they have it good overseas and should make the most of the opportunities there.

The church leader mentioned above, who gave a positive view of the outcomes for overseas-born youth, drew on the classic Christian narrative of redemption in dramatic examples of what he called 'lost children' being saved by being sent to Tonga and returning overseas as much better people. He gave the example of a former drug addict who went home to 'instruct his parents on religious principles' and became a youth worker. The director of a civil society organisation, also an older male, repeated the claim that a high percentage of youth sent to Tonga have positive outcomes. Using the language of rehabilitation he observed: 'I think people see the whole island as a therapy so they assume when they send their kids they will come right'. He added: 'The few lucky ones are the ones whose parents cared enough to send them here. The unlucky ones don't come to Tonga'. He commented sarcastically that perhaps the parents of those 'unlucky' youth think they are safer in prison in Australia or the US.

The students who used this discourse of redemption were usually those who had been sent to Tonga because of concerns about their behaviour. A 16-year-old girl said she was in Tonga 'to suffer from what I was doing back in New Zealand'; a 14-year-old girl, also from New Zealand, admitted: 'the reason why I came is to change my attitude'; and a 15-year-old girl from Australia said she was there 'cause I need to change; change, yeah. Change my ways from before when I was back home'. When reflecting on the impact of their time in Tonga many students used the expression 'my attitude has changed' and when they elaborated, they typically included learning respect, being more obedient, being more helpful with chores and being more responsible in their behaviour. Others talked of a fundamental shift in their sense of self: they had become 'a new person' or 'a better person' or had 'found' themselves in Tonga.

When asked what might have happened if they had not been sent to Tonga most of these students claimed they had been rescued from their 'bad' behaviour becoming even worse. They talked about their siblings and friends 'back home' and how they could have ended up like them: pregnant at 16, drinking, smoking and taking drugs, getting into gangs and so on. They imagined they might have been expelled from school, or 'probably be kicked out of home' and 'out of control'. More dramatically, one boy said 'oh, either in prison or dead!' They had been saved from their former selves; as another boy put it: 'I used to think that I was better than anyone—right now I'm good, I'm all good and yeah, it's better here'.

While some students were convinced their self-transformation was permanent, others were worried about how they might react to returning overseas. A few even said they wanted to stay in Tonga. As one boy admitted: 'I know when I go back I would go back to my old ways'. This concern about leaving Tonga often leads students to extend their time there, even when their families say they can return home. This was the case for Meg, a Tongan woman now in her 30s who grew up in Australia, who described her first year in Tonga as a youth in dramatically negative terms. She was sent to board at Queen Sālote College in her second-to-last year of high school, when her mother was concerned about her becoming rebellious, and her story of that time is full of incidents of hardship and harsh physical punishment from the teachers at the school she described as 'a jail' and 'a different world'. It took nearly a year for Meg to get used to her life in Tonga and to make friends, who were also girls sent from overseas. However, when she went home to Australia for Christmas at the end of that first year and her mother asked what she wanted to do, she replied: 'send me back'. She had been redeemed! She stayed in Tonga for another whole year, by choice, and explains: 'I felt like I needed to learn more. I wanted to understand the whole Tongan way. For me it was like getting down to my roots'.

Reflecting on her experience during her interview Meg cried and said she missed Tonga. She admitted living there taught her to appreciate what she had in Australia and helped her 'find herself'—as if she had been 'lost' before. Nevertheless, she hasn't been back to Tonga since then. She said: 'I haven't gone back 'cause I was traumatised by what I saw—the school, the classrooms, you know, the teachers, the way they are.' Risk and redemption, it seems, are closely interrelated and the need to undergo some form of 'suffering' in the process of claiming an authentic Tongan identity is often implicitly framed around the idea of a rite of passage.

'Learn the Tonga life': Going to Tonga as a rite of passage

Although the discourse around the 'return' of youth to Tonga as a rite of passage is less explicit than that around risk and redemption, there is a common trajectory described by both the youth themselves and the adults observing their experiences that closely fits the classic stages of separation, transition or liminality, and reincorporation (Turner 1967;

Van Gennep 1960). The time spent in Tonga can be seen as a cultural rite of passage or initiation, including the process of 'hazing' by peers and the acquisition of important cultural knowledge through a series of stages leading to eventual acceptance by others as a 'real' Tongan.

Separation: Arrival in Tonga

Even for youth who have frequently visited Tonga before, arriving to stay for a lengthy period can be a daunting prospect and for those who are unfamiliar with life in Tonga it can be what many Tongan adults referred to as 'a huge shock' or 'a culture shock'. For some there is the added emotional impact of feeling abandoned by their parents, when after travelling to Tonga on what they think is a family holiday, they are told they will be staying and attending high school for a while. A 16-year-old boy born and raised in the US said when he arrived in Tonga he was 'mad, angry, unhappy, lonely' and others describe their homesickness, confusion and fears about life in Tonga.

The experiences of youth when they first arrive and begin school can be likened to the 'hazing' common to initiation rituals; it is a time when those in Tonga make it clear these overseas-born youth do not yet belong. A representative from a civil society organisation wryly observed, 'Tongan culture is not a sensitive culture', and it is certainly the case that the students from *muli* (overseas) are frequently teased and mocked by other students, and become the subject of gossip. Due to their poor Tongan language and cultural skills and the fact that they have grown up overseas, they may be derisively called *pālangi* (white), *fie pālangi* (wanting to be white), or *pālangi loi* (pretending to be white). Their clothes and belongings may be taken, particularly if they are in boarding school, and peers will assume that because they are from overseas they are relatively wealthy so will make constant demands on them.

In this 'liminal' stage they are confronted by an unfamiliar environment and their own lack of cultural knowledge. A common claim made by adults in Tonga when discussing diasporic youth was that migrant parents do not teach their children about Tongan culture and daily life; they are supposed to somehow just know. Then, when they get to Tonga, they may find no one there explains anything either; 'basically they feel lost', as a youth worker commented. A 17-year-old female student from Australia said of Tongan culture: 'before Tonga I didn't know what was going on'. In a discussion about this problem of not having anything explained, a 16-year-old girl from New Zealand said: 'I think they think we know, but we don't' and her friend (15, from Australia) added, laughing: 'we don't tell them that we don't know!'

Liminality: 'Learning the culture'

The cultural knowledge that youth lack was described by a senior member of the Ministry of Education and Training as the 'hidden curriculum'. Young people arriving from overseas quickly realise there is a great deal of knowledge they have to acquire in order to be truly Tongan. On their posters the students wrote pleas such as: 'give us time to adjust to the culture' and 'we're different from you so don't expect us to know everything'.

To be accepted and to cope with life in Tonga they have to acquire that cultural knowledge, especially to learn the language, figure out kinship rules and Tongan values and find their place in the social hierarchies with which they have to engage (family, school, church, etc.).[8] They also learn to do hard work and to endure difficult conditions including cold water showers, lack of privacy, insects such as mosquitoes and fleas, and generally far less access to material goods, entertainment and technology than overseas. The students frequently summarised this as 'learn the Tongan life', which they often qualified as 'the hard life'. Both males and females described how they had learned to embody all this cultural knowledge, including their physical mastery of tasks like making an underground oven, building a fire to cook food outside or learning traditional Tongan dances. Their photographs for the project and those they put on their Facebook sites reflect this pride in becoming more Tongan and show them doing typical Tongan chores, or dressed in their traditional dance costumes, in their school uniforms or ready for church wearing formal Tongan clothing.

Despite their obvious pride in what they had learned there were many complaints during the school *talanoa* sessions about 'the hard life'. The students frequently bemoaned the amount of difficult physical work demanded of them both at home and at school—where in most cases

---

8   In a study of 'at-risk' New Zealand born Tongan youth sent to live in Tonga, Adrian Schoone (2008, 2010) has analysed their transformation as 're-scripting' their lives. Schoone describes the way these young people changed their 'personal narratives' through immersion in *anga fakatonga* (the Tongan way).

students are expected to work in the school plantation, keep the grass cut around the school and undertake other maintenance tasks. Another common complaint was poor quality food and general lack of food, particularly from youth in the boarding schools. They described a diet of white rice, flour dumplings and bread, and starchy root vegetables. When asked what they missed most about living overseas an almost unanimous initial response was 'food!' followed by lists of the many varieties of food they could not get in Tonga. When asked what they hated most about being in Tonga, again the typical response was 'the food!'

Getting used to the hard life also entails learning how to manage one's emotions. For boys, this can be particularly challenging when confronted with different expectations around violence. A 17-year-old at Toloa, the boys' boarding school, who had grown up in the US and had only been to Tonga once before as a small child, admitted that when he arrived: 'I wasn't really used to Tongan life. I wasn't used to speaking the language, I wasn't used to like socialising with the kids, like especially [when] they play around. They play around a lot, very, very aggressively'. He observed that in the US if someone hit him hard, he would hit back: 'it's gonna be a fight'. In Tonga, he explained, 'it's just a joke. Like if someone hits, punches you in the ear and it hurts, you just laugh at it'. However, he ended his comments by adding that in the US 'everyone keeps to themselves. Out here everyone's open, everyone's friendly'. Continuing this conversation a 15-year-old boy said that when people mocked him, he had to 'let it go fast' and not react or he would get into trouble, 'so I just tend to control myself'. When asked: 'but overseas, if someone did it you'd knock them out?' the whole group of boys chimed in with an emphatic 'Yeah!'

As mentioned previously, both boys and girls have to learn to deal with the violence associated with physical punishment, although some had already experienced this within their families overseas. Boys tended to underplay this form of violence by joking about it just as they had learned to cope with 'friendly' violence from peers. Some attempted to sound blasé: 'Nah, getting used to it' or 'it's just like a few hidings and that's all'. The girls were less accepting of physical punishment, particularly at school, and one group in particular returned to this topic without prompting during every weekly discussion session and were clearly distressed by their experiences. Nevertheless, most of the students endured this punishment because they saw it as part of Tongan culture—apart from two girls who claimed that every time a teacher seemed likely to hit them they would yell: 'You can't hit me, I'm under New Zealand protection!'

Throughout the school discussion sessions the cultural value the students referred to most often was respect. Part of their acquisition of cultural knowledge was learning to control their bodies in ways that met the cultural requirements for young people to show respect, as well as to be obedient and compliant. When in the presence of adults they had learned to keep their eyes downcast, to speak softly and never answer back, and to sit quietly for as long as required no matter how uncomfortable they may be. A 17-year-old girl from Australia summed it up:

> I learned the Tongan culture by like always going to church and from home to church, home to school—no other place and stuff and I learned—you know how girls are supposed to respect boys too and how boys are supposed to respect girls? It is also about the clothes we wear at home—I have to wear respectable clothes and so I can't wear whatever I want because it might not be respectful to others. That's what I got.

Reincorporation

Not all young people who go to Tonga want to embrace Tongan culture and some struggle against it for their whole stay. Some, like Sela, have to return overseas because they simply cannot adjust to 'the hard life' and many emerge from their experience with a new appreciation of the comforts and opportunities they have in the diaspora. Although few return overseas completely unaffected by their time in Tonga, the experience is not always transformative. The most profound self-transformation is experienced by youth for whom the time in Tonga is effectively a rite of passage, as they acquire Tongan language and cultural knowledge and are eventually accepted as 'proper' or 'real' Tongans. Some wholeheartedly embrace their new status and become what I have previously called 'born again Tongans' (Morton 2002). Others use their experience in Tonga to learn to shift between different personae in order to fit changing contexts, until they are as comfortable with their 'Tonganness' as with their more cosmopolitan selves.

Conclusion

Madeleine Dobson (2009) has discussed how children moving with their families can influence the process of migration even when they have no choice in the move itself. Children separated from their families by migration also influence the outcomes in their own ways: for example, making choices to resist or comply with decisions that affect them; making the most of the experience or reacting with lingering anger and resentment. Much of the literature on youth who 'return' to their parents' homelands focuses on their more negative responses; on their struggles, resentment and alienation. In the Tongan case it also would be easy to focus on the risks and challenges young people face as they cope with their poor language and cultural skills as well as 'the hard life' they encounter. What this would neglect are the more positive outcomes, including in some cases a profound shift in the young person's sense of self and identity.

There are many factors influencing their experiences, in addition to each young person's own agency in coping with life in Tonga. Clearly, boys living out 'in the bush' at Toloa have a much harder life than the students at Tonga High School, a co-educational day school in Nuku'alofa where classes are in English and students are not expected to spend long hours toiling in the school plantations. Yet in each of the schools there were students finding positive aspects of their time in Tonga, particularly their gradual transformation from being mocked as a '*pālangi*' to being accepted by others and, importantly, by themselves as truly Tongan.

Acknowledgements

The project was undertaken through La Trobe University, with funding from the Australian Research Council Discovery Projects scheme, 2012–14. My thanks to the Government of Tonga for permission to conduct this research and to Rebecca Tauali'i and Ebonie Fifita, who did an excellent job of running the school *talanoa* sessions. I am grateful to the students for their enthusiastic participation and to the schools that allowed us to work with their students; as well as to the adult Tongans who also participated. *Mālo aupito* to Meliame Fifita and Hainoame Fulivai for their valuable contributions to the project.

References

Arowolo, O 2000, 'Return migration and the problem of reintegration', *International Migration*, vol. 38, no. 5, pp. 59–80. doi.org/10.1111/1468-2435.00128

Barrow, C 2010, *Caribbean childhoods: 'outside', 'adopted' or 'left behind'. good enough parenting and moral families*, Ian Randle Publishers, Kingston.

Bohr, Y & Tse, C 2009, 'Satellite babies in transnational families: a study of parents' decision to separate from their infants', *Infant Mental Health Journal*, vol. 30, no. 3, pp. 265–286. doi.org/10.1002/imhj.20214

Christou, A & King, R 2006, 'Migrants encounter migrants in the city: the changing context of "home" for second-generation Greek-American return migrants', *International Journal of Urban and Regional Research*, vol. 30, no. 4, pp. 816–835. doi.org/10.1111/j.1468-2427.2006.00697.x

Coe, C 2008, 'The structuring of feeling in Ghanaian transnational families', *City and Society*, vol. 20, no. 2, pp. 222–250. doi.org/10.1111/j.1548-744X.2008.00018.x

Connell, J 1990, 'Modernity and its discontents: migration and change in the South Pacific', in J Connell (ed.), *Migration and development in the South Pacific*, Pacific Research Monograph No. 24, The Australian National University, Canberra, pp. 1–28.

Conway, D & Potter R, 2007, 'Caribbean transnational return migrants as agents of change', *Geography Compass*, vol. 1, no. 1, pp. 25–45. doi.org/10.1111/j.1749-8198.2006.00001.x

Conway, D & Potter, R (eds) 2009, *Return migration of the next generations: 21st century transnational mobility*, Ashgate, Farnham.

Dobson, M 2009, 'Unpacking children in migration research', *Children's Geographies*, vol. 7, no. 3, pp. 355–360. doi.org/10.1080/14733280903024514

Dreby, J 2007, 'Children and power in Mexican transnational families', *Journal of Marriage and Family*, vol. 69, pp. 1050–1064. doi.org/10.1111/j.1741-3737.2007.00430.x

Esser, J 2011, 'From hyperghettoization to the hut: dilemmas of identity among transmigrant tipoti in the Kingdom of Tonga', PhD thesis, University of Minnesota.

Gmelch, G 1980, 'Return migration', *Annual Review of Anthropology*, vol. 9, pp. 135–159. doi.org/10.1146/annurev.an.09.100180.001031

Guarnizo, L 1997, 'The emergence of a transnational social formation and the mirage of return migration among Dominican transmigrants', *Identities*, vol. 4, pp. 281–322. doi.org/10.1080/1070289X.1997.9962591

Hatfield, M 2010, 'Children moving "home"? Everyday experiences of return migration in highly skilled households', *Childhood*, vol. 17, pp. 243–256. doi.org/10.1177/0907568210365747

James, K 1991, 'Migration and remittances: a Tongan village perspective', *Pacific Viewpoint*, vol. 32, no. 1, pp. 1–23.

Lee, H 2003, *Tongans overseas: between two shores*, University of Hawai'i Press, Honolulu.

Lee, H 2009, 'The ambivalence of return: second-generation Tongan returnees', in D Conway & R Potter (eds), *Return of the next generations: 21st century transnational mobility*, Ashgate, Farnham, pp. 41–58.

Macpherson, C 1985, 'Public and private views of home: will Western Samoan migrants return?', *Pacific Viewpoint*, Special Issue: Mobility and Identity in the South Pacific, vol. 26, no. 1, pp. 242–262.

Maron, N & Connell, J 2008, 'Back to Nukunuku: employment, identity and return migration in Tonga', *Asia Pacific Viewpoint*, vol. 49, no. 2, pp. 168–184. doi.org/10.1111/j.1467-8373.2008.00368.x

Matthei, L & Smith, D 1998, 'Belizean "Boyz 'n the 'Hood"? Garifuna labour migration and transnational identity', in M Smith & L Guarnizo (eds), *Transnationalism from below*, Transaction Publishers, New Brunswick, pp. 270–290.

Menjivar, C 2002, 'Living in two worlds? Guatemalan-origin children in the United States and emerging transnationalism', *Journal of Ethnic and Migration Studies*, vol. 28, no. 3, pp. 531–555. doi.org/10.1080/13691830220146590

Ministry of Training, Employment, Youth and Sports 2007, *The Tonga National Youth Strategy 2007–2012*, Kingdom of Tonga, Nuku'alofa.

Moran-Taylor, M 2008, 'When mothers and fathers migrate north: caretakers, children, and child rearing in Guatemala', *Latin American Perspectives*, vol. 35, pp. 79–95. doi.org/10.1177/0094582X08318980

Morton, H 2002, 'Creating their own culture: Diasporic Tongans', in P Spickard, J Rondilla & D Hippolite Wright (eds), *Pacific diaspora: Island peoples in the United States and across the Pacific*, University of Hawai'i Press, Honolulu, pp.135–149.

Orellana, M, Thorne, B, Chee, A & Lam, WSE 2001, 'Transnational childhoods: the participation of children in processes of family migration', *Social Problems*, vol. 48, no. 4, pp. 572–591. doi.org/10.1525/sp.2001.48.4.572

Panagakos, A 2004, 'Recycled odyssey: creating transnational families in the Greek diaspora', *Global Networks*, vol. 4, no. 3, pp. 299–311. doi.org/10.1111/j.1471-0374.2004.00095.x

Parrenas, R 2001, 'Mothering from a distance: emotions, gender and intergenerational relations in Filipino transnational families', *Feminist Studies*, vol. 27, no. 2, pp. 361–390. doi.org/10.2307/3178765

Pereira, N 2011, 'Return[ed] to paradise: the deportation experience in Samoa and Tonga', MOST-2 Policy Paper 21, UNESCO, Paris.

Potter, R & Phillips, J 2006a, 'Both black and symbolically white: the "Bajan-Brit" return migrant as post-colonial hybrid', *Ethnic and Racial Studies*, vol. 29, no. 5, pp. 901–927. doi.org/10.1080/01419870600813942

Potter, R & Phillips, J 2006b, '"Mad dogs and transnational migrants?" Bajan-Brit second-generation migrants and accusations of madness', *Annals of the Association of American Geographers*, vol. 96, no. 3, pp. 586–600. doi.org/10.1111/j.1467-8306.2006.00707.x

Schoone, A 2008, 'Re-scripting life: the experiences of New Zealand-born Tongan "youth at-risk" sent to Tonga', MA thesis, Development Studies, University of Auckland.

Schoone, A 2010, 'Re-scripting life: New Zealand-born Tongan "youth-at-risk" narratives of return migration', *MAI Review*, vol. 1, pp. 1–11.

Suarez-Orozco, C, Todorova, I & Louie, J 2002, 'Making up for lost time: the experiences of separation and reunification among immigrant families', *Family Process*, vol. 41, no. 4, pp. 625–643. doi.org/10.1111/j.1545-5300.2002.00625.x

Tetteh, E 2008, '"My parents are 'burghers'": a study of international labour migration and families in Ghana', PhD thesis, University of Tromso, Norway.

Tsuda, T 2009, *Diasporic homecomings: ethnic return migration in comparative perspective*, Stanford University Press, Stanford.

Turner, V 1967, *The forest of symbols*, Cornell University Press, Ithaca, New York.

Vaioleti, T 2006, 'Talanoa research methodology: a developing position on Pacific research', *Waikato Journal of Education*, vol. 12, pp. 21–34.

Van Gennep, A 1960 [1909], *The rites of passage*, translated by Monika B Vizedom and Gabrielle L Caffee, University of Chicago Press, Chicago.

Wessendorf, S 2007, '"Roots migrants": transnationalism and "return" among second-generation Italians in Switzerland', *Journal of Ethnic and Migration Studies*, vol. 33, no. 2, pp. 1083–1102. doi.org/10.1080/13691830701541614

Whitehouse, B 2009, 'Transnational childrearing and the preservation of transnational identity in Brazzaville, Congo', *Global Networks*, vol. 9, no. 1, pp. 82–99. doi.org/10.1111/j.1471-0374.2009.00243.x

Zhou, M 1998, '"Parachute kids" in Southern California: the educational experience of Chinese children in transnational families', *Educational Policy*, vol. 12, pp. 682–703. doi.org/10.1177/0895904898012006005

Zúñiga, V & Hamann, E 2009, 'Sojourners in Mexico with U.S. school experience: a new taxonomy for transnational students', *Comparative Education Review*, vol. 53, online. doi.org/10.1086/599356

5

Agency and selfhood among young Palauan returnees

Rachana Agarwal

Abstract

This chapter examines the phenomenon of reverse mobility to the Micronesian island of Palau through the perspective of three relatively young Palauan females. The transnational networks that facilitate travel along with key aspects of Palauan social organisation that influence and shape returnees' experiences are described. Importantly, the category of youth is analysed as a culturally constructed subaltern designation within Palauan society, such that those believed to belong to this substratum are structurally subordinated to Palauan elders. In light of the age-related social dichotomy between the younger and the older populations, efforts to exercise agency and assert autonomy by young Palauans transitioning back to life on their home island emerges as a crucial theme. Through extended narratives, I demonstrate how young returnees strive to carve out their own social positions by continuously negotiating their roles in Palauan society. Doing so constitutes an agentive act that is intimately linked to the construction of selfhood. The presented cases are theorised using conceptual tools proposed by Holland et al. Together, they provide insight into the experience of return migration from an age-based gendered lens.

Introduction

Mobility is a familiar theme in Palauan myths and legends. The earliest written record of foreign travel dates from the 18th century and chronicles the journey of a young Palauan of about 20 years of age. This historically significant event dates as far back as 1783 when Lee Boo, the son of a Palauan chief, Ibedul, accompanied Captain Henry Wilson all the way to England (Keate 2002 [1788]; Peacock 1987). Unfortunately, however, he succumbed to smallpox during his stay there and, consequently, his dream to return to his homeland remained unfulfilled. He never set foot in Palau again. Despite its tragic end, it is almost as if Lee Boo's seminal voyage set in motion the modern trend of Palauan youth[1] travelling to distant shores to acquire foreign knowledge and skills. Unlike their predecessor, however, today's youth frequently move back and forth between their homeland and other countries, returning either for short vacations or to finally drop anchor in Palau.

Nowadays, young Palauans chart multiple trajectories to numerous foreign destinations, ranging from the east coast of the US mainland to Taiwan and New Zealand. Their geographic spread and frequency of travel is in keeping with recent scholarship on youth culture and globalisation and exemplifies the observation that contemporary youth traverse local and international boundaries with increasing speed and effortlessness (Dolby and Rizvi 2008; Wulff 1995). Hezel (2001) has noted increasing migration trends in Micronesia (2001: 144–145), and Nero and Rehuher (1993) comment on gender-based migration patterns, pointing out the slightly higher number of Palauan females pursuing education abroad (1993: 251). While educational endeavours, employment, enlistment in the American military and living with relatives overseas are the key reasons that pull youth away from Palau, their motives to return are more diverse: to care for ageing kin members, meet familial and customary obligations (*siukang*), retain land ownership, pay off student loans, for holidays, because of financial and circumstantial reasons, to experience a sense of belonging lacking elsewhere or to finally realise their original intent to resettle in their homeland.

---

1   I use the terms, 'youth' and 'young Palauans/returnees' interchangeably for convenience and to connote how such persons are perceived by Palauan elders. However, these relatively young persons, most of whom are in their 20s or early 30s, may not all perceive themselves as 'youth'. They are nevertheless defined as such in the Palauan sociocultural context where adulthood is signalled at 35 or 40 years of age.

However, homecoming may not be a smooth and seamless process for all youth. Aside from individual particularities, underlying sociocultural factors, such as the cultural construction and social position of youth within multiple scales of hierarchy, may complicate the transitional life back home. In normative terms, youth maintain a markedly subordinate position to those categorised as mature adults and elders. Importantly, however, the social categories of young and elderly Palauans, while distinct, are not static or immutable. Many Palauan elders today may have sojourned overseas in their youth and would likely have been exposed to alternative lifestyles. In fact, they may continue to travel abroad for conferences, workshops, medical treatments or to visit their children and relatives residing outside Palau. Nevertheless, upon return, they often become gradually steeped and invested in Palauan customs and politics, and thereby come to embody an intensely hierarchical social system. Palauan elders may be keen to exert local authority and maintain the status quo as they benefit from it. Their adherence to Palauan social norms effectively continues to privilege elders and may be perceived as oppressive by some youth.

The culture of deference towards elders (*omengull*), a linchpin of Palauan society, relegates young returnees to uncomfortable and structurally disadvantageous positions. This includes cases when returnees are deemed subaltern despite attaining impressive academic qualifications elsewhere or being single parents well into their 30s and wishing to raise their children in their homeland. Readjusting to life in Palau involves inhabiting or reinhabiting a socially designated position determined largely on the basis of clan ranking order and kinship, especially one's maternal ancestry (Barnett 1949; Smith 1983; Parmentier 1987). Young people are usually considered extensions of their families and not independent individuals in their own right. Being constantly perceived as such upon return may result in a conflicted identity or a subtle shift in one's sense of self as the young person struggles to confine him or herself to a predetermined and externally imposed social role. Therefore, the reception of young returnees in Palauan society emerges as a cogent determinant of their lived experiences at home and has an enduring influence on self-construction. After an initial period of adjustment, some returnees find the sense of belonging, rootedness and contentment they may have been seeking. Others report feelings of discontent, disillusionment, frustration and ambivalence resulting from factors such as how youth are generally perceived, their unmet expectations of an imagined homeland, local politics, nepotism, and the difficulty of readjustment to the work culture as well as the social environment in Palau.

I draw on data gathered from two preliminary fieldtrips to Palau in 2006 and 2007, and extended fieldwork from 2008 to 2009, to present three individual narratives of young Palauan female returnees. All three, Hannah, Diana and Dilumang,[2] were highly educated, unmarried young women at the time. Diana was in Palau for an extended visit— one of many such circular transnational movements. Hannah and Dilumang, on the other hand, had chosen to permanently resettle in Palau. Gendered experiences of mobilities of return are especially significant in light of the matrilineal emphasis in Palauan social organisation. All three females, two of whom were then in their mid-20s and one in her early 30s, came from privileged backgrounds, in the sense that their respective families could comfortably provide for their needs and education, hire domestic help and make arrangements for foreign travel and even employment for their daughters. Two of the families were quite prominent socially and enjoy elevated rank in the clan system. In sum, they represent the elite of Palauan society.

As this chapter demonstrates, despite their socially structured subordination, young returnees do not passively accept the position that is expected of them. Instead, they actively negotiate their roles in society and strive to assert autonomy and individuality while at the same time integrating into the community hierarchy. When examining individual narratives, I conceptualise agency and selfhood as closely related analytic constructs, such that the self may be continually fashioned, contested, validated and transformed through actions of the individual and through interactions with social relations, such as kin and community members. I draw on the theory of identity proposed by Holland et al., defined as emotionally imbued 'self-understandings'[3] (1998: 3), and their concepts of positional identities, agency as improvisation and the balancing of culturalist and constructivist principles in the construction of selfhood, all of which are explicated in some detail later. Within this framework,

---

2 All names are pseudonyms and I have deliberately concealed and changed some revealing details about my Palauan interlocutors to maintain anonymity.

3 Since selfhood is implicated in the very definition of identity, Holland et al. sometimes use 'identity' and 'self' interchangeably. I mostly use selfhood instead of identity, even though both are assigned the same conceptual and analytic meaning.

the central goal of this chapter is to examine the constellation of sociocultural, political, economic and transnational structural forces that enable, shape and restrict young Palauans' choices, and identify elements of youth agency as they navigate life in Palau.

Perhaps reflecting the socially inferior position of youth in Palauan society, youth perspectives are virtually absent in the ethnographic literature on Palau (Agarwal 2013). By contrast, my intent here is to emphasise the individual voices of my young interlocutors. Hence, I present extended narratives and excerpts from recorded conversations to highlight their unique, emotionally resonant 'self-understandings'. In doing so, I hope to highlight the act of narrating one's story as an important agentive process. To background this agency, I begin with a description of various transnational and local structures involved, followed by a discussion of some patterns of recent reverse mobilities in Palau.

Structures of transnational relations and social hierarchies

A confluence of transnational and local sociocultural factors set the parameters for youth mobility. As a nation, Palau maintains different political-economic alliances, and such international ties not only shape, but actually 'create' the possibility of transnational migration. Two of these relations, one with Japan and the other with the US, stem from Palau's complex and extensively documented colonial history (Gale 1979; Heine 1974; Hughes and Lingenfelter 1974; Leibowitz 1996; McHenry 1975; Nevin 1977; Kiste 1993).

Japan colonised Palau between the two world wars until its eventual defeat at the end of the Second World War led to the advent of the American administration in Micronesia. Since decolonisation in the mid-1940s, Japan has resumed cordial political-economic ties with Palau, which is manifested through, among other measures, the provision of scholarships and grants for educational pursuits. This allows young Palauans to travel between the two countries with relative ease. After the Second World War, various Micronesian states, including Palau, were declared United Nations Trust Territories to be administered by the US. Charged with the task of 'developing' Micronesia, the US cultivated a persistent economic dependence on the islands that was formalised through the

Compact of Free Association, which, for Palau, came into effect with political independence in 1994. Under this agreement, Palau has received staggering amounts of financial assistance from the US, with a trust fund valued at $147 million set up since the last comprehensive review of the Compact in 2010 (US Department of State website). This strategic relation continues to enable Palauans to travel, study and work freely in the US. Palauans also enlist in the American military and may attain dual citizenship. Academic pursuit in the US is one of the main reasons for youth mobility, however, and numerous sources of financial support make this avenue a realistic and affordable one. In addition, youth also travel frequently to the Philippines, Taiwan, New Zealand, Fiji and other nations to study.

Complementing such opportunities, the Palauan government has established the Palau National Scholarship Board (PNSB), a state apparatus that provides educational loans, scholarships and grants to Palauan citizens. Importantly, PNSB conditions stipulate the return of citizens to serve in their homeland for specified lengths of time. Thus, youth may be obliged to return to pay off student loans and may find it necessary to secure employment in Palau for many years to do so.

While financial incentives from foreign entities and Palau's own national resources facilitate the transnational movement of youth, social organisation within Palau critically impacts young returnees. Palauan social structure may be divided into two broad categories, including *klou el chad*, elders and mature adults, on the one hand, and *kekerei el chad*, children and young people, on the other (Parmentier 1987). This division creates a fundamental hierarchy such that the young must defer to elders and give them obeisance (*omengull*). Consequently, youth are expected to constantly police themselves and be mindful of their behaviour, speech and actions, especially when in the company of elders. Indeed, on an island such as Palau, where there is intense social and spatial proximity because of its relatively small population and limited geographic size, heightened surveillance and lack of anonymity impacts everyone regardless of age.

In Palau, a person's agency and identity is heavily defined by her or his socially designated position and the responsibilities and rights that such positioning entails. The concept of positional identity defined by Holland et al. (1998) is particularly applicable to the Palauan context as it operates on the premise that a person's identity is founded within existing social hierarchies. They maintain that, 'positional identities are about acts that constitute relations of hierarchy, distance, or perhaps affiliation' (Holland et al. 1998: 128). Youth's positional identities are established by a confluence of factors: age, primogeniture, genealogy, rank of clan, village, state and gender being some of the most important determinants. All Palauans occupy specific social positions, of course, but in the case of youth, their age subjugates them to Palauan elders. The culture of deference imposes a tangible yoke on youth and limits their actions both publicly and privately. It permeates their relationships with elders and may sometimes create a socially stifling or oppressive environment.

Operating within such social hierarchies involves the dynamic interplay of individual desires and societal expectations. This is encapsulated in two approaches offered by Holland et al.— the culturalist approach that emphasises the influence of social norms in regulating behaviour, and the constructivist approach that underscores agentive improvisation by individuals. From the culturalist perspective, behaviour is guided by the expectation of social conformity such that an individual 'seeks to conduct herself so as to do right by a preconstituted, culturally given, moral world' (1998: 13). However, actors are bound to encounter situations 'that do not fit the rules' (Holland et al. 1998: 13), in which case they will be compelled to improvise and act in ways that may not be foreseen or dictated by cultural convention. Hence, according to Holland et al., the culturalist approach does not account for improvisation whereas, 'constructivists think of improvisation as an expected outcome when people are simultaneously engaged with or pushed by contradictory discourses' (1998: 17). Applied to the Palauan context, the culturalist paradigm may grant youth 'greater or lesser access to spaces, activities, genres, and through those genres, authoritative voices, or any voice at all' (Holland et al. 1998: 127–128). In the Spivakian sense, strict adherence to culturalist principles may not allow youth the 'space' to voice their thoughts, feelings and concerns or exercise agency when immersed in Palauan society (Spivak 1988).

One of my interlocutors, Diana, who I introduce in more detail below, once mentioned a Palauan phrase that is sometimes used to derisively remind a woman of her social position by likening the person to her mother. This remark, 'Ke kora di ua delam' ('You are just like your mother'), is considered an insult and can be extremely provocative. This is especially the case given the matrilineal context, where one's maternal ancestry[4] commands reverence and must not be casually discussed in public. Diana translated and explained the phrase in the following words: 'You're just like your mother, because usually peoples' opinions of you are based on your family; not on what you do, like as an individual, but who your family [is]'. This instant identification of a female with her mother, and consequently her maternal lineage, positions a person along lines of descent within the larger social matrix. Youth are expected to comprehend and internalise their social position so as to appropriately behave and interact with other Palauans, especially elders. A Palauan's social position therefore informs her (or his) sense of self in fundamental ways.

Another crucial social determinant relating to lineage is the identification of a child with the maternal or paternal matrilineage. Although descent may be traced bilaterally (Barnett 1949), the emphasis on matriliny dictates that a 'child of the woman' (*ochell*) is entitled to primary rights whereas a 'child of the man' (*ulechell*) has secondary rights (Smith 1983: 42). A youth may be able to exercise greater agency in his or her maternal home(s) in comparison to the paternal one(s). Beyond the hierarchies of age and genealogy, each clan in every village, every village in each state, and all 16 Palauan states are also ranked (Vidich 1949; Parmentier 1987). Therefore, youth are expected to be cognisant not only of their age and maternal and paternal affiliations, but also of the social order of their clan, village and state when calibrating their social status in relation to other community members. All of these sociocultural factors constitute the structural forces that influence the everyday lives of Palauan youth.

Using the analytic tools developed by Holland et al. (1998), I present three cases of female returnees, describing their adaptive processes in Palauan society. These are not intended to be representative of young returnees at large. Instead, their voices are those of a gendered and educationally accomplished segment of Palauan society that has the resources to facilitate transnational mobility. Furthermore, the narratives I present capture only partial fragments of their lives. The primary aim is to spotlight how they perceive themselves and their roles in Palauan society.

---

4   Various female kin, such as aunts and grandmothers, may take on caregiving roles and occupy the same position of maternal authority.

Trends in return mobilities

In recent history, Micronesian migration trends have soared since the 1960s, primarily because of the policy changes introduced by the US Kennedy administration (Nero and Rehuher 1993). Following an initial period of 'benign neglect' (Kiste 1993: 70), the eventual American investment in the 'development' of Micronesia and Micronesians generated considerable opportunities for islanders to not only travel to the US for educational pursuits, but also to return to their island homes to find employment, particularly in various administrative capacities (Nero and Rehuher 1993). Palauans benefited enormously in this regard, and a large proportion returned to Palau in the 1980s, a period in which a sense of national identity was heightening. Many were employed in the government as well as the growing private and service sectors in the emerging Palauan nation. One of my older male interlocutors reported that he had chosen to return to Palau in his youth many years ago because he felt like a 'nobody' in Hawai'i, while he had the comfort of a recognised social position in Palau. Likewise, many people in the contemporary population of elderly Palauans have previously lived abroad, especially in the US, for lengthy periods before finally resettling in Palau. Numerous political figures in the elected government, highly respected authorities and titleholders in the chiefly system, teachers, medical professionals, educational administrators, entrepreneurs and local social scientists, among others, have had prior experience in the American military or substantial exposure to overseas educational systems. Such persons, who may be recognised locally as successful returnees, have, in effect, created a now well-trodden path for all kinds of foreign pursuits followed by eventual return to the homeland. They have set forth a pattern of 'chain migration' and have provided a 'living demonstration to young adults in the community' of the possibilities of mobility (Gmelch 1980: 153; Lee-Cunin 2005: 125.) In conversations, I observed that many Palauan youth do, in fact, perceive such socially established figures as role models and attribute their success to their foreign-earned credentials.

Over the years, Palauans have established extensive networks of social relations stretching across and beyond the Pacific Ocean to facilitate international mobilities. Asang employs the Palauan linguistic term *klaingeseu* to refer to the process of mutual assistance and social support for foreign travel, and describes it as 'a tapestry of helping hands' (2000: 371). Youth mobility for educational pursuits is heavily encouraged by most Palauans. Parents consider their foreign-educated children a form of social capital and their success overseas is equated with greater prestige for the family. This trend is in keeping with traditional practices of sending youth outside the home or village to gain foreign skills and knowledge and use them for the benefit of the kin group upon return. Lee Boo, introduced in the opening paragraph, embarked on his voyage with Captain Henry Wilson with exactly this intent.

Unlike the initial wave of migrants who returned and secured employment in newly opened administrative positions in the developing government, job opportunities may not be as easily available for contemporary returnees. Therefore, some believe that Palauans who have found work stability outside Palau would be better off not resettling in their homeland. Instead, they could serve their families and nation by living abroad and sending remittances back home. Many, however, especially parents, want their children to eventually re-establish their base in Palau, where they can find a Palauan partner, start a family and live close to their natal kin. Familial ties often constitute a strong 'pull factor' (Gmelch 1980) for youth to re-establish themselves in Palau. Re-entry may be voluntary and intentional, motivated by long-term resettlement, it may involve several transitory visits and vacations while living abroad, or it may be reluctant or forced because of circumstantial necessity.

The manner in which the Palauan community may receive returnees tends to change with the passage of time. Initially, returnees may be welcomed but also 'othered' to some degree, and may be perceived as outsiders or newcomers on the social scene (Conway et al. 2005: 15). Sometimes this may be manifested linguistically, by addressing a person by her English-derived name, such as Diana or Hannah, instead of the more socially intimate Palauan name, such as Dilumang.[5] The general view held by Palauan resident elders of returnees is that they are young, fresh and confident with new ideas, and need to be reintegrated into the community by relearning social norms and acceptable codes of conduct. For instance, dressing conservatively and not provocatively, especially for women,

---

5   With a few exceptions, most Palauans I met had two first names: one foreign, English-sounding name and one Palauan name. I did meet some Palauans who had only a Palauan name, but none who had only a name of foreign origin. The foreign name is mostly used in public or formal settings, such as in school, at work and so on, whereas, the Palauan name is usually known to kin members and very close friends. It is usually derived from the individual's maternal or paternal genealogy. Hence, the Palauan name is imbued with a familial, intimate, personal meaning and symbolises a person's social link with the matrilineage.

displaying humility and deference to elders, and being proficient in Palauan are all desirable qualities for successful reintegration into Palauan society. Some returnees cross this threshold of cultural appropriateness more easily than others and in doing so may experience more harmonious transitions.

From a cross-cultural perspective, gender has emerged as an important analytic category in the literature on return migration (Conway et al. 2005; Gmelch 1980; Koning 2005; Lee-Cunin 2005; Nero and Rehuher 1993; Pérez 2005; Potter and Conway 2005), and its significance is conspicuous in the Palauan case as well. For instance, findings by Caribbean scholars reveal that female returnees may experience isolation, disenchantment and frustration because of their confinement to the domestic sphere (Pérez 2005: 192–193), and may report 'the loss of the gendered gains made in metropolitan societies' (Potter and Conway 2005: 285). In the Indonesian context, Koning (2005) foregrounds the 'clash of values' (Koning 2005: 166) that Javanese female migrant labourers experience when attempting to reconcile divergent rural and urban values regarding motherhood and marriage in their lives. Nero and Rehuher (1993: 251) discuss the demands of customary obligations and the considerable social responsibilities saddled on women once they return to Palau. The three cases studies that follow complement such scholarship and offer some insight into the individual struggles of young female Palauan returnees.

Hannah: 'It was my choice'

Hannah was a 27-year-old computer studies teacher in a school in Palau, who had strong ties with her paternal family. She had lost her biological mother in her early teenage years and had subsequently been raised by her father and her paternal grandparents. In fact, she had come to think of her paternal grandmother as her mother and that was how she addressed her. Having left Palau in 1998 to pursue computer science on the west coast of the US mainland, she had returned to Palau for a holiday in 2001, and was scheduled to leave for the US right after the September 11 incident. On this occasion, her grandmother expressed deep concern for her safety and advised her to stay in Palau, get married and find employment instead of returning to the US. However, Hannah was determined to resume her academic training and stood her ground by deciding to return to the US. She reassured her family that if the situation in the US worsened, she would call home every day to remain in constant touch with them. She was emphatic in her assertions to her family and confidently told me: 'It was my choice'. She explicitly framed her decision to continue her studies in the US as a manifestation of her agency. In this instance, her agency emerged in opposition to the wishes of her family as she chose to adopt the constructivist paradigm over the culturalist one that her family preferred. Similarly, she decided of her own accord to return to Palau in 2004. In her words:

> After I graduated [from] college I decided that I had to move back home. And just spend as much time as I had with my grandmother before she passed away because [brief pause] I don't want to have to feel the same feelings that a lot of Palauans go through when you're in the States and a loved one passes away and you just come here for the funeral. I wanted to spend some time with her before she passed away. So, yeah, it was really my choice. I actually just graduated and a week later I flew out. I didn't really care about my stuff. I just gave them up for free because I just wanted to just come back home.

I asked if her family had been surprised with her decision and she affirmed that they had. She moved in with her grandmother and shouldered all her responsibility by taking care of the expenses, and she even assumed the duties of the Filipina domestic helper whom her sister had hired to attend to her grandmother. Hannah appeared to be very content with her decision and did not seem to think of it as a sacrifice at all. Over time, her desire to play a particular social role and her family's expectations of her had become aligned. She wholeheartedly embraced the culturalist paradigm and recognised her choice to do so as a self-agentive act.

It is possible that Hannah's decision to eventually return to Palau was motivated by strong pull factors, such as her affection for her grandmother and the internalised cultural obligation of intergenerational reciprocity, according to which the caregiving of ageing kin members is expected from offspring in return for the care received by them in formative years. However, Hannah emphasised her conviction that her movements between Palau and the US were a direct product of her own agency and not a consequence of succumbing to social pressure. She identified the prioritisation of her social obligations in Palau as a marker of her agency, just as much as her decision to continue studying computer science in the US.

Dilumang: 'What you think of yourself is not how people see you'

I first met Dilumang at an educational institution in Koror where she was an adjunct faculty member. When I expressed my desire to contact her later she handed me her business card imprinted with the emblem of a distinguished American university, establishing her as a PhD candidate in a social science department. Our first substantive conversation took place in September 2008, when we met for lunch at a local restaurant. We talked about a Palauan historic preservation symposium that we had both attended. Dilumang remarked on the presence of students at the symposium, which she noted was setting a precedent of sorts since conventionally only adults, mostly Palauan elders, participated in such events. It was gradually becoming clear to me that she was fairly critical of the structural subordination of youth in Palau. She commented that with regard to her own academic accomplishments she refrained from openly announcing her doctoral candidacy since she had returned to Palau, as elders would be quick to put her in her place. Although she was in her early 30s, her experiences had led her to believe that she was still categorised as a young person in Palauan society. She complained that even though she worked multiple jobs and had a steady income, her relatives treated her as a youth and would not let her contribute financially in *siukang* (Palauan customs). She considered this an upsetting affront because she thought of herself as an economically independent adult, a single parent and someone who was striking out on her own without exploiting the clout her family had in Palauan society. Moreover, she was eager to participate in customs to better integrate into Palauan society since she had lived abroad for many years. She surmised that, had she been married, her relatives would have expected her to contribute financially. But because she stood on her own, her relatives believed the family should extend support to her instead of the other way around.

Our mutual interest in the social sciences eventually steered our conversation to our respective scholarly pursuits. It seemed to me that her academic training had enhanced and mobilised her political consciousness about Palau's standing in the world as an independent nation-state, and provided her with a vocabulary to articulate her stance on issues pertaining to cultural revitalisation, especially in the face of Palau's ongoing relations with powerful foreign countries. We shared a postcolonial perspective and she remarked that subaltern theory, especially the work of the Indian scholar, Gayatri Spivak, resonated with her. I found it fascinating that although she had devoted herself intellectually to the promotion of Palauan cultural nationalism while a student in the US, her lived experience in Palau was fraught with ambivalence and frustration. Her narratives revealed a profoundly knotty relationship with her kin members and Palauan society at large, complicating her sense of self and belonging in the midst of people who were constantly putting her at arm's length in terms of her involvement in the community.

Upon request, Dilumang offered a detailed account of her coming of age in a fractured family. The first two decades of her life were characterised by familial rupture, discord and locational instability. Her parents had a difficult marriage, which was followed by divorce and a complete severing of ties between the maternal and paternal sides of her family. Living periodically with either her mother or father after their divorce, or a relative, she had shuttled back and forth between the American Midwest, Hawai'i, Guam and Palau. Unavoidably, she slipped in and out of many schools in these places, sometimes every couple of years, depending on which parent she was living with at the time. Legal custody had been granted to only one of the parents and consequently she was expected to completely dissociate herself from the other parent. Eventually, she was able to exercise her will and live with the parent who most keenly attended to her needs and interests. That she managed to keep an impressive academic record despite domestic strife, frequent transitions and changing educational environments, all factors beyond her control, demonstrated her incredible resilience. I wondered aloud if people in Palau recognised her accomplishment of having defended her dissertation proposal. She responded:

> No. So that was a very personal thing for me … establishing that faith in myself … It had nothing to do with what I felt people would perceive of me … the fact that I'm ABD [all but dissertation] now, nobody really understands what that means here. And it's not important. But the fact that I understand what it means and what it's meant for me, gives me the confidence to be here and ah, actually function day to day, as myself. You know, I didn't feel like I had that, uh, stability before. Yeah, I feel like I am grown up now. [Chuckles.] You know, like I can stand on my own two feet and not constantly have to say that 'Oh yeah, I am my dad's daughter and my mum's daughter' for that to give me some kind of grounding …

So a lot of people are actually very intrigued by the fact that I chose this moment to return. And … I can't explain it to them because it's a very personal thing that they probably can't understand, you know.

Dilumang explained that her uncles constantly questioned her determination to complete her doctoral studies. 'Just forget it' and 'you don't need it', were usually the sort of comments she received with regard to her degree. Her relatives wondered what she would 'do' with a PhD when she resettled in Palau. This was why her brother, who resided in the US, had expressed misgivings about her decision to return, afraid she may lose sight of her educational goals. Dilumang asserted, 'I need it [the PhD] for myself. It's something that I need to do for me. I've started it and I want to finish it'. Her doctorate was imbued with a deeply personal, symbolic meaning and was a source of self-validation. Education was a way of exerting agency and getting a sense of control in her otherwise chaotic life. It was an opportunity for her to reconstruct herself, or improvise, to use Holland et al.'s term, outside the constraining parameters of the Palauan social environment. Every milestone in her academic trajectory was a source of strength and self-confidence that emboldened her to face the emotional and psychological demands of life in Palau. Consider the following dialogue in which she describes her efforts to reposition herself in Palauan society:

> **Dilumang:** … it was always uncomfortable for me to return home, and walk around on this island and not even know anybody. And I would be walking by my relatives and they'd be like, 'Oh, are you so-and-so's daughter.' And I'd be like 'Yes, I'm sorry I don't know who you are. I should know, you know.' I was always constantly apologising for not knowing something about something or somebody. And, so I wanted to be able to have some grounding before I returned home. And have something to contribute. And once I defended my proposal I felt like I had the tools, um, to come back and be able to learn without being afraid to learn … That's why I felt comfortable coming home. Even though everybody that I knew [relatives in the US] discouraged me … And then everyone here [in Palau] kept saying, 'It's about time [you returned to Palau]. But now that you're here what are you gonna do?' You know, so they've all been sort of waiting and anticipating my next move. And watching me. [pauses] And everyone always says, 'Oh you're so stubborn', you know. And it's because I don't wanna, ah, manoeuvre in society because I am related to so-and-so. I want it to be based on my merit, my work, my brain … me. And so, me not getting assistance from some of my family, ah, has been like me turning my back. They think I'm stubborn and [pauses]

Rachana: Did they offer assistance?

Dilumang: Oh yeah.

Rachana: You declined.

Dilumang: Graciously. [Laughs] Graciously.

She continued:

Dilumang: There were all these different offers. But I really just didn't wanna [pauses briefly] get a job like that. So I've been struggling to find work on my own … It's been very difficult to sell myself here because people know who I am automatically. And so I think they are suspicious about why I am not affiliated with my family and why I would wanna work in places where I have applied … But then some of, um, I've been participating in different things and so some people are talking to me and realising, you know, that I am actually interested in other things. And so, I've been getting other kinds of offers lately, which is kind of nice. Which is how I found out about this particular job opening … And then my Dad asked me to help him work in _____ [his home state]. And that is no way anywhere near what I wanna do.

Dilumang's polite refusal to accept financial assistance from her family or to capitalise on their social influence to secure a job illustrates the claim by Holland et al. that 'identities are hard-won standpoints that, however dependent upon social support and however vulnerable to change, make at least a modicum of self-direction possible' (1998: 4.). Her insistence on defining herself as a separate individual with her own mind and ability to make her own decisions, despite being a part of her natal family, demonstrates her agency. The associations that Palauans 'automatically' made between her and her family, despite her efforts to establish herself independently, explain her comment: 'What you think of yourself is not how people see you'. She yearned to be recognised as an accomplished scholar and an independently contributing member of Palauan society, but was usually perceived with paternalism as a child of her family. Although aware of it, she was not deterred by the unceasing scrutiny to which she was subjected. Nor was she dissuaded by the social pressures her well-wishers feared she would encounter in Palau. She emphasised: 'I want to create a niche on my own', and she persevered in doing so upon returning to Palau.

Diana: 'I can't say I'm a hundred per cent Palauan anymore because … living abroad has changed me'

Diana had one foot in Palau and the other in Hawai'i; in the former she was her parents' daughter and the latter a graduate student. Her transnational lifestyle had made her acutely sensitive to the distinct behavioural codes and expectations she observed in the two places as she constantly shifted cultural gears to readjust to each. She lived in Hawai'i for long stretches of time, which were periodically interrupted by return trips to Palau, especially during the holidays. Although this to-and-fro movement across the Pacific occurred with ritualistic regularity, uprooting from one place and transplanting to the other had not become easier over the years. Returning to Palau always signalled a careful change in her presentation of self, especially when in the company of Palauan elders, which she explained in a style characteristic of Goffman (1956):

> **Diana:** You have to act, act, um, differently [in Palau]. Slower in your movement, the way you talk. Make sure you talk at the right time. Um, don't come out too strong. Don't speak your mind. Respect what they say even if you think it's wrong. Don't be too opinionated, you know … Even when you're walking, there's a way … [to] hold yourself. I mean, if they're [Palauan elders] around you and you're walking make sure you always bow. You cannot walk straight up.

In these vivid details, Diana accentuates the performance of deference towards elders and how it is embodied in practice. A change in behaviour with every transnational move is not merely a superficial change in performance at that moment but requires a subtle shift in her sense of self as she plays culturally distinct roles. Diana believed that living abroad for extended periods of time had made her 'a diasporic person', and that such an experience 'sets you in a different space'. Hence, she claimed, 'I can't say I'm a hundred per cent Palauan anymore because … living abroad has changed me'. She reflected that one of the outcomes of such a transformation was that when in Palau, she felt most at ease with people who had, like her, been exposed to the world outside for substantial periods. On one occasion, we were discussing the subject of social acceptance in Palau and how comfortable both she and I felt when spending time with her friends. However, she did not think this was as simple a matter as I made it out to be. She clarified:

Diana: People you hang out with are not typical Palauans. Not, oh no, let me rephrase that. That's, that's problematic. Not that they're not typical Palauans, but they've been outside so they're more open-minded to, like, me. I'm comfortable because I can express myself … and they're okay with it, you know, because they're the same way. Or they know what it's like out there, knowing how you've changed. Like I cannot speak to like just regular Palauans that way. They'll look at me weird, or like 'Wow! This is a new _____ [name of speaker]!' You know! So when I speak to like *mechas* [elderly Palauan women] and you know my aunties then I have to try my best to speak Palauan because they respect you more … Maybe it's just me thinking that if I talk Palauan more I'll be more accepted. I don't know. I talk Palauan and be more respectful to them. It's [a] different me.

Diana's qualifications of Palauans as 'typical', 'regular', 'more open-minded', and her comments regarding herself as 'new' or 'different' point towards the varied constructions of self as a consequence of transnational mobility. Regarding her proficiency in Palauan, she lamented not knowing some of the Palauan words that those residing in *honto*[6] (Babeldaob, big island in Palau) used so casually. And to add to this, 'even my accent is kind of off a little bit'.

She perceived life in Palau as not changing at the same rate as the world outside and believed that studying abroad offered her an opportunity to exercise agency and keep pace with global trends. She stated: 'Well … if you'd ask me, I'd say that going out and being educated is kind of my way of controlling things, you know'. Yet, she claimed she wanted to eventually disentangle herself from the trappings of all 'American things' and 'live a Palauan life' in *honto* where she could attend to her taro patch.[7] As a child she had been very close to her now deceased maternal grandmother who had lived in *honto* and whom Diana would accompany to the taro patch. She reminisced that during those days there were no showers, or electricity or refrigerator, but she loved that life and wanted

---

6   'Honto' is a Japanese word appropriated by Palauans to refer to the big island of Babeldaob in Palau. *Honto* may be used in contrast to the commercial district of Koror to connote a more rural or traditionally Palauan lifestyle free of modern conveniences, such as electricity.

7   Tending the taro patch (*mesei*) is a cultural practice of Palauan women. The quality of taro (*kukau* or *brak*) may signify a woman's worth in the social system, in which women are expected to contribute starchy foods (*ongraol*) to complement the meat or fish (*odoim*) provided by men. Nowadays, some *mechas* (elderly women) continue to take pride in tending their taro patch, while many others hire foreign labour to grow their taro.

to return to that idyllic past. She seemed to have a romanticised and static image of the 'old-fashioned' Palauan way of life from which she and her present reality were far removed.

Strikingly, like Dilumang, Diana also had strong postcolonial research interests with an emphasis on culturally relevant pedagogy. Intellectually, she was most keen to investigate Palauan efforts towards cultural revitalisation and passionately advocated that Palauans ought to take pride in their genealogy and history and their ties to the land. However, ironically, while studying abroad had equipped her with the theoretical and linguistic vocabulary to express her views, and further politicised her in the process, it had also created a cultural and linguistic lag between Diana and those she perceived to be 'true Palauan'. Her experience in Palau every time she returned from Hawai'i betrayed her ambivalence and discomfort with readjustment to life in Palau. It seemed to me that transnational mobility had left her in some sort of limbo. She articulated her liminal predicament quite clearly:

> **Diana:** It's a struggle. It's a struggle. I mean it's good to know you have two homes but having to constantly like transition, or, um, you know, adjust yourself to both environments and expectations that come from it. I mean especially coming to Palau. You know you have to reposition yourself back into the culture … after living in Hawai'i for a long time when you come back here you really have to change how you act. It's different. It's really different.

For Diana, life in Hawai'i afforded her the opportunity to improvise and reconstruct her sense of self. However, her return to Palau required her to subsume her improvisational transformations to the culturalist principles prevalent in Palau; in her words, she had to 'reposition' herself 'back into the culture', which had proven to be challenging. Therefore, the continuous shifting of cultural paradigms was a source of considerable stress for her.

Theorising the agentive self: A comparative analysis

Constructing the self is an ongoing process that is shaped by personal choices and actions and through relational interactions in the inhabited sociocultural and global environments. It may be as much a personally meaningful imaginative craft as it may be a product of societal norms and expectations and foreign influences. For Palauan youth, travel abroad may hypothetically offer an escape from cultural constraints and provide youth with more permissive spaces that allow for greater agency, improvisation and the refashioning of self, as aligned with the constructivist stance. However, upon return to Palau, youth may be expected to relinquish their newfound agency and slip into previously inhabited positional identities once again. They may experience customary obligations as burdensome and the constant subjugation of self under the dictates of Palauan society frustrating.

While this may indeed be the case for some, the conflation of life at home with the culturalist principle and lack of agency, and that of mobility with the constructivist position and manifested agency, may be far too simplistic and misleading. Individuals may choose to operate within a culturalist paradigm even when away from home, just as they may challenge imposed social roles and improvise on established norms when living in Palau. At times, the adoption of the culturalist perspective, for instance, in a global setting such as a foreign, multicultural university, may reflect agency, whereas improvisation may become a conditional necessity, rather than an act of deliberate intent.

Moreover, the culturalist and constructivist positions are not mutually exclusive and may overlap, coexist, bear different weight and be assigned alternative meanings in distinct phases and situations in a person's life. An individual may improvise to some degree while largely embracing a culturalist paradigm or vice versa. Choosing and balancing these paradigms may itself be a marker of agency, and one's choices may change with the passage of time, enabling fluid and 'continuous self-fashioning', as explained by Holland et al. Instances of cognitive dissonance—such as when a person may intellectually align herself with a particular paradigm but experientially prefer another in her daily life—as observed in the cases of Diana and Dilumang are especially revealing. In such cases, the coexistence of culturalist and constructivist paradigms may be fraught with tensions and ambivalence.

The narratives of both Diana and Dilumang demonstrate that their postcolonial leanings and intellectual allegiance to their homeland may not align smoothly with the experiential outcome upon return. Both experienced an unsettling cognitive dissonance between their imagined homeland and the reality of life in Palau. Their perception of a noticeable cultural and linguistic disconnect displays their self-reflexivity and keen awareness of the differences in the cultural worlds they inhabited. They believed that their academic achievements, or improvisational accomplishments, had empowered them to face Palauan society, bolstered their sense of self and encouraged them to reengage with their community, intellectually and more personally. However, both longed for unconditional acceptance from Palauans at home.

Dilumang wanted to accept the culturalist paradigm by re-establishing herself in the Palauan community and raising her children in her homeland. Returning to Palau was a definite marker of her agency for her because she did so on her own terms, against the advice and resistance she received from some of her relatives. But the culturalist principles that were imposed on her did not allow for an easy reconciliation with her constructivist scholarly self. Her academic accomplishments were belittled and despite being a single parent, she felt infantilised by community members. Her example provides an interesting contrast to the common refrain of customary obligations being burdensome for locals. While many Palauans, young and old, would rather extricate themselves from the trappings of *siukang*, Dilumang was keen to participate in such customs to consolidate her position as a productive member of Palauan society.

On the other hand, Hannah was able to successfully inhabit the culturally accepted position of a caring granddaughter. Her agency was reflected in the timing of her choice since she returned to Palau on her own accord and not when her grandmother wanted her to stay behind. Her example illustrates that travel abroad and improvisation need not be the only indicators of a person's ability to act even in highly structured social systems; a wilful decision to adopt the cultural paradigm may very well reflect individual agency.

Displays of agency by young returnees may not be restricted to self-construction. Palauan youth may effectively serve as agents of social change, who may be uniquely positioned to 'remake the world' they encounter in their homeland (Inden 1990: 23 quoted in Holland et al. 1998: 42). They may introduce fresh ideas about human rights, gender and sexuality, present alternative career paths and lifestyles, and broaden and redefine the imaginative boundaries of younger generations.

References

Agarwal, R 2013, 'Asserting identity: youth culture, education and nationalism in contemporary Palau', Unpublished thesis, Brandeis University, Massachusetts.

Asang, I 2000, 'Remaking footprints: Palauan migrants in Hawai'i', *The Contemporary Pacific*, vol. 12, pp. 371–384. doi.org/10.1353/cp.2000.0040

Barnett, HG 1949, *Palauan society: a study of contemporary native life in the Palau Islands*, University of Oregon Publications, Eugene.

Conway, D, Potter, RB & Phillips, J 2005, 'The experience of return: Caribbean migrants', in RB Potter, D Conway & J Phillips (eds), *The experience of return migration: Caribbean perspectives*, Ashgate, Farnham, pp. 1–25.

Dolby, N & Rizvi, F (eds) 2008, *Youth moves: identities and education in global perspective*, Routledge, New York & London.

Gale, R 1979, *The Americanization of Micronesia: a study of the consolidation of U.S. rule in the Pacific*, University Press of America, Washington DC.

Gmelch, G 1980, 'Return Migration', *Annual Review of Anthropology*, vol. 9, pp. 135–159. doi.org/10.1146/annurev.an.09.100180.001031

Goffman, E 1956, *The presentation of self in everyday life*, University of Edinburgh, Social Sciences Research Centre, Edinburgh.

Heine, C 1974, *Micronesia at the crossroads: a reappraisal of the Micronesian political dilemma*, University of Hawai'i Press, Honolulu.

Hezel, FX 2001, *The new shape of old island cultures: a half century of social change in Micronesia*, University of Hawai'i Press, Honolulu.

Holland, D, Lachiocotte Jr, W, Skinner, D & Cain, C 1998, *Identity and agency in cultural worlds*, Harvard University Press, Cambridge, Massachusetts and London, England.

Hughes, D & Lingenfelter, SG (eds) 1974, *Political development in Micronesia*, Ohio State University Press, Columbus.

Keate, G 2002 [1788], *An account of the Pelew Islands*, KL Nero and N Thomas (eds), Leicester University Press, London & New York.

Kiste, R 1993, 'New political statuses in American Micronesia', in V Lockwood, T Harding & B Wallace (eds), *Contemporary Pacific societies: Studies in development and change*, Pearson.

Koning, J 2005, 'The impossible return? The post-migration narratives of young women in rural Java', *Asian Journal of Social Science*, vol. 33, no. 2, pp. 165–185. doi.org/10.1163/1568531054930839

Lee-Cunin, M 2005, 'My motherland, or my mother's land? Return migration and the experience of young British-Trinidadians', in RB Potter, D Conway & J Phillips (eds), *The experience of return migration: Caribbean perspectives*, Ashgate, Farnham, pp. 109–133.

Leibowitz, AH 1996, *Embattled island: Palau's struggle for independence*, Praeger Publishers, Westport, Connecticut and London.

McHenry, DF 1975, *Micronesia, trust betrayed: altruism vs. self interest in American foreign policy*, Carnegie Endowment for International Peace, New York and Washington.

Nero, KL & Rehuher, FK 1993, 'Pursuing the dream: historical perspectives on Micronesian movement patterns', in G McCall & J Connell (eds), *A world perspective on Pacific Islander migration: Australia, New Zealand and the USA*, Pacific Studies Monograph no. 6, Centre for South Pacific Studies, The University of New South Wales, Australia, pp. 239–255.

Nevin, D 1977, *The American touch in Micronesia*, WW Norton & Company, New York.

Parmentier, RJ 1987, *The sacred remains: myth, history, and polity in Belau*, University of Chicago Press, Chicago.

Peacock, DJ 1987, *Lee Boo of Belau: a prince in London*, University of Hawai'i Press, Honolulu.

Pérez, GM 2005, 'A gendered tale of Puerto Rican return: place, nation and Identity', in RB Potter, D Conway & J Phillips (eds), *The experience of return migration: Caribbean perspectives*, Ashgate, Farnham, pp. 183–205.

Potter, RB & Conway, D 2005, 'Experiencing return: societal contributions, adaptations and frustrations', in RB Potter, D Conway & J Phillips (eds), *The experience of return migration: Caribbean perspectives*, Ashgate, Farnham, pp. 283–287.

Smith, DR 1983, *Palauan social structure*, Rutgers University Press, New Brunswick.

Spivak, G 1988, *Can the subaltern speak?* Macmillan, Basingstoke.

Spivak, GC 1994, 'Can the subaltern speak?' in P Williams & L Chrisman (eds), *Colonial discourse and post-colonial theory: a reader*, Columbia University Press, New York, pp. 66–111.

US Department of State, viewed 25 October 2015, www.state.gov/r/pa/ei/bgn/1840.htm

Vidich, A 1949, *Political factionalism in Palau: its rise and development*, Coordinated Investigations in Micronesian Anthropology, Report no. 23, Pacific Science Board, Washington.

Wulff, H 1995, 'Introducing youth culture in its own right: the state of the art and new possibilities', in V Amit-Talai & H Wulff (eds), *Youth cultures: a cross-cultural perspective*, Routledge, London & New York, pp. 1–18.

6

(Be)Longings: Diasporic Pacific Islanders and the meaning of home

Kirsten McGavin

There's nothing like when you're flying into PNG, when you're flying over Port Moresby and you're landing in Jackson's airport and the wheels touch down; it's sort of like, I'm just at ease, I'm at rest. There's nothing like it, you know, this is where you belong. Australia's sort of like my waiting room. It's my home as well and I love Australia, but when you land in Papua New Guinea, your heart sinks into the land and you're like, 'This is where I'm from'.

Rick,[1] 20, born in Australia, of PNG and Australian descent and visiting Papua New Guinea regularly since age 11.

Abstract

For diasporic Pacific Islanders, journeys 'back to home' islands bring different consequences and have varied impacts upon identity and sense of belonging and 'home'. The purpose of these journeys plays a significant role; within this article, I compare the influence of 'homecoming' (specifically designed trips with cultural reconnection as a major impetus) and 'non-homecoming' (e.g. holidays, weddings, birthdays etc.) trips. As people's identities in 'home' islands are scrutinised, negotiated and

---

1   All informants are provided with aliases in order to preserve their anonymity.

contested, two things happen: the boundary between socially defined and self-defined identity becomes increasingly marked; and people's sense of belonging, their idea of 'home'— both in the Pacific Islands and in the diaspora—fluctuates, morphs and/or solidifies. Indeed, identity, home and belonging are highly personalised concepts, shaped in the nexus between experience and expectation. Further, identity becomes defined through a complementary duality of categories, oscillating between a fixed construction of ethnicity/'blood' and a more interpretable idea of behaviour/performance. This is a dichotomy which I have termed 'being' versus 'doing', in which both elements must be present in order to establish an 'authentic', almost indisputable Pacific Islander identity.

Introduction

The very nature of a diaspora relies on the notion that the people 'contained' within it identify—or are perceived to identify—with a distant homeland (Delanty, Wodak and Jones 2008). In many cases, there is a paradisiacal view of the homeland; romanticised, historicised and solidified by family stories about the 'good old days' and things 'back home'. For Pacific Islanders living in Australia, this sense of transnationalism is further reinforced by others asking questions like: 'Where are you from? No, I mean, where are you *really* from?'; 'Have you been home?'; 'What's [your island] like?'. Such questions establish a subtle social distancing of Pacific Islanders from their 'diasporic home' in Australia and situate them instead in terms of their island homeland. Emplaced identity (that is, identity positioned within a particular location)—and its related sense of belonging—provides its bearer with an idea of 'home'. However, for many migrants and/or descendants of migrants, 'home' can be a multivalent concept, fluctuating throughout time and adhering in various degrees to one or more sites and localities (Kleist 2013; Kuah and Davidson 2008; Radhakrishnan 2008; Sawyer 2002; Spickard, Rondilla and Hippolite Wright 2002; Waite and Cook 2011). That is, 'home' can be a *combination of belonging* to the diaspora *and* to the homeland. This is certainly the case for Sam, a 25-year-old who was born in Samoa and grew up in New Zealand and Australia. He says, 'Australia is home now. And New Zealand is home too. Well, they're types of home, but the big home, the real home is Samoa. I guess it depends on how you define it, because when I went to Thailand for my holidays, I came home to Australia.'

For Pacific Islanders in Australia, nothing shapes this sense of belonging—and ipso facto their ethnocultural identity—more than physically visiting the island or islands of their origin. This is a key point, with the importance of the journey 'home' also reflected in Christou and King's (2010: 642) study on German-based Greek diaspora, Chambers' (1994) research on migration and identity, and Papastergiadis' (2000) work on migration and the resultant hybridity of identity (see also Jones 1980; Lubkemann 2004; Markowitz 2007; Markowitz and Stefannson 2004). Indeed, throughout this article, I explore the important interaction between 'return'[2] trips, identity and belonging by focusing on two distinct types of non-permanent journeys 'home': homecomings and non-homecomings. I define 'homecomings' as those trips to the homeland specifically undertaken by the person, and usually accompanied by a senior family member, to learn more about their heritage and family history. 'Non-homecoming' journeys include visiting homelands for more recreational purposes, including events such as general holidays, weddings and birthday parties. I argue that the distinction between homecomings and non-homecomings is an important one as, through my research, I found that each *type* of journey back to homelands usually results in a set of experiences unique to that type, which in turn affects identity and sense of belonging in a particular way. Although Pearce (2012) also examines the effect of *intentionality* of travel on people's experiences and relationship with concepts of home, his focus is on 'visiting home and familiar places' as a subset of the formal visa category of 'visiting family and friends'.

It is important to note that within this article, I focus on Pacific Islanders in Australia rather than on a smaller, discrete Pacific Islander community, for example, Fijians who live in Brisbane or Samoans who live in Sydney. This is because I use my previous work (McGavin 2014), in which I describe the circumstances under which panethnic labels of identity are important to diasporic communities in Australia, as a foundation for my current research.[3] As such, this article centres not only on the effect on identity of the short-term journeys to homelands but also on the effect when people return to their Australian 'homes'.

---

2   Like Tsuda (2009: 1), I problematise the idea of 'returning' or 'going back' to the homeland, because for many people, this is their first visit.

3   I also acknowledge the maintained ethnocultural diversity within diasporic use of categories such as 'Pacific Islander'. This sense of simultaneous togetherness and separateness is also found within homeland regions. As Hall (1990: 227) states of the cultural and historical differences between Islands and Islanders in the Caribbean, 'It positions Martiniquains and as both the same and different. Moreover, the boundaries of difference are continually repositioned in relation to different points of reference'.

For Pacific Islanders, especially those of Melanesian ancestry, the concept of a 'homeland' is often anchored in notions of *peles* (McGavin 2014). McCall and Connell (1993: 263) concur with the sentiment, stating that 'A central quality of Micronesian identity is the strong cultural attachment to home and land, as it is among many Pacific Islanders and other traditional peoples throughout the world'. *Peles* is a multivocal term indicating a person's place (usually a village, but it can also refer to an urban centre, province or island) of Indigenous origin. *Peles* refers not just to the physical landscape, but also to the seascape and starscape and to the less-tangible spheres such as the spiritscape (McGavin 2014). *Peles* is important because, regardless of birthplace or time spent away, a person inherits this affiliation and is said to always belong to and feel welcome in their *peles*. Indeed, some informants describe this connection as being 'carried in their blood',[4] particularly because links to *peles* are defined through matrilineal or patrilineal lines of descent. If these bonds with place are the 'being' part of Islander identity, then behaviour, attitude and performance are its 'doing' component. Indeed, my research has shown that both elements are expected of an 'authentic' Pacific Islander identity, and it is often the 'doing' component which is the most frequently scrutinised by others in the Islander community. Importantly, this is one reason which drives some diasporic Pacific Islanders to journey 'back' to their homeland—because visits to *peles* are perceived as enabling people to *remember* and therefore put into action their cultural knowledge (see McGavin, 2016).

Of course, the urge to reconnect with an ancestral 'home'—and the problematic nature of the reconnecting visits—are not unique to diasporic Pacific Islanders. Maruyama and Stronza (2010) describe Chinese Americans' desires and subsequent travel experiences 'back' to China—and the disillusionment that sometimes follows. 'Chinese Americans, born and raised in the United States … revealed that their imagined personal connection to the ancestral land was often contested in the actual encounter. The differences in language, class, family structure and gender roles overpowered a sense of affinity' (Maruyama and Stronza 2010: 23). While Christou and King (2010) explore similar stories of diasporic German-based Greeks' experiences of 'returning home', they also tell how, for one informant in particular, 'other aspects of the Greek diaspora homeland experience—landscapes and soundscapes, a profoundly

---

4   I realise that many people contest the idea that ethnicity or 'race' is carried within 'blood', but I use this term as an emic descriptor.

ontological sense of belonging—override the disappointments' (Christou and King 2010: 643). Certainly, while 'return' journeys allow Australian-based Pacific Islanders to gain a greater sense of awareness that the homeland is not always the paradise that they had previously envisioned it to be, they also provide people with a stronger sense of ethnocultural identity and belonging—whether socially or self-defined. (I explain the importance of this latter point in a later section of this article.)

I acquired data for this article through conducting interviews and participant observation within diasporic Pacific Islander communities in Australia, as well as in New Zealand and the New Guinea Islands, between 2012 and 2014. Informants were current residents of Australia and were between the ages of 18 and 84. I made no distinction between first, second or subsequent generation migrants and although I do list birthplace when describing an informant's background, it is more to provide readers with a clearer understanding of the participant's cultural knowledge than to highlight the influence of birthplace itself. This is because of my own ethnocultural identity and socialisation as an Australian of Pacific Islander descent, and my consequent knowledge of the importance of concepts of *peles* to Pacific identities. Participants were an even mix of male and female. All informants were Pacific Islanders, which, for the purposes of my study, I define as being anyone with Melanesian, Micronesian and/ or Polynesian descent. I include in this group New Zealand Māori and Australian South Sea Islanders, but I do not include Torres Strait Islanders because of their Indigeneity to Australia.[5]

This article is set out into three major sections. In the first, I provide an exposé of models of identity and 'home' and relate these to the Pacific Islander experience. Secondly, I present three case studies, through which I describe people's journeys to their 'home' islands and investigate the impact each trip 'home' has had on their identity and sense of belonging. Part of this involves the gauging of people's feelings before, during and after the 'home event'. In the third section, I analyse these accounts and reinforce my understanding of them by drawing on data collected from other informants. Here, I examine the socio-politics of the 'return' journey to the Pacific.

---

5   I acknowledge that my definition of 'Pacific Islander', my inclusion of New Zealand Māori and Australian South Sea Islanders, and my exclusion of Torres Strait Islanders from this category may be problematic for some. I realise that in other studies, this use of the term 'Pacific Islander' (and its inclusions and exclusions) may be contested.

I turn now to an exploration of theories of identity and home, in order to establish a framework for understanding the case studies that follow.

Theory and methodology

On identity

As Hall (1990: 222) says of identity, it is 'a "production" which is never complete, always in process ...'. It is vital to develop an awareness of different facets of identity because visits to homelands provide the perfect opportunity for people's identities to come under close inspection. Indeed, the journey 'home' (that is, to the 'homeland') shows Pacific Islanders whether what they have been longing for in terms of 'home' actually exists, and if their connection to it can be supported by a feeling of belonging or weakened by a social rejection of their self- or diasporic-defined identity.

As highlighted above, 'authenticity' vis-à-vis Pacific Islander identity is determined by the presence of two elements, which I have labelled 'being' and 'doing': an Indigenous connection to place, often described in terms of 'blood' and *peles*; and the performance of this descent, through behaviour, attitude and the putting into action of cultural knowledge. In a way, this theory of identity is similar to that put forward by Linton (1936), who explained social organisation in terms of ascription and achievement. According to Linton (1936: 115–116, 128), elements of 'ascription' refer to any characteristic that a person displays that is 'ascertainable at birth', whether socially or biologically constructed (one's sex or 'race' is an example of this), while components of 'achievement' involve 'baits for socially acceptable behavior' and performance. While Linton (1936) used his theory to explain overarching social systems and to describe classifications of social status in general terms, my theory of 'being' and 'doing' is more culturally specific, applying only to individual Pacific Islanders and generated only from my academic interactions with Pacific Islanders through the course of this research and by my socialisation as a person of Pacific Islander ancestry. However, both Linton's (1936) and my theories acknowledge the geopolitics of identity (that is, the ways in which identity is interpreted in various locations/ settings) and recognise the existence of socio-political contestations and negotiations of and over identity construction.

Although a person may seem to have a 'fixed' identity in a particular location (for example, Australia), that same person may have a different identity in another place (for example, Fiji, Hawai'i, Samoa, Tonga etc.). For example, Spickard (2002: 44) argues that Pacific Islander identity—at least in the US—is 'situational', using the example of a woman of mixed Hawaiian, Filipino and Portuguese descent who identifies as: Portuguese when with her grandmother, Filipina if with her paternal aunts, and Hawaiian when on the mainland America. This is a key point, because it highlights the effect that 'return' homecomings and non-homecomings may have on Pacific Islanders' identities, whether socially or self-defined. It is clear that a person's identity—or at least perceptions of it—may flex and change according to the geopolitics of particular localities (Basu 2004: 28; Bhatia and Ram 2009: 142; Brown 2011: 229). For example, Schramm (2009) describes individuals' constructions and negotiations of their racial identities as a response to visits 'home' in Ghana. Indeed, the varying socio-politics of identity from location to location are such that a person may attain a greater understanding of the difference between socially and self-defined identity and during this process, recognise that self-definitions of identity are the most stable.

Hall and du Gay (1996) discuss the stability—and perceived instability—of some elements of identity, particularly the difference between self-determined and socially determined identity. They (Hall and du Gay 1996: 4) state, 'identities are never unified and [are] increasingly fragmented and fractured; never singular but multiply constructed across different, often intersecting and antagonistic, discourses, practices and positions'. Giddens (2013: 188) takes this one step further, positing that others' definitions of an individual are not intrinsically alienating or oppressive—or positive—and that self-defined and socially defined identities are interactive and influence each other. Shotter and Gergen (1989: 4) concur, arguing that identity does not 'begin with two independent entities, individual and society, that are otherwise formed and defined apart from one another and that interact as though each were external to the other'.

As mentioned previously, visits to *peles* are often perceived as allowing diasporic Pacific Islanders to *remember* rather than acquire or learn cultural knowledge; so to reach a position where 'authentic' Pacific Islander identity is the outcome, the 'doing' is dependent on the 'being'.

It is important to remember that, unlike other authors (for example, Tonkinson 1990; Watson 1990) who focus on locally constructed identities in a specific, defined, 'contained' area (for example, Indigenous

Fijian identity in Suva), this article examines a broad, panethnic identity (that is, Pacific Islander) and attempts to theorise the ways in which that identity—or those categories of identity 'contained' within it (for example, Papua New Guinean, Samoan, Tuvaluan)—is interpreted across and between homeland and diasporic 'boundaries'. To that point, although many of my informants used the panethnic term Pacific Islander as one of several categories of self-identification and others did not, their 'return' journeys to 'home' islands showed patterns of similarity—both in terms of how the journey shaped their identity and, in turn, how that affected their sense of belonging and ideas about 'home' after they returned to Australia.

On home

What is 'home'? According to Markowitz (2004: 22), 'home' is 'an everchanging and slippery concept' but one which is related to people's identities and belongings; a place (or places) which provides 'intimate familiarity' and comfort. She argues that 'home' is a beginning *and* end point, where 'people "have to take you in" while understanding that the "have to" is not a matter of externally imposed law but an automatic response to similitude' (Markowitz 2004: 24). Note that Markowitz (2004: 22) also acknowledges that home might be found in multiple locations. This is an especially salient point for people in diaspora who, to various degrees and under certain circumstances, may perceive both the diasporic 'home' and the ancestral 'homeland' as equal in the levels of personal belonging that the places generate for them (Weingrod and Levy 2006: 693).

Tsuda (2009: 3) describes reasons for diasporic homecomings in relation to permanent 'ethnic return migration', whereby people whose family may have lived for several generations in diaspora decide to move back to their homeland. Although this article examines non-permanent journeys 'home', many of the underlying motivations for this type of travel are the same, that is, to rediscover 'ethnic ties to ancestral homelands [and to follow] a nostalgic desire to rediscover ethnic roots' (Tsuda 2009: 3).

For diasporic Pacific Islanders, part of the construction of 'home'—and by extension, ethnocultural identity—relies on cultural memory, which Mageo (2001: 1) describes as involving the 'valorization of certain aspects of the past, as well as amnesia about other aspects'. This process is one via which the romantic, and not always accurate, idea of the homeland may be created and perpetuated (Herbert 2012: 298). Often, diasporic people's notions of the homeland also include ideas about homeland-based people. For example, Gershon (2012: 17) describes how Samoans in New Zealand perceive Samoans in Samoa as being 'pure', 'untainted' and ethnoculturally homogenous, even though this is not the case. Importantly though, cultural memory may also include origin stories, which are entwined with 'family landmarks that Pacific people have long inscribed themselves upon their islands' (Mageo 2001:19). This highlights and reinforces the importance of concepts such as *peles* and the environment, as discussed above. It is important to note, however, that cultural memory is differentiated from the type of 'remembering' of cultural knowledge that is perceived to occur when a person visits their *peles*.

Case studies

In these case studies (each chosen because they demonstrate different aspects of the effect of the *type* of return journey on identity), I detail the experiences of three Australian-based Pacific Islanders, relating to their visit to their 'home' islands. For ease of flow, I have edited these accounts so that they appear as monologues rather than the two-way conversations that were had between the informant and me. In doing so, I aimed to preserve the participants' expression and believe I have presented a true version of their stories. The informants describe the feelings associated with their 'return' journeys, how others interacted with them and the impact their visits had on their ethnocultural identities, both in the homeland and back in their diasporic 'home'.

Case study one: Shaun

Shaun is a 37-year-old male who, at the time of our interview, had been living in Australia for nine years. He was born in Papua New Guinea and grew up there. Each of his parents identifies as being 'mixed race' and Shaun is of Papua New Guinean, German, Chinese and Indonesian descent. He says:

> I wish I could go home [to Papua New Guinea] more often but it's too expensive—and I'm not just talking about flights. Yes, the flights are expensive—well, better than they used to be, but still expensive. It takes so long to save up because you have not only the flights, but also the other expenses. I mean, it's free accommodation when you go back home,

because you're staying with family. But when you stay with family, you've got all these other things to think about too. All these other obligations. Your parents, your cousins, your *wantoks* [people from the same *peles* or from the same language group; your kinsmen or countrymen], sometimes *wantoks* you don't even know—they all want money. Which, I don't mind. But I don't have money to give! They think because you live in Australia you're made of money, but it doesn't work that way. I wish I could go home all the time, but … I just can't.

I came this time for my cousin's wedding, but everyone's so busy— I'm so busy going to all these family events and driving people around and organise everything. It's one thing after another, it's like we're not even back in PNG, but could be anywhere. Don't get any free time. Not relaxing at all.

Anyway, maybe next time I come back, I'll come when there's no event, no big event on, like a wedding or whatever … so I can just have all free time and do my own stuff, spend time with the place. Have a real holiday. Then again, is it possible? And will it be as much fun?

It's funny, because when I'm in Australia, I'm homesick for PNG. But now that I'm here [in PNG], I'm homesick for Brisbane! For the first time! I want my house, my TV, good roads, good shops, movies, I want my own bed. PNG is always 'home' for me. But now, I think Australia is becoming … 'A' home, kind of like a home, but it's not the same.

I'm *very* secure in my PNG identity. Those ones living in Australia [Pacific Islanders], the ones born there and grew up there, especially, those ones definitely should go back home [to the Islands]—they have to! I hate seeing these ones saying, 'Oh, I'm Samoan', 'I'm PNG', 'I'm Fijian'—and yet they've never even been there! They don't speak the language, they don't know *kastom* ['traditional' customary practices], they don't know anything about who they think they are. Yes, they have the blood, they need the blood, but they also need something else as well. They need to come back.

Case study two: Mia

Mia is a 21-year-old female who was born in Australia and also grew up here, between Perth and Melbourne. Her mother is Tuvaluan and her father is Middle Eastern. She says:

When people ask me where I'm from, I tell them, 'I'm Polynesian and Middle Eastern'. Occasionally, I'll say I'm Australian, but when they ask, 'Where are you from?', they're really asking, 'Where are your parents from?'. I can speak English and … I wouldn't say Tuvaluan, 'cause it's not fluent. I can understand it fluently and I can only speak just sort of the basic stuff, like questions and answers. I learnt it here, in Australia. Mum spoke it to us when we were younger and then in Tuvalu we got more exposed to it so I picked it up a little bit more.

I've only been to Tuvalu once and it was recently, like 2012 or something like that, when I was 19, I think. For Christmas. I went back with Mum and my younger sister and brother. We were planning that trip for a long time, well, Mum was planning it for a long time. We were there for five weeks and spent a week in Fiji on the way back to Australia. We've got relatives in Fiji as well, but we didn't stay with them. Mum wanted to take us to Tuvalu because she wanted to see her family and wanted us to see her family. She hadn't been back in 21 years or something like that and her siblings and her mum are there—and I hadn't seen my grandma since we were living in Perth. Mum wanted us to see where we're from, where she grew up. I wanted to go just to see what it was like and to see the family.

Going to Tuvalu made me feel *less* Tuvaluan than I did before I ever went there. Growing up here in Australia and with my Australian family— my Polynesian Australian family here—we're more Westernised than the people there, everything's totally different: what we eat, how we work, you just feel like an outsider, like you don't fit in. As soon as we arrived at the airport, some of the cousins who picked us up, the girl cousins, they started talking about us in Tuvaluan, calling us *pālangi* [White people]. And when they said something else, my sister and I turned around to them and responded in Tuvaluan and they were like, 'Holy shit, they can understand us!'. Then you realise, when you go to the *maniapa* (the family functions at the gathering place, with food on the side and entertainment), you just sort of see everyone in the island when you go there. We had one for Christmas and another one, like a feast for New Year's, and another one for all the Australians—all the Tuvaluans from Australia. It's such a small island, everyone knows everyone's business. Anyway, you go to the *maniapa* and we look different, dress different, topics of interest are different too—and they were talking about us until they realised we understood. Even when you go to the nightclub and everyone will come up to you and then they realise you're related. Like, some boys came up to us and then my cousins told them who my grandmother was and they back off. People are more welcoming when they realise who we are—still don't know you personally, but they know who you're related to. Otherwise they will look and stare. And you have to be careful what you do, because of all the gossip. I was talking to my cousin about this yesterday, like when I was riding the motorbikes (around Tuvalu) and then all the questions come: why are you out, where are you going, who are you with, who are you going to see? And it gets back to my family and I wasn't even doing that!

One day when I was there, I went to the shop and tried to buy 'cake', which actually was some kind of tobacco in the tin that the ladies would roll up and sell, but I didn't know! I thought it was cake! I forget the name of the tobacco … Anyway, the look on the ladies' faces when I asked for it, it was like a scandal or something—and she must have been a cousin of my mum's because someone told my grandma because the next day she asked about it—and I didn't tell her! They all thought I smoked!

All my aunties just wanted me to stay at home because I'm a girl. But I wanted to go out to the beach and go on the bikes and go fishing. I told my mum, 'I'm not staying at home! I didn't come all the way to Tuvalu just to wash dishes in the kitchen. I want to go hunting and fishing and do all the fun stuff! I want to get a tan!' And then one of my aunties told me that some of the other aunties had been gossiping about me, saying I wasn't a 'good girl'—that I was 'too Australian' [sighs]. Of course my sister was perfect though. She was happy to just stay in the kitchen all day. All day! Doing nothing! Why bother going to Tuvalu?

Did I feel at home there, like I belonged? To a degree, but I don't know, just the traditional things, clothing, food … When we ate the traditional food, Mum cooks it better at home. It sounds bitchy to say but it [hesitates] wasn't up to my … standard of what I'm used to at home. It just wasn't nice, they have no fresh produce and stuff. And they don't know how to eat healthy. They have taro and stuff, they grow that there, and they have chicken too but I didn't eat any chicken. And they cook taro leaves. But all the fresh produce—all the fruit and everything, you have to wait for the next boat to come from Fiji—and when I was there, the boat didn't come! They have coconut and mango and stuff like that, but no other fresh stuff!

I do think I'll go back to Tuvalu again, but not for as long—I'd go for a shorter time. I'd always wanted to go to see what it was like. I kind of knew what to expect because I'd been to the New Guinea Islands before and I thought it would be a bit similar to that to be honest, and it is, but some aspects are different. I guess I only really thought about the island itself, the airport, the houses, the food. But before I went to New Guinea, I had no idea what to expect. I think, since coming back from Tuvalu, being exposed to it, I do feel more Tuvaluan now than before. Now I can compare my holidays, with other Tuvaluans and Islanders and you do pretty much the same thing when you're there, 'cause there's not much to do there.

Case study three: Beth

Beth is a 36-year-old female who was born in Belgium and grew up between Australia, Germany and Papua New Guinea. Beth is of Papua New Guinean and white Australian descent and she has been living in Australia for approximately 20 years. She says:

Dad is from Poiam, in the East Sepik, near Dagua, so when anyone asks, I always say Dagua, because no one knows the village, but there's a clinic in Dagua, so most people know about that. My mum is from Warragul in Victoria. When people ask me where I grew up, I always say Port Moresby. I don't usually say the rest [Belgium, Germany, Australia] 'cause it takes too long, it's too complicated and I just don't want to get into all of that.

I don't usually say I'm from Australia—only when people say to me, 'Oh, you've got a really good, strong, Australian accent' or 'You speak English really well'. And I explain that my mother's white, that she's Australian. And that I've lived here for 20 years! It's mostly like older people in Australia who say those kinds of things to me, like, people who might have lived in PNG, like in the '70s, you know? When people ask me where I'm from, I know they're asking based on what they're looking at. They see a family photo and they say, 'Who's that?' And when I tell them, 'That's my mum', they say, 'I didn't know your mum was white!' or 'European'. Nobody, nobody ever thinks I have a white mother! Other people in PNG look at me and think I'm mixed, I think.

I feel mixed, I'm proud of my Australian heritage and I'm proud of my Papua New Guinean heritage. I'm proud to be of convict stock even though I think convicts or at least those early settlers killed lots of Aboriginals, which is terrible, but I like that my relatives came over on the First Fleet. I feel like I should feel more Australian than I do, 'cause I feel like, my ancestry goes back 10 generations or something, to the first boat. Actually, I think they came over on the second boat. On the other side, I'm also really proud that I come from a big, long line of chiefs. Even though I'm pretty sure they also did some bad things, like killing people as well—but I'm proud to have PNG heritage.

In the last 20 years, since I've been living in Australia, I've been back to Papua New Guinea about 10 times, sometimes with my parents, sometimes by myself; most of the time by myself to go and see my parents (who were still living there) and mostly for weddings or funerals.

My first time back as an adult was when I was 18. I went on a scuba diving holiday with a bunch of Aussies, really rich Aussies, and travelled from Milne bay to Madang. For two weeks. And when we were diving, travelling up the coast, it was just amazing. We went into villages and the villagers would come out in their canoes to meet us and for me, that was really amazing because I'd never seen anything like that before, you know, mostly being in Port Moresby, and I realised how much I'd missed out on—how much I thought I'd missed out on. Like, when I was in Germany, I'd forgotten so much about PNG, language mostly. And you know, from the ages of about 14 to 18, a lot of people make huge transitions, but I was really trying to work out where I was from. It probably would have been different if I was living in PNG, but I was really feeling like, 'Where do I fit in? This is shit [not knowing where she fit in]. I've got to work this out'. That first visit back when I was 18 really made me understand what I needed to do. So I went back again to try and work it out, to get my identity sorted.

I went back (to my dad's village) for two months when I was 21 or 22 I think, to try and you know, learn about the culture and stuff 'cause I was feeling really disconnected. And when I got back to Australia, I had major culture shock; everything was just so loud and fast, too much information. I went to a party the first night back in Australia and I couldn't stay, I had to go and sit on the steps outside. It was just so different. I said I'd go back to PNG again, but I just caught up with work, caught up with getting married and having children, so it was a long time before I went back to the village. If you have family here to remind you of it—PNG—you know, aunties coming over and cooking and speaking Pidgin, it would be different. Like, I don't even do much PNG cooking and Mum never did either. If I had that here, it wouldn't be so easy to forget and start feeling insecure about my PNG identity. Language plays a huge part in whether or not you fit in, and when you go back you pick it all up again and you feel good about it.

This time, when I went earlier this year [for a relative's funeral], I'd forgotten again, so I was disconnected again, and needed that … reconnection. It hasn't been all good though. Some of the aunties still call me *misis* [white woman] and this time my cousin reprimanded them for it and I was embarrassed because I didn't want to make the aunties feel embarrassed, but they got it. And I got to polish up on my Tok Pisin and the cultural stuff and I realised it's already something within me. I feel better about it. In the last couple of years, I had felt so disconnected from my identity that I got myself involved in all these PNG and Pacific Island community groups, hoping that that would give me my cultural connection, but I don't really feel like I need that anymore. I was looking for a general PNG connection—as a nation—but now I have a stronger connection to my village and my clan, and *that's* what I want to look into more. I feel like I've found a little category for myself now. I have a stronger sense of identity.

I feel more comfortable about my PNG identity now that I've been back, but if you ask me that in two years time and I haven't been back again, I might see it in a different way, I think [laughs]. I don't hold it up there on a pedestal now like I did before, because I can see and I'm more … aware about everything now than I was before. I see a lot more of the negatives now than I did before. Actually going back and making a plan of building a house in the village, for the boys [her children], it does scare me a little bit. I don't wanna get dragged back into all the village crap; even if you don't want to, it will happen. You can fight it, fight it, fight it, but they will make you … an accomplice. And I do think about whether about I want my boys being dragged into that. The village, it's more complicated than I was … I was pretending it wasn't. Village politics, gossip, and half of it's so irrational; little-town mentality that you'll get anywhere in the world.

I suppose when you feel like you belong somewhere, it's because other people are saying you belong there with them. Like, my relatives back at the village will say to me, '*Yu meri Poiam*' [you're a Poiam woman], but I think they're just being polite. Like, they don't look at me the same way they look at each other, they don't talk to me the same way they talk to each other or behave or react the same way towards me as they do to each other. So I don't really feel like I belong there, or here either. I feel like, when I'm in Australia, I always have to prove myself. I don't feel like I belong anywhere, because of the way people make me feel. Dad always used to say we were 'citizens of the world'. I think that was his way of saying, 'you can belong wherever you want. You don't have to be limited to one place'.

The socio-politics of return

As Tsuda (2009: 26) argues, 'most diasporic descendants imagine their ancestral homelands from afar in rather idealized romantic, if not mythical ways'. People long for a place where they belong, where they can feel 'at home'; and this is the impetus for many homecoming and non-homecoming trips. However, as Shaun's story in the case studies above shows, there may be hesitation about going 'home': financial costs, social obligations, familial responsibilities. And, as both Mia's and Beth's stories demonstrate, the paradisiacal view of the homeland does not always manifest upon 'return': disagreeable social mores, culture shock and exclusion based on perceived 'race', culture or language barriers. All of these factors impede the visitor from experiencing what they had been longing for, what their cultural memory had told them was there.

In Shaun's case, for the first time during a visit back to his homeland, he developed homesickness for Australia, longing for the infrastructure, material goods, facilities and activities available to him here. It was at that point that he realised, 'Australia is becoming ... 'A' home, kind of like a home, but it's not the same'. He is not alone in his use of this terminology. Time and again throughout my research, even when informants told me that Australia was their 'home', it came out in their choice of words that their homeland was 'home' and Australia was 'a home'. This was not surprising, as I realised how important concepts like *peles* were to Pacific Islander identity, and *peles* serves as an anchor for ethnocultural belonging. It is the reason that Beth chose to go back to Poiam, her father's village (rather than to anywhere else in the country), to reconnect and energise her identity as a Papua New Guinean. Likewise, the connection to the homeland was also highlighted in informants' talking about 'going back' or 'going home' even if they had never actually been to their 'home' island before. Another example of this is from Ricky, a 32-year-old woman of Cook Islands and Fijian descent who was born and grew up in Australia. She says, 'My parents moved [to Australia] before I was born. I've always wanted to go back [to Fiji and the Cook Islands] but I haven't had the chance. It was the money and now my kids. But one day I'll get back home.'

I argue that during visits that are specifically established as homecoming journeys, the visitor's identity as a Pacific Islander is under great scrutiny, and as a result, feelings of social rejection and isolation are more likely. The overall experience is likely to be a negative one. Mia's story illustrates this point perfectly. She says, 'Going to Tuvalu made me feel *less* Tuvaluan than I did before I ever went there'. The cultural divergences between Australia and Tuvalu were the biggest hurdle for Mia, with gender roles and assumptions about her knowledge (that is, her 'doing') as a Pacific Islander playing a significant role. Beth had a similar experience, through her series of homecoming trips, with relatives referring to her as 'white' (whether based on her appearance or her ability to socioculturally integrate into village life) or her feeling that her relatives were merely being polite or complimentary when they referred to her as '*meri Poiam*'. This is contrasted with Beth's positive experience when she was a dive tourist in Papua New Guinea. Jacquie, a 45-year-old woman of ni-Vanuatu descent who moved to Australia when she was four has a similar story. She says,

I didn't go back to Vanuatu until I was an adult [22 or 23] and it was a terrible experience. I went back with Dad, who could still understand the language and all the customs, but he hadn't taught me or my brothers and sisters anything about any of that stuff. We went back to the village and met with all our relatives. I felt totally rejected … by everyone and everything about the village life. I just didn't fit in at all.

However, Jacquie went on to say that a few years later, she went back to Vanuatu for an Australian friend's wedding. 'It was a much better time, staying at the resort. Even the locals who were working there seemed to accept me more than my own relatives did when I went to the village.'

Indeed, I contend that the non-homecoming journeys are more likely to be positive experiences, because visitors' identities are not as much the focus and the 'holiday' activities are more likely to present the paradise that people had been longing for. Beth's dive trip, for example, and the interaction with villagers as a tourist, she describes as 'amazing'. It was this trip that made her realise that she was a part of Papua New Guinea and that she needed to 'return' to *peles* to reinforce that part of her identity. We see through Shaun's story, however, that despite being 'home' as part of a non-homecoming (that is a relative's wedding) his social obligations and duties as a family member became burdensome, resulting in his feeling, not any less Papua New Guinean, but rather homesick for Australia, while longing for a real holiday on his next visit to the country. This demonstrates that the distinction between 'homecoming' and 'non-homecoming' is not always clear, especially in relation to visits for a ceremonial occasion during which a visitor might be expected by a relative to behave in a certain way. Indeed, a visit with friends to home islands, initially pegged as a 'non-homecoming', may develop—either fully or sporadically—into a 'homecoming' experience depending upon the extent to which a relative has expectations of the visitor to display cultural knowledge and practical expertise.

The feelings of negativity associated with homecoming journeys lead to people developing a greater awareness of the difference between self-defined and socially defined identity. Note that Beth creates a 'category for herself', based more on her relationship with her clan and *peles* than with a country-wide connection. Often, the first connection a person makes is between the visitor and the place, rather than the visitor and the people in the homeland. When the divergence between self-defined and socially defined identity becomes clearer—usually due to experiencing both kinds of social systems of interpretation of identity—a person realises that what remains stable is their self-defined identity.

Importantly, the journey 'home'—and perhaps surprisingly, *especially* the homecoming visit—was ultimately viewed in the diaspora as extremely positive, regardless of whether aspects of the actual homeland visit were negative. Visits to the homeland helped to reinforce Pacific Islander identity and sense of belonging amongst other Pacific Islanders in the diaspora. As Mia notes, despite feeling *less* of a Tuvaluan during her homeland visit, 'since coming back from Tuvalu, being exposed to it, I do feel more Tuvaluan now than before. Now I can compare my holidays, with other Tuvaluans and Islanders and you do pretty much the same thing when you're there'. Shaun too, says that for diasporic Pacific Islanders, journeys 'home' were a necessary part of identity maintenance. For many, Australia becomes 'a home' but not the only 'home' and often not *the* 'home'. 'Being' a Pacific Islander (that is, having Islander 'blood' and *peles* and heritage) sets up expectations of a person, particularly in terms of what cultural knowledge they have, or are perceived to have. Even when Beth and Mia were called white, it was meant as a commentary on their lack of knowledge of Pacific Islander culture and their adherence to Australian or European customs, rather than to mean they were not Islanders. Whether or not you performed the 'right' actions, the 'correct' behaviour, reinforces this notion and effects, whether negatively or positively, how others view visitors in the homeland or back in the diaspora.

Conclusion

In what ways does a journey to their homeland affect a person's identity, sense of belonging and their interpretation of 'home'? Throughout this article, I have differentiated between homecoming and non-homecoming trips because I argue that each type of visit results in a different set of outcomes for the visitor.

Homecoming journeys (that is, those specifically designed to enable the visitor to 'reconnect' with their homeland as well as those in which someone is expected to behave in a culturally appropriate way in a ceremonial context) tend to place greater scrutiny on the person's identity. Homeland-based friends and relatives are more likely to perceive—and vocalise—the cultural differences between themselves and the visitor which, in turn, makes the visitor question their own 'authenticity' as a Pacific Islander. The awareness of cultural differences is made greater by the fact that the visitor is usually accompanied by a senior family member (who tends to be more readily able to 'shift' between homeland and diaspora mores) and an easy comparison is drawn between the culturally competent senior family member and the less knowledgeable visitor. Many informants whose 'return' journey involved a homecoming described the experience as being a negative one, particularly because they had previously assumed that the homeland would be where they would fit in the most, over and above all other places.

By comparison, non-homecoming journeys (for example, holidays with friends) place less pressure on visiting people's identities and as a result, they tend to feel as though their identity in the homeland remains 'authentic' and secure—if not *more* secure than previously because they have just visited their homeland, an act which many perceive to strengthen Pacific Islander identity. Of course, for many people in the diaspora, there is an idealistic view of 'home': it is beautiful, fun and paradise. Although the actual homeland experience does not always live up to these 'memories' or 'longings', positive experiences in the homeland (whereby the 'authenticity'—or 'inauthenticity'—of the person's ethnocultural identity is neither highlighted nor questioned) reinforce the romantic, paradisiacal view.

In many cases though, it does not matter whether the journey is a homecoming or non-homecoming one; when the person returns to Australia, their fellow diasporic Pacific Islanders and members of the wider general community tend to think of them as having gained cultural savvy and a reinforced legitimacy to their claim to identity as a Pacific Islander. As mentioned above, the act of 'return' is itself an important one, allowing the visitor to *remember* rather than to learn cultural knowledge. This highlights the connection between inherited ethnocultural identity (through a descent connection to *peles*) and the performance of that identity through actions and behaviour, elements which I have labelled 'being' and 'doing'. Both 'being' and 'doing' are necessary components of 'authentic' Pacific Islander identity, at 'home' and in the diaspora.

Whether people are longing for a place or its people, longing for a 'home' that no longer exists or a 'home' they have never been to, it is clear that 'home' in all its forms is related to identity and sense of belonging. Because of this, people have and experience a range of 'homes' and 'home'-like states that come to the fore in different circumstances; 'home' is not defined by an opposing dichotomy between homeland and diaspora. Connections to 'home' can be multiple, tangible and/or intangible; they are not as simple as merely longing for the 'other' place where you wish you were.

Home, identity and belonging are very personalised and shift focus where and when experience and expectations meet. Therein, of greatest importance to the relationship between identity and journeys 'home' is individuals' reconciliation of the ways in which they respond—*externally* and *internally*—to the manner in which they are defined and treated by others during their visits to Island homes.

Acknowledgements

This research was made possible through the support and guidance of colleagues at the University of Queensland's School of Social Science, and the Association for Social Anthropology in Oceania. I'd also like to acknowledge the advice and financial support received from Ms Leslie Bryant.

References

Basu, P 2004, 'My own island home: the Orkney homecoming', *Journal of Material Culture*, vol. 9, no. 1, pp. 27–42. doi.org/10.1177/1359183504041088

Bhatia, S & Ram, A 2009, 'Theorizing identity in transnational and diaspora cultures: a critical approach to acculturation', *International Journal of Intercultural Relations*, vol. 33, no. 2, pp. 140–149. doi.org/10.1016/j.ijintrel.2008.12.009

Brown, J 2011, 'Expressions of diasporic belonging: the divergent emotional geographies of Britain's Polish communities', *Emotion, Space and Society*, vol. 4, pp. 229–237. doi.org/10.1016/j.emospa.2011.01.004

Chambers, I 1994, *Migrancy, culture and identity*, Routledge, London. doi.org/10.4324/9780203182093

Christou, A & King, R 2010, 'Imagining "home": diasporic landscapes of the Greek-German second generation', *Geoforum*, vol. 41, pp. 638–646. doi.org/10.1016/j.geoforum.2010.03.001

Delanty, G, Wodak, R & Jones, P (eds) 2008, *Identity, belonging and migration*, Liverpool University Press, Liverpool.

Gershon, I 2012, *No family is an island: cultural expertise among Samoans in diaspora*, Cornell University Press, Ithaca. doi.org/10.7591/cornell/9780801450785.001.0001

Giddens, A 2013, *Modernity and self-identity: self and society in the late modern age*, Stanford University Press, Stanford.

Hall, S 1990, 'Cultural identity and diaspora', in J Rutherford (ed.), *Identity: community, culture and difference*, Lawrence and Wishart, London, pp. 222–237.

Hall, S & du Gay, P 1996, *Questions of cultural identity*, Sage Publications, London.

Herbert, J 2012, 'The British Ugandan Asian diaspora: multiple and contested belongings', *Global Networks*, vol. 12, no. 3, pp. 296–313. doi.org/10.1111/j.1471-0374.2012.00353.x

Jones, Y 1980, 'Kinship affiliation through time: Black homecomings and family reunions in a North Carolina county', *Ethnohistory*, vol. 27, no. 1, pp. 49–66. doi.org/10.2307/481627

Kleist, N 2013, 'Flexible politics of belonging: diaspora mobilisation in Ghana', *African Studies*, vol. 72, no. 2, pp. 285–306. doi.org/10.1080/00020184.2013.812883

Kuah, K & Davidson A (eds) 2008, *At home in the Chinese diaspora: memories, identities and belongings*, Palgrave Macmillan, New York.

Linton, R 1936, *The study of man: an introduction*, Appleton-Century-Crofts, New York.

Lubkemann, S 2004, 'Diasporas and their discontents: return without homecoming in the forging of Liberian and African American identity', *Diaspora: A Journal of Transnational Studies*, vol. 13, no. 1, pp. 123–128. doi.org/10.1353/dsp.2006.0007

Mageo, JM 2001, *Cultural memory: reconfiguring history and identity in the postcolonial Pacific*, University of Hawai'i Press, Honolulu.

Markowitz, F 2004, 'The home(s) of homecoming', in F Markowitz & A Stefansson (eds), *Homecomings: unsettling paths of return*, Lexington Books, Oxford, pp. 21–33.

Markowitz, F 2007, 'Ethnic return migrations –(are not quite)– diasporic homecomings', *Diaspora: A Journal of Transnational Studies*, vol. 16, no. 1, pp. 234–242. doi.org/10.1353/dsp.2007.0006

Markowitz, F & Stefannson A (eds) 2004, *Homecomings: unsettling paths of return*, Lexington Books, Oxford.

Maruyama, N & Stronza A 2010, 'Roots tourism and Chinese Americans', *Ethnology*, vol. 49, no. 1, pp. 23–44.

McCall, G & Connell J 1993, *A world perspective on Pacific Islander migration: Australia, New Zealand and the USA*, Centre for South Pacific Studies, Sydney.

McGavin, K 2014, 'Being Nesian: Pacific Islander identity in Australia', *The Contemporary Pacific*, vol. 26, no. 1, pp. 126–154. doi.org/10.1353/cp.2014.0013

McGavin, K 2016, 'Where do you belong? Identity, New Guinea Islanders and the power of *peles*', *Oceania* vol. 86, no. 1, pp. 1–18. doi.org/10.1002/ocea.5112

Papastergiadis, N 2000, *The turbulence of migration: globalisation, deterritorialization and hybridity*, Polity, Cambridge.

Pearce, P 2012, 'The experience of visiting home and familiar places', *Annals of Tourism Research*, vol. 39, no. 2, pp. 1024–1047. doi.org/10.1016/j.annals.2011.11.018

Radhakrishnan, R 2008, 'Ethnicity in an age of diaspora', in J Evans Braziel & A Mannur (eds), *Theorizing diaspora: a reader*, Blackwell Publishing, Oxford, pp. 119–131.

Sawyer, L 2002, 'Routings: race, African diasporas and Swedish belonging', *Transforming Anthropology*, vol. 11, no. 1, pp. 13–35. doi.org/10.1525/tran.2002.11.1.13

Schramm, K 2009, 'Negotiating race: blackness and whiteness in the context of homecoming to Ghana', *African Diaspora*, vol. 2, pp. 3–24. doi.org/10.1163/187254609X430795

Shotter, J & Gergen, K (eds) 1989, *Texts of identity*, Sage Publications, London.

Spickard, P 2002, 'Pacific Islander Americans and multiethnicity: A vision of America's future?', in P Spickard, J Rondilla & D Hippolite Wright (eds), *Pacific diaspora: Island peoples in the United States and across the Pacific*, University of Hawai'i Press, Honolulu, pp. 40–55.

Spickard, P, Rondilla, J & Hippolite Wright D (eds) 2002, *Pacific diaspora: island peoples in the United States and across the Pacific*, University of Hawai'i Press, Honolulu.

Tonkinson, ME 1990, 'Is it in the blood? Australian Aboriginal identity', in J Linnekin & L Poyer (eds), *Cultural identity and ethnicity in the Pacific*, University of Hawai'i Press, Honolulu, pp. 191–218.

Tsuda, T (ed.) 2009, *Diasporic homecomings: ethnic return migration in comparative perspective*, Stanford University Press, Stanford.

Waite, L & Cook, J 2011, 'Belonging among diasporic African communities in the UK: plurilocal homes and simultaneity of place attachments', *Emotion, Space and Society*, vol. 4, no. 4, pp. 238–248. doi.org/10.1016/j.emospa.2010.08.001

Watson, JB 1990, 'Other people do other things: Lamarckian identities in Kainantu Subdistrict, Papua New Guinea', in J Linnekin & L Poyer (eds), *Cultural identity and ethnicity in the Pacific*, University of Hawai'i Press, Honolulu, pp. 17–42.

Weingrod, A. & Levy, A 2006, 'Paradoxes of homecoming: the Jews and their diasporas', *Anthropological Quarterly*, vol. 79, no. 4, pp. 691–716. doi.org/10.1353/anq.2006.0057

7

Adding insult to injury: Experiences of mobile HIV-positive women who return home for treatment in Tanah Papua, Indonesia

Leslie Butt, Jenny Munro and Gerdha Numbery

Abstract

This chapter explores the personal experiences of mobile HIV-positive indigenous women from Tanah Papua, Indonesia who returned to their home communities in need of social support and treatment. Little is known about the experiences of HIV-positive women returnees in general, and the contours and effects of the moral expectations and boundaries within home communities in particular. This paper draws on close-grained analysis of in-depth interviews and fieldwork conducted between 2009 and 2013 to suggest Papuan women returnees suffer a reduced quality of local network relations, and sustained stigma and gender-based discrimination. We illustrate how the inevitable struggles over belonging that returning young adults face are intensified by the intersection of seropositivity, shifts in the quality of social networks and gendered judgements about mobility. Women returnees are unable to rely on affective networks, and Papua's poorly developed HIV treatment programs magnify these challenges.

Introduction: Mobility and HIV

Increasing numbers of women leave rural communities in search of work, educational or relationship opportunities. Evidence is compelling across the globe that such journeys increase the risk of exposure to HIV (Whiteside 2006; Welaga et al. 2009). Having HIV, in turn, encourages further mobility, including among infected persons who choose to return home for treatment (Clark et al. 2007; Berk et al. 2003; Davis and Stapleton 1991). Despite this strong association between mobility and HIV, there have been surprisingly few studies outside of US contexts exploring the experiences of HIV-positive men and women who return to their home communities. Studies do show that HIV-positive returnees tend to go home because they are seeking support from family, often elderly parents, to go on treatment (Knodel et al. 2010; Carrasco 2011; Elmore 2006). However, little is known about the emotional nature of the relationships between women returnees in particular, and the moral expectations and boundaries of the communities to which they return (compare Salazar and Smart 2011). In communities such as Tanah Papua (a term used by indigenous persons to describe the Indonesian provinces of West Papua and Papua), where high rates of HIV infection add to strong stigmatisation of HIV-positive women, a return may be fraught with unmet expectations on both sides.

In Tanah Papua, as in Melanesia more broadly, the trajectory and growth of HIV has been interwoven with changing patterns of mobility in local moral perceptions. In particular, HIV plays into community-wide understandings of 'risk' behaviour based on mobile women, in which movement is understood as a vehicle for at best unmonitored and at worst unrestrained sexuality, which is understood to result in infection with HIV. This moral script plays into both local evangelical Christian and ancestral understandings of the complex relationship between sickness, morality and sexuality (Wood and Dundon 2014). Christian interpretations view AIDS as the 'scourge' of God; and ancestral logic views responsible sexual behaviour as the only appropriate and effective platform for the continued health and wellbeing of people and their families and villages (for example, Lepani 2012; Dundon 2010).

Regrettably these local moral interpretations have meant that while newer practices of mobility for women have often provided greater access to educational and employment opportunities away from home, or opportunities for different kinds of sexual experiences and marriage than those usually experienced in home villages, the negative association of mobility with HIV has had a significant impact on the quality of nurture and care available to women when they return home as HIV-positive persons seeking compassion and support. This paper explores the personal experiences of mobilities and of return for adult HIV-positive women from Tanah Papua, Indonesia. Many of the 33 indigenous women we interviewed between 2009 and 2013[1] returned home after finding out about their status in order to seek treatment and care.

We situate the returnees' expectations of family nurture and support within a wider context of migration and its impact on social networks. In other contexts, affective networks help migrants retain positive associations with home communities while women are away from home. Remittances, cell phone contact, social media, webcams, and personal networks help maintain a sense of closeness (McKay 2007, 2012). Home, for many women, is understood as a place of refuge and an idealised site of safe affective networks. Yet for those who remain away, the quality of networks does not necessarily remain intact despite consistent efforts, rigorous routines around social media or diligent efforts by migrants to meet the expectations of home communities (for example, Madianou and Miller 2011). Returning home often means trying to reinvigorate distant and fractured family and extended kin relations. Mallett (2004) suggests home has multiple meanings for the world's migrants, not all of them positive. For mobile Papuan women in particular, the home they left often falls short of their nostalgic imaginings and memories. Further, women who leave are often targets of suspicion associated with their status as mobile persons, especially if their return is viewed as a failure, or if they did not live up to family expectations while away (for example, Lindquist 2009; Williams 2007). Despite opportunities for young Melanesian women to

---

1   Leslie Butt and Gerdha Numbery worked with a Papuan research team to conduct a total of 32 in-depth interviews with HIV-positive Papuans in 2009–10 in the central highlands region of the province of Papua. Sixteen of those interviews were with adult women, ranging in age from 18 to 40. In collaboration with local Papuan-run NGOs, Jenny Munro conducted nine interviews with HIV-positive women in Manokwari, in the province of West Papua, in 2011, and eight interviews with HIV-positive women in the highlands of the province of Papua in 2013 as part of a broader project on indigenous experiences of HIV care and education provided by Papuan organisations. Interviews were conducted in Bahasa Indonesia by Munro and Numbery, and were translated by Butt and Munro. All women in all sites were diagnosed as being HIV-positive at least six months prior to their interviews. All the women in all sites were connected to the HIV healthcare system either through a clinic or an NGO; most were either on antiretroviral therapy (ART) or Cotrimoxazole (for treatment of tuberculosis), although their commitment to drug regimens varied widely.

be more mobile than in the past, and the discourses of empowerment that aim to place women at the centre of development, significant tensions surround women's mobility (Wardlow 2006; Spark 2011; Cummings 2008). Mobility away from more conservative, watchful rural sites opens up the possibility of women making decisions, however constrained, about sex and relationships in ways that challenge norms of patriarchal dominance over women's sexual engagements.[2]

Because of these dynamics, this paper explores the particular case of Papuan women (for men, see Butt 2015) asking if, and how, their HIV status compounds the challenges of fitting in that they already face as mobile returnees. We suggest the Papuan women we interviewed suffer a reduced quality of local networks as a result of being away, and they also suffer the stigma and discrimination that are often directed towards women who are viewed as the source of HIV infection and the target of accusations (for example, Hammar 2008). We ask whether the complex negotiations around belonging that young Papuans inevitably face are compounded by local expectations of community solidarity and sociality. Long-term absences may undercut the quality of social networks and the intensity and depth of affective relations.

We further ask how HIV status challenges the work of maintaining social relations on a daily basis once returned home. In Indonesia, HIV-positive persons are termed *ODHA (orang dengan HIV/AIDS*, or persons living with HIV/AIDS), and upon being so defined by a positive diagnosis, enter into 'HIV-land'. Klitzman and Bayer (2003) coined the term 'living in HIV-land' to describe the universe of languages, treatments and protocol that HIV-positive people experience after accepting a diagnosis. Being an *ODHA* means living in HIV-land, but it is a life that must typically be masked. Like other Indonesians, Papuan *ODHA* must engage with kin and community, all while dealing with the health and lifestyle requirements of a demanding treatment regimen (compare Boellstorff 2009). The challenges of returning home are magnified by Papua's HIV treatment program, typical of many resource-constrained communities globally, which is poorly developed. We suggest this confluence of factors exacerbates stigma for all HIV-positive returnees. After briefly reviewing the political context and patterns of HIV infection and treatment in

---

2   In Indonesia more broadly, conservative government and Islamic influences also strongly influence gender and sexual space along boundaries of public and domestic domains (Slama 2012: 314; see also Robinson 2009; Davies 2015).

Papua, we describe through the voices of mobile women in three case studies the daily challenges they face. We describe the importance of secrecy and of adopting more traditional social roles because these two strategies allow women to maintain and strengthen the social relations necessary for their wellbeing.

Tanah Papua: Seropositivity and the curtailment of mobility

Tanah Papua has a complex colonial history which distinguishes it from the rest of Indonesia, and shapes the experiences and decisions of mobile people (see Figure 1). Brought under the mantle of Dutch colonialism in the 19th century along with the rest of what is now the independent nation of Indonesia, the geographically challenging western half of the island of New Guinea is made up of approximately one million indigenous Papuans from over 200 distinct language groups. Accelerated development, oppressive political conditions and militarisation characterise ongoing colonialism by Indonesia since a 1969 fraudulent vote found indigenous Papuans coerced into the Indonesian nation (Braithwaite et al. 2010). Many Papuans leave the provinces not, as Indonesia would like, to participate as full citizens in the nation, but in order to acquire education and skills in other Indonesian provinces, which will allow them to return to Tanah Papua able to further the political objective of independence from Indonesia (Munro 2013).

Tanah Papua has one of the fastest growing rates of HIV infection in Asia. Estimated infection rates in 2013 suggest 2.9 per cent of the indigenous population is HIV-positive (Integrated Biological and Behavioral Surveillance cited in Munro 2015a). In Tanah Papua, unlike the rest of Indonesia where intravenous drug use is a common source of HIV infection, HIV is widely understood to be contracted primarily by heterosexual contact. Farmer (1997) has argued that HIV follows along the 'fault lines' of society, reinforcing vulnerabilities and hardening inequities along the lines of income, race and gender. As indigenous migrants travel, they encounter risks to sexual health, such as novel sexual opportunities, novel ways to spend newfound money and exposure to new high-risk lifestyles. In addition, in urban settings dominated by non-indigenous migrants their status as racialised indigenous persons widens 'fault lines' and exacerbates risk.

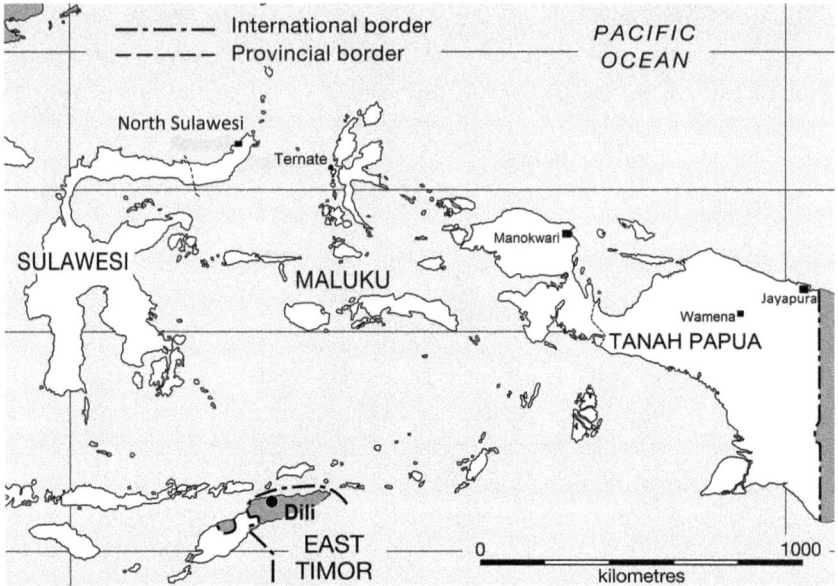

Figure 1: Tanah Papua, eastern Indonesia

Source: © The Australian National University, College of Asia and the Pacific, CartoGIS.

The experience of HIV-positive returnees appears to be shaped more by hopes for compassionate care than by expectations of competent medical care. HIV testing and treatment in Tanah Papua until 2007 was poor or non-existent (Rees and Silove 2007; Butt 2011) and since then has become increasingly available but is erratic and regularly affected by volatile political conditions, stereotypes about indigenous patients and local forms of discrimination (Simonin et al. 2011; Butt 2012; Munro and McIntyre 2016). Testing and treatment travels with 'baggage', namely protocols and guidelines about who, when and how to provide treatment (Hardon and Dilger 2011: 136; Sullivan 2011). In particular, protocol demands treatments remain in a fixed locale. Thus people have to travel to clinics to get drugs and care. For an HIV-positive woman who has returned to Tanah Papua or to her natal town or village for family support, accessing treatment can mean having to relocate from where her family and kin live to one of the larger towns where the few established treatment centres have been set up.

Another challenge to receiving competent care lies in divergent ideas about personal responsibility. Protocol exacerbates the gap between expectations by global agencies that an *ODHA* can respond to testing, counselling and treatment in a way that is independent of social context (Eves and Butt

2008). In Tanah Papua, the grounded reality, where local context strongly shapes behaviour, decisions and assessments about quality of treatment, puts social relations at the forefront. There is a powerful disconnect between what global AIDS narratives promote, namely treatment, and the genre of debates taking place locally, which are primarily grappling with moral, religious and cultural understandings of HIV deservedness (Eves 2012, 2010).

Among local cultural expectations, genealogical ties to land and access to it are strong features of social organisation. These ties must be constantly asserted, and maintained, by using the land, by assisting others in working land or making decisions about land, and by sharing the produce and benefits gained from land. In Melanesian communities sociality is maintained typically through regular displays of gift-giving, nurturance and social assistance; engaging in exchange relations and helping to build and maintain affective networks, which can offer a protective home space for persons who need it. Obligations to family to assist in nurturing the wellbeing of others are constant. When a Papuan woman leaves the region, expectations are raised that she will continue to provide support and reinforce solidarity, with those in the home community often displaying little patience or understanding of the challenges of supporting social relations from afar. Even migration from the highlands to the coast, about 220 kilometres by plane, can have significant consequences for a young woman's ability to maintain strong relations with family at home. At the same time, women face something of a double bind in that while national and local development objectives support education and modernisation, they also emphasise that a woman's most important role is as a sedentary, home-based mother and supportive wife (Nilan 2008).

Thus, for Papuans living in HIV-land, cultural expectations combine with structural limits on treatment to enhance the value of staying in one place. For women, this can mean a complicated dance of trying to overcome the many costs of having left in the first place, engaging anew in local forms of sociality and gift-giving, and making regular visits to a health centre for treatment without disclosing HIV status or disrupting the flows of everyday life and expectations of people around them. The following sections summarise how women we interviewed view their time away and their return home.

Narratives of mobility, contagion and secrecy

Women's explanations and understandings of how they contracted HIV were linked in almost every case to their own mobility. It has become the norm in the past decade for young Papuan women to leave remote rural communities and travel 20 or 30 kilometres by taxi or truck to regional towns to get an education. Spurred on by their parents who want their children to benefit from the province's rapid development, young women leave the village and live in rudimentary student dormitories or with family in town. A fortunate few go on to university, some travelling thousands of kilometres by ferry or by plane to study in other provinces in Indonesia, notably North Sulawesi and Central Java. Away from the protective mantle of close kin, women's sexuality can shift from a set of values primarily created and enacted within rural, clan-based systems that strongly value women's role as the source of brideprice, and as mother to valued offspring, to ones more dominated by individualism, sexual desire and desires for companionate relationships within monogamous marriages (Munro 2012). Being away from home may also introduce a new level of complexity in decisions around sex that women have not previously encountered.

For women, dangers resulting from an HIV diagnosis were local, familial and domestic. Women mainly feared the reactions of those in the home community to which they returned. Women we interviewed were afraid to disclose their status to anyone. Women disclosed on average to only one person, typically the healthcare worker, a spouse or a parent (Butt et al. 2010), a figure that is much lower than global norms, where typically people disclose to parents, spouses and siblings early on, and to increasingly large numbers of people as time passes (Klitzman and Bayer 2003; compare Zhou 2007). The secrecy of these women around HIV is a constructive strategy, a 'generative mechanism for constituting self' that allows them to create safer identities at home (Herdt in Jones 2014: 54). On one hand, secrecy is an effective strategy for managing fragile social relations and for creating confidence. Yet, because secrets by their very nature are made meaningful only because they exist as unspoken within a public domain, their source as a form of protection is always fragile, and secrets are potentially always about to be disclosed. For Papuan women, the choice to keep secrets is a highly compelling, if fraught strategy for coping with moral judgements, avoiding ostracism and remaining socially connected to family (Butt et al. 2010). For women, the home community was an unsafe place where their status had to be guarded very carefully.

Women's sense of their own material worth shaped their determination to keep secrets. Several women said a decrease in their physical wellbeing was a threat to good relations in the family, not just because of brideprice considerations and possibly the loss of culturally significant reproductive capacities, but also because of lost productive capacities as domestic labourers, income earners, market vendors or gardeners. Being criticised for their weak bodies made women feel unworthy, as these statements by HIV-positive women interviewed in 2009 exemplify:

> So now my family is mad, because they say to me you are our capital, now that you are sick all the time, our investment is not paying off.

> My brother says, 'Why are you always sick like this? … you sick like this, it's our loss, we could lose our investment'.

> For four months I have not been taking medicines. When I don't take the medication my body gets thin … I also can't work in the garden much, because I get tired very quickly. I don't have money to buy medicine. My brother says 'there's medicine but it's expensive, five doses is one million rupiah ($US100)' … So my body is getting thin again, and I can't work well. And often my brother says, 'Ayaah, our investment is all gone, right?' According to my brother, in Dani culture we believe the woman is the family's future capital.

In the above statements, interviewees explain that relatives—notably men—are concerned with what they may or may not receive through brideprice payments, and what productive labour has been lost. A groom's family will pay more brideprice for a wife who is educated, who is seen as pious, who performs domestic duties well, and who is seen as sexually innocent—a cornerstone of a 'good' reputation. Walking with or being seen talking to an unrelated male might cause a woman to gain a reputation for being sexually active, especially if she is young and unmarried. Unmarried women with HIV face an additional social imperative to behave and appear 'normal' in order to avoid judgements or questions about their reputation.

If a woman's behaviour deviates from the norm, or is likely to be perceived as deviating from the norm, she is more likely to keep her HIV status a secret. Strikingly, we observed that women who maintain a reputation as a 'good woman' are more likely to confide in their husbands than women who fear their reputations have been damaged. Women with good reputations have earned their husband's trust, and thus hope and expect to receive support from him.

Women also keep secrets because they want to avoid judgements along religious lines. Women whose parents or husbands are involved in church matters were extremely concerned about revealing their status. When women were involved in negotiations around cultural sanctions—for example, brideprice disputes or domestic violence payments—they remained silent to avoid losses to their families and their husbands' families if their status became known. Women also keep secrets to avoid punishment, in particular physical violence at the hands of their husbands or their fathers. Last, but most frequently noted by women, women choose secrecy because they want to avoid ostracism. Ostracism can happen when a family wants to maintain their good name, especially in church circles. If a woman is seen going alone to the clinic or the hospital she may be ostracised: the woman is shunned, limited in her movements and mocked.

As a result, the women we interviewed showed themselves to be experts at hiding their status. When women reveal their status, they tend to do so to persons who are 'safe' in structural terms. For example, we found that women only reveal their status to their boyfriends or husbands if they have already paid the brideprice to their family. Women hide their status by drawing on a strong determination to remain active, contributing members of society. Women work hard to maintain their secrets by increasing their participation in the domestic realm. As one respondent noted:

> They all suspect something, so I have changed my behaviour so I don't lose my husband. Before I got sick, if I did something wrong I always ran away to my mum's house … Now, I am sick but I try really hard to work at selling stuff so that money can come in. I'm afraid, if they know, they won't want to live with me, they won't want to eat my leftover food … So that people don't suspect me, I have to act as though everything is normal. I eat the same as normal with my children and my siblings, I work in the garden like normal, I sell in the market, just like regular healthy people. In the house, my husband treats me like normal. I eat leftover food like everyone else, we sleep together, I breastfeed my child.

Women on medication maintain secrecy about their drug regimen in quite specific ways. Many women obtain medication secretly, by dealing with nongovernmental organisations (NGOs) who pick up and hand out medicines for women, instead of going directly to the hospital. Several women said that if they had to go to the hospital for drugs they would not go. In order to access the medicines, women will lie to husbands about where they are going. They avoid people they know when they are in places where their status might be revealed (for example, at the HIV treatment centre). They hide medication in a safe, personal space within the home, notably wrapped in plastic in their netbags, and take drugs secretly when everyone is out. They do all of these things to maintain their social role as valued members of their family and community, and to avoid the potential shame and pain of stigmatisation.

As the following case study of one young mobile returnee shows, women who return home for care are required to mediate familiar social networks such as church communities or family expectations. We suggest that for women, secrecy is essential because they rely on social support in the domestic domain to live productive lives. Veronica's[3] story shows how strategic, and demanding, is this work of secrecy.

Case study Veronica: 'This secret is non-negotiable'

Veronica was born and raised in Manokwari, the capital of West Papua province, but her family hails from the island of Biak off the north coast of Papua. Her parents were school teachers and she was a university student until 2011 when her pregnancy began showing. She lived with her boyfriend, a non-Papuan man from Ternate (see Figure 1), whom she referred to as her husband (*suami*) although they were not married. She also lived with her mother, father and her younger sisters in a two-bedroom house in a close-knit neighbourhood full of other people of Biak heritage.

In 2007 while at university in North Sulawesi, she fell sick. She described,

> I got so sick, my skin was full of white spots and boils … I left and went straight home on my own and went to the doctor by myself … I thought it was just a regular disease so I had some medicine but it didn't help, then I went to the tuberculosis room and the doctor said let's just do a complete blood work. He said I had HIV … My reaction was … stress, and fear. But the doctor gave me medicine right away so I felt I was doing something about my sickness.

No one in Veronica's family knew of her HIV status. She was emphatic that the secret must be kept at all costs. 'This secret is non-negotiable (*harga mati*) for me.' Her parents would be so ashamed, she said: 'They heard

---

3   All names are pseudonyms.

about someone else who got HIV, and they talked so badly about that person, I can't imagine if they found out their own child was HIV-positive.' She picked up her medication at the Manokwari district hospital and told her family she had a chest infection. Keeping her status a secret most of all, for Vero, involved 'watching my mouth': 'If the neighbours are talking about HIV, I just listen, I just follow along.' Veronica said,

> The hardest thing for *ODHA* is to watch what we say. What would happen if we got engrossed in a conversation and we just said it out loud, 'I've got HIV', well, right away, we better look for somewhere else to stay.

Veronica also described some of the changes in her life and personality she had experienced since her diagnosis, 'I used to get together with friends, take part in activities, but not anymore. I'm afraid they'll find out, or I'll feel like telling them, but I can't if I want to maintain my life, even if it's just like this.'

Veronica and her boyfriend were raising her older brother's child, a girl who was born in 2010. Veronica said that within the family the baby is seen as hers and her responsibility. Vero's parents gave her the task of raising her brother's child while she was studying at university, a move that would seem to contradict cultural and Christian norms concerning marriage and the importance of education. While intrafamily adoption is not uncommon in Papua, handing the baby over to an unmarried university student is unusual, and may be viewed as an attempt by her parents to curb Veronica's mobility and sexual freedoms. Unmarried young women are often expected to look after children in order to teach them to become 'good' wives and mothers, but in Veronica's case it was clear she was given total responsibility, with attendant loss of freedom, increase in responsibility, and heightened gender expectations of conformity and domesticity that come attached with the full-time care of a child. Veronica's father insisted that her boyfriend move into their house as well, so that they might act and appear married, even if they were not. HIV has disrupted Vero's life in that she abandoned her university studies, and depended on performing the hard work of being a housewife and caregiver to earn her keep in the family. Her daily routine revolved around household and childcare duties, including cooking special meals for her ailing father. Social support appears to be most readily obtained through Vero's act of resuming traditional domestic tasks in a fixed locale, and by downplaying personal desires for mobility and education in favour of security.

Punishment, immobility and ostracism

Not all women are as adept at keeping secrets as Veronica. For some, disclosure happens because persons in positions of power reveal a woman's status to the wider community. Disclosure by persons of influence we suggest is more likely to occur when a woman returns home seeking care and support but lacks the deep, ongoing social networks that would make it easier to negotiate relationships and protect secrets. Our second case study profiles a young woman who was unable to keep her status a secret. The fragile nature of HIV care networks surface in this account. What also stands out is the capacity for discrimination at the family level and how judgements about mobility may come to shape how a woman's HIV status is understood.

Case study Nelly: The punishment of loneliness

Nelly was diagnosed with HIV in July 2013 in the regional highlands centre of Wamena, in Papua province, after she became sick while attending university in the coastal capital Jayapura. As Indonesia's easternmost capital, highlanders commonly travel to Jayapura in search of relatives, opportunities or to escape trouble for a while. Although Jayapura's HIV treatment and support facilities are regarded as superior to what Wamena offers, highlanders with ailing health may return home to be close to relatives or to seek traditional medicines. 'I was just about to graduate, I was supposed to graduate in August, but I got sick. I got so skinny and I had diarrhoea. So I came home to Wamena and I didn't graduate', Nelly explained sadly. She described how when she was in Jayapura she struggled financially (*susah uang*) and started hanging out with and having sex with a married man who was older than her. As she said, 'He would call me up and invite me. Then we would get together and have sex, and he would give me money for things. I didn't have money for tuition.'

Nelly described hearing her diagnosis. 'I was scared, I'm going to die … but the nurse said I could take medication and live, and be healthy again.' Nelly lived in a house with her sister and brother-in-law in Wamena where she could access treatment. She told her sister and brother-in-law that she has HIV. 'They know I'm sick and they don't want to talk to me any more … I tried to ask for their understanding, I'm sick right now and I can't work, I can't do anything … I don't have money to even take a pedicab (*becak*) to the clinic … Sometimes I just stay alone in my room, hungry.' Nelly also noted, voice quivering, that her sister refused to take her to the clinic. She recalled, 'The nurse asked me, "Nobody accompanied you!?"'

Nelly is clearly devastated by her unfortunate return to Wamena just weeks before she was to graduate. Nelly had strongly embraced the aspirations embedded in the very act of leaving home, including her hopes for personal success, her family's hopes, as well as the expectations of the wider community (Lindquist 2009; Munro 2015b). Many young women who start university do not get past their initial year or two before they get married and/or pregnant, usually to a fellow university student. That Nelly managed to get so far into her degree, without actually finishing, perhaps contributes to the rejection, lack of compassion and ostracism her sister and brother-in-law displayed towards her upon her return. When Nelly went away to study in Jayapura, like many students, she was expected to live independently from her family, to protect herself, to stay on the moral path and to achieve results amidst trying conditions. That she returned HIV-positive and ill means Nelly is not able to gain employment and is likely seen as having no prospects for marriage. Nor is she able to perform domestic duties because she is too ill. There is the shame and stigma of HIV, but there is also the shame of going back home in a worsened personal situation. When her family refused to take her to the clinic, they forced her to go alone: to do anything alone, be it stay in a room in the house or go out in town, is a particularly strong expression of disapproval and form of exclusion in a place where people rarely eat, sleep or walk around on their own. Her ostracism on the domestic front drives home the fragile balancing act young women must maintain in order to be mobile and modern while at the same time establishing their status as grounded, community-oriented 'good women'.

The final case study highlights the heartache of having secrets exposed to the wider community. Tina's story reinforces how women who have spent time away from their homes find it hard to establish and maintain the successful social relations necessary to shield themselves from stigma and discrimination when they return.

Case study Tina: 'Hey kids, don't play near her'

Tina was born and raised in a rural district near Wamena, but she moved with her family to attend high school in Wamena for two years. She married a local man and had twin girls at a young age, living continually with her parents and eventually divorcing her difficult and irresponsible first husband. Tina promptly married again, to a soldier who accused her of infidelity when she travelled to a dance in another region without him. Tina was heartbroken at his constant abuse, leaving her children behind to travel alone to the coastal capital of Jayapura for several months.

After falling sick while on the coast, she returned home to Wamena a year later and underwent HIV tests at her father's insistence. Her father was a trained healthcare worker and had learnt about the symptoms of HIV at a training workshop in 2007. She was diagnosed with HIV, and received moderate support from her family who knew about her status from the outset because the lab worker had communicated results to Tina and to Tina's father, who then told the remaining members of their household. Both her parents and her older sister humanely provided nurture and care, cooking foods she could eat and helping her with medications. By and large her family accepted the situation: 'My father wasn't mad at me, he only thought, "this is my daughter, my young daughter, she likes to go out and about (*jalan-jalan*), she doesn't like to listen to her parent's advice, she doesn't look after herself." But my mother, she was very angry at me.'

As is typical of others living in HIV-land, Tina was immersed in the life of her medications, carefully naming and itemising the drugs she had to take and their side effects. But her regular trips to the health centre and her obvious physical symptoms of extreme weight loss and skin lesions led to many questions in the community. Because of a healthcare worker's disclosure, Tina's status became public knowledge. As a result, neighbours and extended kin have shunned her, and her former husband's family in particular have actively marginalised her.

While her father's position in the health sector made it impossible to truly shun her, as he is a person of some renown in the community, she had nowhere else to stay. Living in her father's house in health worker housing in the centre of town, she was unable to guard her secret from the wider community. Similarly, because she was too sick to care for herself, she was unable to retreat to an isolated rural home and withdraw herself, a respected local response to illness. In town, in front of neighbours, she was exposed to constant, overt stigmatisation. 'The worst are the neighbours', said Tina. She would sit outside and the neighbours would come out of their house and just stare at her. They would then shoo the children away, Tina recounted: '"Hey kids, don't play near her", they say, or "Why are you just sitting there?" so the kids don't play in front of my house, it really hurts my feelings.'

Tina said the health worker who did her blood test was from the same clan as her. He helped her choose her foods and gave advice on staying healthy. But inadequate training around confidentiality led to him disclosing her status to many others within the wider community.

> He makes it really clear he doesn't care anything about me. When he comes by he just looks at me with half an eye, like he is afraid to come into my house and talk to me. It makes me very sad … So I sit in the house only, if I ever leave the house people from around the house are afraid to see me, they run away from me. If I am sitting here and the health worker walks by, he ignores me. He looked after me at the clinic, but now he just gives me a dirty look.

Tina's case reinforces the importance for women of having a safe domestic space they can count on. Treatment itself reimposes constraints on women's mobility, and, as enacted through local health workers, also becomes a form of moral recovery through domestic confinement and compliance with gender norms. Confinement and compliance are, in local understandings, contrasted with Tina's former preference to 'go out and about' (*jalan-jalan*), or to travel alone to the coast, both of which are associated with a negative and promiscuous sexuality.

Discussion: Living in HIV-land

This paper has explored the challenging experiences of women who return to their home communities with HIV. Rather than home being a place of solidarity and refuge for care and HIV treatment, women may be stigmatised, ostracised, denied support or forced into secrecy to avoid these eventualities. Family commitment cannot be guaranteed. Stalwart community networks such as church congregations, and respected public figures such as healthcare workers, may not turn out to be reliable sources of support and forgiveness. The case studies of Veronica, Nelly and Tina signal the anxieties and challenges Papuan women face as they suffer through the consequences of a diagnosis that, for most Papuans, is still a death sentence. Their stories tell us that choosing to leave their homes has long-term negative effects when they return with HIV. All our respondents strived for belonging through retaining or re-establishing social roles that had been transformed by their 'failed' mobility. The social roles they could achieve were further dependent on whether or not their HIV diagnosis was kept secret. The management Veronica and Nelly deploy to maintain their social networks *and* their secrets fill their days.

The enmity Tina and Nelly experienced was of that directed at a relative outsider, someone whose return to the home community set in motion resentment and retribution perhaps for the wider project of having left, of having sought an education or opportunities elsewhere, or of implicitly challenging some of the social and sexual norms of local social life. In other words, being a returning migrant is hard, being a female return migrant is harder still. Being *ODHA* and at 'home' just adds insult to injury.

Women's experiences of HIV and mobility are best understood in relation to their ventures outside the domestic sphere and away from the guardianship of close kin. The women in this paper were not only spatially mobile but also socially mobile—they made sexual choices, relationship choices and life choices—and the subsequent treatment they received from others around them reflects not just the stigma of HIV but ambivalent views of women's mobility in spite of empowerment discourses, middle-class aspirations and pro-development conditions. When women's status is in transition, the violence against them and efforts to control or stigmatise their behaviour are at their peak (Spark 2011). Veronica, Tina and Nelly left home to seek opportunities elsewhere, in pursuit of education, broader social networks and other opportunities. Negative or at best ambivalent views of young women's mobility contribute to the vulnerability that they ultimately experience when they return home HIV-positive. Furthermore, if low social support is a determinant of HIV risk in other contexts (Weine and Kashuba 2012), then mobile women in Papua are already more vulnerable to HIV transmission in the first place because their mobility is almost certainly going to be judged as inappropriate or will cause them to lose kin networks. The women's experiences also affirm the findings of Olwig (2012) that women migrants often feel compelled to narrate their mobility in positive moral and gendered terms, and as deserving of social recognition by the community in an effort to deflect preconceived negative attitudes, and, we also suggest, to protect social support and kin networks.

Living in HIV-land forces an identity as an *ODHA* that requires secrecy and deception as an everyday feature of life. The mobile women we interviewed have the chance to construct and reconstruct identities and opportunities with a degree of self-consciousness not always available to those who do not leave their home villages and towns. But as Lindquist (2009) documents for other parts of Indonesia, opportunities are not always forthcoming: many mobile aspirants return home empty-handed, the lure of middle-class status unattained. Opportunities are even less readily available for the return Papuan HIV-positive women. The mere act of requiring care, rather than giving it, may test local gender expectations where women are the caregivers and expected to sacrifice their own well-being.

Mobility and opportunity have resulted, ultimately, in immobility. Papuan women are forced to stay put to access care where stigma is perpetuated, yet are unable to strengthen social relations, or invoke a caring support network, because the mechanisms of social control within the home community privilege those who remained in place and built local connections and solidarities. The divergent experiences of Nelly, Veronica, Tina and others, and the central importance of secrecy in their everyday lives, challenge simplistic notions that a strong Melanesian safety net based on traditional kinship systems will somehow override the stigmatising potential of HIV. The cultural aspirations for belonging and solidarity of our respondents are, however, not diminished. The denial of forms of sociality they have previously enjoyed in their communities is particularly hurtful. At the same time, based on their experiences, we ask how much not being able to access support at home is a cultural phenomenon, and how much it relates to the broader formulation of HIV responses, which have neither engaged Papuan values nor created space for conversations about how Papuans might, or would like to, support *ODHA* in their families and communities. Dominant responses to HIV in Tanah Papua have tended to overlook the complexity of Papuan lives, gender relations and inequalities, not least because Papuan research, leadership and experiences have been overshadowed by a politically motivated preference for simplified and standardised international HIV policies and interventions (Munro and Butt 2012). To improve care and support for HIV-positive Papuan women, especially return migrants, local moral judgements *and* inflexible HIV strategies need to be challenged. Papuans are already acknowledging and critically reflecting on these complexities, but they would benefit from more partners in development agencies and government who support efforts to build appropriate local treatment and support. Appropriate public health interventions need to view HIV-positive women less in terms of their adherence to treatment protocols and more as persons whose survival may depend on social support. They will need to tackle the hard truths that existing systems of social support may exacerbate problems of stigma and secrecy, and may contribute significantly to the challenges of accessing adequate HIV treatment and effective care for the deserving Papuan women who have returned home looking for it.

Acknowledgements

We would like to thank the Social Sciences and Humanities Research Council of Canada (Butt, Numbery), the CIHR Postdoctoral Fellowship Program and the former Canadian International Development Agency (Munro) for funding this research. The Centre for Population Studies (PSK) at Cenderawasih University under the leadership of Jack Morin provided important research support in Papua. Assistance from the NGOs Pacific Peoples Partnership, Pt Peduli Sehat, Yukemdi, and Humi Inane facilitated fieldwork. We are especially grateful to our respondents for sharing their experiences and stories with us.

References

Berk, ML, Schur, CL, Dunbar, JL, Bozzette, S & Shapiro, M 2003, 'Short report: migration among persons living with HIV', *Social Science and Medicine,* vol. 57, no. 6, pp. 1091–1097. doi.org/10.1016/S0277-9536(02)00487-2

Boellstorff, T 2009, 'Nuri's testimony: HIV/AIDS in Indonesia and bare knowledge', *American Ethnologist,* vol. 36, no. 2, pp. 351–363. doi.org/10.1111/j.1548-1425.2009.01139.x

Braithwaite, J, Braithwaite, V, Cookson, M & Dunn, L 2010, *Anomie and violence: non-truth and reconciliation in Indonesian peacebuilding,* ANU E Press, Canberra.

Butt, L 2011, 'Can you keep a secret? Pretences of confidentiality in HIV/AIDS counseling and treatment in Eastern Indonesia', *Medical Anthropology,* vol. 30, no. 3, pp. 319–338. doi.org/10.1080/0 1459740.2011.560585

Butt, L 2012, 'HIV/AIDS testing, treatment and the sedimentation of violence in Papua, Indonesia', *Western Humanities Review,* vol. 66, no. 3, pp. 35–57.

Butt, L 2015, 'Living in HIV-land: mobility and seropositivity in highlands Papua', in M Slama & J Munro (eds), *'Stone age' to 'real time': exploring Papuan mobilities, temporalities and religiosities*, ANU Press, Canberra, pp. 221–242.

Butt, L, Morin, J, Numbery, G, Peyon, I & Goo, A 2010, *Stigma and HIV/AIDS in highlands Papua*, Pusat Studi Kependudukan, Jayapura.

Carrasco, LN 2011, 'Who cares? HIV-related sickness, urban–rural linkages, and the gendered role of care in return migration in South Africa', *Gender and Development,* vol. 19, no. 1, pp. 105–114. doi.org/ 10.1080/13552074.2011.554028

Clark, SJ, Collinson, MA, Kahn, K, Drullinger, K & Tollman, SM 2007, 'Returning home to die: circular labour migration and mortality in South Africa 1', *Scandinavian Journal of Public Health,* vol. 35, 69 sup, pp. 35–44.

Cummings, M 2008, 'The trouble with trousers', in L Butt & R Eves (eds), *Making sense of AIDS: culture, sexuality, and power in Melanesia,* University of Hawai'i Press, Honolulu, pp. 133–154. doi. org/10.21313/hawaii/9780824831936.003.0008

Davies, SG 2015, 'Surveilling sexuality in Indonesia', in LR Bennett & SG Davies (eds), *Sex and sexuality in Indonesia: sexual politics, diversity and representations in the Reformasi era*, Routledge, London, pp. 30–61.

Davis, K & Stapleton, J 1991, 'Migration to rural areas by HIV patients: impact on HIV-related healthcare use', *Infection Control and Hospital Epidemiology*, vol. 12, no. 9, pp. 540–543.

Dundon, A 2010, 'AIDS and "building a wall" around Christian country in rural Papua New Guinea', *The Australian Journal of Anthropology,* vol. 21, no. 2, pp. 171–187. doi.org/10.1111/j.1757-6547.2010.00077.x

Elmore, K 2006, 'The migratory experiences of people with HIV/AIDS (PWHA) in Wilmington, North Carolina', *Health and Place,* vol. 12, no. 4, pp. 570–579. doi.org/10.1016/j.healthplace.2005.08.009

Eves, R 2010, 'Masculinity matters: men, gender-based violence and the AIDS epidemic in Papua New Guinea', in V Luker & S Dinnen (eds), *Civic insecurity: law, order and HIV in Papua New Guinea*, ANU E Press, Canberra, pp. 47–80.

Eves, R 2012, 'Resisting global AIDS knowledges: born-again Christian narratives of the epidemic from Papua New Guinea', *Medical Anthropology*, vol. 31, no. 1, pp. 61–76. doi.org/10.1080/01459740.2011.594122

Eves, R & Butt, L 2008, 'Introduction: gender, sexuality and power in Melanesia', in L Butt & R Eves (eds), *Making sense of AIDS: culture, sexuality, and power in Melanesia*, University of Hawai'i Press, Honolulu, pp. 1–23. doi.org/10.21313/hawaii/9780824831936.003.0001

Farmer, P 1997, 'Social inequalities and emerging infectious diseases', *Emerging Infectious Diseases,* vol. 2, no. 4, pp. 259–269. doi.org/10.3201/eid0204.960402

Hammar, L 2008, 'Fear and loathing in Papua New Guinea', in L Butt & R Eves (eds), *Making sense of AIDS: culture, sexuality, and power in Melanesia*, University of Hawai'i Press, Honolulu, pp. 60–79. doi.org/10.21313/hawaii/9780824831936.003.0004

Hardon, A & Dilger, H 2011, 'Global AIDS medicines in East African health institutions', *Medical Anthropology,* vol. 30, no. 2, pp. 136–157. doi.org/10.1080/01459740.2011.552458

Jones, GM 2014, 'Secrecy', *Annual Review of Anthropology*, vol. 43, no. 1, pp. 53–69. doi.org/10.1146/annurev-anthro-102313-030058

Keusch, G, Wilentz, J & Kleinman, A 2006, 'Stigma and global health: developing a research agenda', *The Lancet,* vol. 367, pp. 525–527. doi.org/10.1016/S0140-6736(06)68183-X

Klitzman, R & Bayer, R 2003, *Mortal secrets: truth and lies in the age of AIDS*, Johns Hopkins University Press, Baltimore.

Knodel, JE, Hak, S, Khuon, C, So, D & McAndrew, J 2010, *A comparative study of antiretroviral therapy assistance from parents and family members in Cambodia and Thailand*, Population Studies Center, University of Michigan, Ann Arbor.

Lepani, K 2012, *Islands of love, islands of risk: culture and HIV in the Trobriands*, Vanderbilt University Press, Nashville.

Lindquist, JA 2009, *The anxieties of mobility: migration and tourism in the Indonesian borderlands*, University of Hawai'i Press, Honolulu.

Madianou, M & Miller, D 2011, 'Mobile phone parenting: reconfiguring relationships between Filipina migrant mothers and their left-behind children', *New Media and Society,* vol. 13, no. 3, pp. 457–470. doi.org/10.1177/1461444810393903

Mallett, S 2004, 'Understanding home: a critical review of the literature', *The Sociological Review,* vol. 52, no. 1, pp. 62–89. doi.org/10.1111/j.1467-954X.2004.00442.x

McKay, D 2007, '"Sending dollars shows feeling" - emotions and economies in Filipino migration', *Mobilities,* vol. 2, no. 2, pp. 175–194. doi.org/10.1080/17450100701381532

McKay, D 2012, *Global Filipinos: migrants' lives in the virtual village,* Indiana University Press, Bloomington.

Munro, J 2012, '"A diploma and a descendant!" Premarital sexuality, education and politics among Dani university students in North Sulawesi, Indonesia', *Journal of Youth Studies,* vol. 15, no. 8, pp. 1011–1027. doi.org/10.1080/13676261.2012.693592

Munro, J 2013, 'The violence of inflated possibilities: education, transformation and diminishment in Wamena, Papua', *Indonesia,* vol. 95, pp. 25–46. doi.org/10.1353/ind.2013.0008

Munro, J 2015a, '"HIV is our problem together": developing an indigenous-led response to HIV in Tanah Papua', SSGM In Brief 2015/5, State, Society and Governance in Melanesia Program, The Australian National University, Canberra.

Munro, J 2015b, '"Now we know shame": malu and stigma among highlanders in the Papuan diaspora, in M Slama & J Munro (eds), *'Stone age' to 'real time': exploring Papuan mobilities, temporalities and religiosities,* ANU Press, Canberra, pp. 169–194.

Munro, J & Butt, L 2012, 'Compelling evidence: research methods, politics and HIV/AIDS in Papua, Indonesia', *The Asia Pacific Journal of Anthropology,* vol. 13, no. 4, pp. 334–351. doi.org/10.1080/14442213.2012.694467

Munro, J & McIntyre, L 2016, '(Not) getting political: indigenous women and preventing mother-to-child transmission of HIV in West Papua', *Culture, Health and Sexuality*, vol. 18, no. 2, pp. 156–170. doi.org/10.1080/13691058.2015.1070436

Nilan, P 2008, 'Youth transitions to urban, middle-class marriage in Indonesia: faith, family and finances', *Journal of Youth Studies*, vol. 11, no. 1, pp. 65–82. doi.org/10.1080/13676260701690402

Olwig, KF 2012, 'The "successful" return: Caribbean narratives of migration, family, and gender', *Journal of the Royal Anthropological Institute*, vol. 18, pp. 828–845. doi.org/10.1111/j.1467-9655.2012.01794.x

Rees, S & Silove, D 2007, 'Speaking out about human rights and health in West Papua', *The Lancet*, vol. 370, pp. 637–639. doi.org/10.1016/S0140-6736(07)61318-X

Robinson, K 2009, *Gender, Islam and democracy in Indonesia*, Routledge, London.

Salazar, NB & Smart, A 2011, 'Anthropological takes on (im)mobility', *Identities*, vol. 18, no. 6, pp. i–ix. doi.org/10.1080/1070289X.2012.683674

Simonin, A, Bushee, J & Courcaud, A 2011, 'Social, cultural and political factors in the design of HIV programmes with Papuan highland communities', *Culture, Health and Sexuality*, vol. 13, supp. 2, pp. 185–199.

Slama, M 2012, '"Coming down to the shop": trajectories of Hadhrami women into Indonesian public realms', *The Asia Pacific Journal of Anthropology*, vol. 13, no. 4, pp. 313–333. doi.org/10.1080/14442213.2012.699089

Spark, C 2011, 'Gender trouble in town: Educated women eluding male domination, gender violence and marriage in PNG', *The Asia Pacific Journal of Anthropology*, vol. 12, no. 2, pp. 164–179. doi.org/10.1080/14442213.2010.546425

Sullivan, N 2011, 'Mediating abundance and scarcity: implementing an HIV/AIDS-targeted project within a government hospital in Tanzania', *Medical Anthropology*, vol. 30, no. 2, pp. 201–221. doi.org/10.1080/01459740.2011.552453

Wardlow, H 2006, *Wayward women: sexuality and agency in a New Guinea society*, University of California Press, Berkeley.

Weine, SM & Kashuba, AB 2012, 'Labor migration and HIV risk: A systematic review of the literature', *AIDS and Behavior*, vol. 16, no. 6, pp. 1605–1621. doi.org/10.1007/s10461-012-0183-4

Welaga, P, Hosegood, V, Weiner, R, Hill, C, Herbst, K & Newell, ML 2009, 'Coming home to die? The association between migration and mortality in rural South Africa', *BMC Public Health,* vol. 9, no. 1, p. 193. doi.org/10.1186/1471-2458-9-193

Whiteside, A 2006, 'HIV/AIDS and development: failures of vision and imagination', *International Affairs,* vol. 82, no. 2, pp. 327–343. doi.org/10.1111/j.1468-2346.2006.00534.x

Williams, CP 2007, *Maiden voyages: eastern Indonesian women on the move*, Institute of South-east Asian Studies, Singapore.

Wood, M & Dundon, A 2014, 'Great ancestral women: sexuality, gendered mobility, and HIV among the Bamu and Gogodala of Papua New Guinea', *Oceania,* vol. 84, no. 2, pp. 185–201. doi.org/10.1002/ocea.5054

Zhou, YR 2007, '"If you get AIDS … you have to endure it alone": understanding the social constructions of HIV/AIDS in China', *Social Science and Medicine,* vol. 65, pp. 284–295. doi.org/10.1016/j.socscimed.2007.03.031

8

Urban castaways: The precarious living of marooned islanders

Thorgeir Kolshus

Abstract

On Mota island in north Vanuatu, the attitude towards urban migration has changed significantly over the past 20 years. Due to rapid population growth and consequent pressure on already scarce land resources, leaving for the two urban centres of Luganville (Santo) and Vila has become a livelihood strategy for entire households rather than a temporary arrangement usually involving young unmarried men. With conflicts over land rights on the rise, long-term absentees find it difficult to defend their claims. This challenges their safety net and consequently exacerbates their sense of precarity: if they can't make it there, they can't make it anywhere. This chapter shows how various factors involved in decision making, such as education, cash crop prices, droughts, urban sorcery, job opportunities and sheer adventure-seeking, fluctuate and cause constant reassessment among the urban-dwelling Motese of whether to stay or return to the island.

Introduction

The inhabitants of the island of Mota in the Banks Islands in north Vanuatu have always been ambivalent towards urban life, yet throughout the 150 years for which we have historic records, young women and men have left the island in search of adventure and an unlikely pay-off.[1] In the latter half of the 19th century, people from Mota were eager recruits for the Anglican Melanesian Mission's Central School, first in Auckland and later on Norfolk Island. Much to the mission's dismay, they also enthusiastically signed up for the 'blackbirding' labour trade, citing the prospects of adventure and change of scenery rather than financial gain as prime motivations (Kolshus and Hovdhaugen 2010). In those days, Mota was itself a centre of the Anglican Melanesian world of northern Vanuatu and the south and central Solomon Islands. Being the site for both the mission's Summer School and for the experimental Christian village Kohimarama, Mota had the attention of a mission with a distinct cosmopolitan flavour, manned as it was by Oxbridge-educated Englishmen of noble birth (Armstrong 1900; How 1899; Kolshus 2013, 2014). The language of Mota was used as the mission's lingua franca, serving as the medium of teaching in the extensive Anglican school system and as the language of the Bible, the Book of Common Prayer and the much-cherished Hymns (Firth 1970); and Mota figured prominently in the imagination of the Melanesian Mission's numerous supporters, both in the British homeland and in the antipodean colonies.

But at the stroke of the pen that in 1893 erected the first of the expanding boundaries between the British Solomon Islands Protectorate and its neighbours, and cemented by the establishment of the Condominium of the New Hebrides in 1906, Mota found itself moved from the centre of an island world with immediate global connections to the periphery of a peripheral political unit. This process of gradual marginalisation continued after Vanuatu's independence, an experience that has been particularly discouraging to the Motese and the other Banks Islanders after being the most solid pro-independence supporters of all of Vanuatu's regions.

---

1   In pre-contact days, canoe expeditions would have served the same purpose, although not of the scale nor the regularity of the visits to Mota from Tikopia, a Polynesian outlier some 200 kilometres north-east of the island (see Kolshus 2013).

In this chapter, I address some of the changes in how people on Mota imagine life in *taon* ('town'), and how they act in accordance with these changing imaginaries. I have no theoretical axe to grind: I do not apply any distinct analytical framework exogenous to the ethnography itself, and I do not engage the misrepresentations, alleged or real, of previous scholarship. I aim for little more than presenting a historically informed, multi-temporal, ethnographic account of how the prospects, promises and perils of travelling to and living in an urban setting are conceived by the 1,000 people living on a small island at the periphery of a small Pacific state and by the 400 who live on other islands but still hold that 'home' is elsewhere (cf. Rousseau 2015: 24).[2] I intend to show how their choices of whether, and when, to stay or to go are informed by a multitude of factors, some of which are structural—ecological, demographical, economic, political—while others relate to worldview-based[3] risk assessment, adventurism or sheer opportunism. I show how a gradually increasing disenchantment with the promises of a more 'refined' city life has brought a new conviction that staying put is the better option. Partly, this is affected by the realisation that few Motese possess the combination of being well-educated and confident that gives them the edge in a labour market characterised by 'diploma disease'. But it also coincides with the increase in urban sorcery that has become the topic for a number of recent publications, both from urban Vanuatu and elsewhere in Melanesia. This has brought a sense of entrenched uncertainty that is particularly severe to people from Mota, whose island is sorcery-free. Combined, these developments have triggered a revaluation of the virtues of the 'simple life on the island' that on the one hand strengthens their pride, but also serves to limit their options. Given an increasingly dire shortage of land, exacerbated by climatic hazards like droughts and cyclones, such a limiting of options might in the long run prove unfavourable.

---

2   It is based on 'dual-synchronic' long-term fieldworks in 1996–97 and 2002–03 and a five-week fieldtrip in 2012, 23 months of which were spent on Mota and two months among Motese in Luganville and Vila, Vanuatu's two main urban centres.

3   In recent anthro-speak, my use of 'worldview' would translate into 'ontology'. I readily admit to be less than enchanted by the multifarious strains that are subsumed under the heading of anthropology's 'ontological turn'. I find the critical realism of the likes of Andrew Sayer (2000), recently modified to cater to anthropology by David Zeitlyn and Roger Just (2014) and David Graeber (2015), both infinitely more constructive and appealing. This also informs my continued belief that ethnography has a different epistemological status than mere 'experience', given that on an interpersonal level, some experiences obviously are less, well, idiosyncratic than others. For a lively critique of the epistemological foundations of critical realism, see Martin (2015).

Santo city lights

Since the 1960s, Luganville, colloquially referred to as 'Santo', has been the destination of choice for Motese on urban adventures. Here they immediately learn from resident Motese that people from most other islands are temperamental fighters; and that sorcery is omnipresent, mainly because of the large Ambrymese contingent (see Rio 2007). Eventually, they learn from experience that it is hard to eke out a living without an established network, and that 1,000 vatu[4] does not go a long way. They also find that the 'ways of the town', '*ō matevui tape taon*', are characterised by haughtiness and lack of any expressed sociality beyond the boundaries of the household. 'Contrary to the custom of the island', they say, 'people will only stare at strangers, never greet them or invite them in'. Thus strengthened in their belief in the virtues of island living, for which the lack of material goods is far outweighed by the companionship and sense of feeling safe in an island that has been free of sorcery since the 1950s,[5] they return to Mota with some perishable merchandise and the much more cherished stories, which grow with every retelling. The ones who linger are those who marry someone from another island. Hardly any mixed couples choose to settle on Mota. This might be due to the matrilineal transfer of land rights, which, in spite of the customary practice of adoption of newcomers, might leave a Mota man and his foreign wife too reliant upon his matrilineal land and the children of the union with contestable land claims (Kolshus 2008). But the Motese insist that the reluctance of other ni-Vanuatu (as citizens of Vanuatu are called) to settle on Mota is due to the island being regarded as far too remote and backward. Many Motese take this disparaging outsider's view lightly. It is simply a validation of the virtues of an island life that is independent in its own right. But to the youngsters and those with tertiary education, it used to sting. This is because it reminded them that everywhere else, people were moving ahead. Also, even though they appreciated the strong

---

4   Approximately US$10.

5   To fully appreciate how exceptional this is, one needs to take into account how sorcery elsewhere in Vanuatu shaped the traditional sociocultural landscape (see for instance Hess 2009; Rio 2007; Eriksen 2008; Rio and Eriksen 2013), and the recent hike in sorcery accusations and extension of the phantasmagoric repertoire in urban contexts characterised by increasing social inequalities (Rio 2011, 2014; Mitchell 2011; Taylor 2015; Rousseau 2015). Cases that resemble the Mota situation can be found in south-east Ambrym (Tonkinson 1981) and Akhamb (Bratrud 2011). *Talking it through*, a recently published collection of articles (Forsyth and Eves 2015), gives ethnographic examples of sorcery from various parts of Melanesia.

position of Mota traditions and their regard for historic connections, they frequently expressed a sense of their options as steadily shrinking (cf. Knauft 2002).

Since I started my work on Mota in 1996, leaving for Santo has acquired an ever stronger tinge of necessity. A rapid population growth of 4 per cent annually for the past four decades has made land scarce for several matrilineages, and in particular land suitable for growing coconuts in order to produce copra, which is the only available cash crop. The shortage has been exacerbated by frequent droughts, with both 1997 and 2003 being El Niño years. Consequently, in the village of Lorovilko, some 20 kilometres outside Santo town, more than 60 Motese had by 2003 established a hamlet of their own, growing tobacco, kava and vegetables for sale in the Santo market house. Most of them belonged to the same lineage, which had simply too many members to provide for on Mota. When I visited them in 2003, they admitted that relations with their Lorovilko neighbours were strained, to say the least. Those local villagers had vehemently opposed selling the piece of land that enabled the Motese to settle. And in the recent past there had been numerous physical attacks made by them. Stones were regularly thrown into the hamlet, houses had been torched, and people had been assaulted on their way to their gardens.

Over and above these physical attacks, their main concern was sorcery. Several of their adversaries were renowned and feared sorcerers, who during earlier conflicts in the East Santo area had proved their willingness to harm or even kill people in order to have things their way. Faced with such intangible threats, the Motese had sought the assistance of the *tasiu*, 'brothers', of the Melanesian Brotherhood, an indigenous Anglican order. Anglicans hold that because of their close association with the bishop the *tasiu* have access to particularly powerful *mana*, extra-human agency (Kolshus 2013), which is believed by people of all denominations to be highly effective in counteracting sorcery.[6] The brothers had prayed and performed various rituals that established a protective perimeter around their hamlet. Conventional attacks, such as garden plundering, arson and assaults, had not stopped. But at least they were now safe from the dangers of sorcery that they had neither the experience to detect nor the knowledge to defuse. Everybody seemed to agree that they would much rather lead

---

6   In an article titled 'The ecology of faith', currently undergoing peer review, I address the role played by the Anglican Church, and the Melanesian Brotherhood in particular, in manipulating weather conditions and protecting people against sorcery.

a less refined life on Mota than endure the menaces of Lorovilko. This option was not available to them, however, since virtually everyone belonged to land-deprived matrilineages. If they were to return, they would have to rely on relatives whose resources were already stretched to the limit during the critically long period between clearing and planting new gardens and their first harvest.

They had left home in search of a new life and now they were stuck. But, they said, at least we have enough food and water. From what they had heard from me and others, the drought on Mota made life difficult. There was a measure of solace in others' misfortune, or perhaps rather in knowing that at least for the time being, their lot seemed the more attractive.

In terms of subsistence, the situation of the Motese living in the actual town of Luganville was different from that of the Lorovilko settlement. There, virtually everyone was engaged in the urban equivalent of hunting and gathering. This involved a perennial search for short-term employment in a labour market increasingly characterised by the developing world's 'diploma disease', in which the usually poorly schooled Motese consistently fell short of the better educated contestants from less peripheral islands. Very few of these town dwellers stayed on for more than a year or two before returning to Mota, richer in histories but otherwise with little to show for their urban adventures.

But some managed to secure more steady employment, or find spouses who did, and consequently spent many years in Luganville. One of these was Ata[7], who had lived there permanently since 1982. His household, next to the bridge crossing Side River, was a landmark and social anchorage for all Motese arriving in Espiritu Santo. When I last met him as an octogenarian in 2003, he insisted that life in Luganville had been good to him. But lately, he said, interisland violence had been on the rise, and the dramatic increase in sorcery and sorcery accusations was particular cause for concern. The culprits were mainly men from Ambrym, and people from other islands were forced to seek preventive measures. Anglicans like Ata relied on the assistance of the clergy and the *tasiu*, who also would help members of other churches who came to them for advice and protection. But as a supplement, many sought the services of sorcerers from the mainly Anglican island of Maewo,

---

7   Most of the names in this chapter are pseudonyms.

whose magic was considered to be even more powerful than that of the Ambrymese. Nonetheless, anyone walking alone in Luganville after dark would be exposed to attacks of a kind that in Mota is called *varalōlōqōñ*, (lit. 'unconscious steps'), by which the victim later falls ill and usually dies with no recollection of what has happened because the sorcerer has erased the victim's memory. All Motese were careful never to let anyone move around unaccompanied. Even though I as a non-Melanesian most likely was safe from harm, which according to local exegesis is due to my use of deodorant, they insisted on following me home after nightly kava sessions, keeping a watchful eye out for any item along the way that might resemble a charm or a harmful substance (cf. Taylor 2015: 39–40). These were skills the Motese had to acquire as soon as they arrived in Luganville.

Luganville, nine years on

Shortly into my five-week fieldtrip to Mota in June 2012, news of the death of Mark, a man in his early 20s, came through from Luganville. As people mourned, snippets of new information trickled in regarding the circumstances of his death. It seemed that he had hanged himself following a quarrel with his Ambrymese girlfriend. His mother Anne, overwhelmed by grief, insisted that he never would have ended his life this way. Her brother Woros, on the other hand, was of a different opinion: Mark had a troubled relationship with his girlfriend and her parents, and had in his despair chosen to end his life. Casually, bordering on callous, Woros stated in front of the mourners, amongst them Mark's father and me, that the young man would never enter '*Paradaes*', the afterlife where all believers in Christ shall meet again.[8] But in the days that followed a richer background story expanded, which endorsed Anne's refusal to accept the initial accounts. Mark's fiancée had indeed found him dead with a noose around his neck, but, the story went, a number of factors indicated that this had been the work of sorcerers. They would need an official autopsy to confirm, but three diviners, in Bislama called *kleva*, from Maewo discovered leads suggesting that Mark had fallen victim to one of the most dreaded sorcery methods: he had been killed and his inner organs were removed and replaced with leaves before he had been magically brought back to life and sent home only to die five days later.

---

8   According to the logic of the Mota kinship system, as Mark's mother's brothers, Woros and his brother Baddeley are heads of the matrilineage.

The guiding hand behind the young man's suicide had not been Mark's. Even though the autopsy results allegedly were inconclusive, people had no doubt: Mark had been killed by Ambrymese sorcerers, commissioned by his father-in-law.

In addition to preparing the regular mortuary feasting cycle, the days that followed were filled with attempts to reach relatives in Luganville, who, it was believed, were now living in the utmost danger. Making matters worse, this was not the first fatal attack by Ambrymese on Motese living in Luganville. Mark's elder sister had been killed by sorcerers 10 years earlier, allegedly because her Ambrymese partner's kin did not want to pay the brideprice that was required to seal their union in marriage. Christina, Mark's mother's sister's daughter, who had left Mota a few months earlier, sent us a message pleading for someone to buy her a return ticket. According to her, the Motese on Santo were in constant fear of what the Ambrymese would come up with next. They took refuge in the homes of the permanent residents, while those who were in a position to return looked for a way home. People on Mota were deeply worried about their diasporic relatives. Califord, one of just a few young men who held a secondary school diploma and who also had lived for several years on Malekula and consequently knew the ways of the world, was adamant: those who did not study or were otherwise occupied should return immediately! Amidst all these worries, the fact that Mark had actually been killed and that his soul of baptism, *ō atai tape vasōgōrōñō*, consequently would find peace in heaven was cause for some comfort. His life soul, *ō atai ta lō marama*, would find its way home to Mota and eventually dwell on its matrilineal land.

A couple of weeks later, I spent a day in Luganville with Stella, Mark's mother's sister, and her son, Fisher Young. Stella had been widowed around 1994, after which she married a carpenter from Maewo and moved to Luganville, while Fisher Young had joined the Melanesian Brotherhood as soon as he was old enough and served seven years as a *tasiu* on various islands, including Maewo, before he settled in Luganville with his mother. Once off the island, most Motese would become more socially restrained and less outgoing. Not so with Fisher Young, who apparently had adapted to the more fluid relationships of the town. His conviviality and social skills secured short-term engagements with various building firms, and he was consequently able to support his wife and small child as well as his mother and now-retired stepfather. On the wall of their kitchen house was written 'Keep your heart save [sic] from evil spirit and whichcraft [sic]'. I asked him what they did to protect themselves from sorcery, or *malagagapalag*, (lit. 'harmful schemes'). He immediately mentioned the members of the Melanesian Brotherhood. In addition to the Brothers, individual prayers were also effective, he said. He was vaguer when he talked about the third means of protection, but it gradually became clear that he referred to the *kleva*. With a stepfather from Maewo and an extensive social network from his long service there, he personally felt safe. But he quickly acknowledged that most Motese had reason to be afraid, since they lacked his experience and consequently would be easy targets. Young women like Christina, with no regular employment, should return to Mota as soon as possible. Luganville was no longer a place for Motese in search of adventure.

The rise and fall of Patteson Roy

On 22 September, 2014, after an unprecedented eighth round of voting, the Vanuatu electoral college managed to come to agreement on a new head of state. *Mama*[9] Baldwin Lonsdale from Mota Lava, Mota's northern neighbour, was elected to serve as president of the Republic of Vanuatu for the next five years. In Torba, the news was greeted with celebrations across the province. Throughout Vanuatu's time as an independent nation, people in Torba have harboured a strong sense of being ignored by the rest of the nation, due to the province's relatively few inhabitants, peripheral location, and lack of economic significance. With only two MPs and unpredictable lines of communication between the province and the capital, there was a general feeling that their concerns were not heard and, more certainly, never met. So the choice of a Torba man as the head of state came as a very welcome surprise. And the fact that *Mama* Baldwin was an Anglican priest gave additional cause for celebration in a province that 150 years ago became the cradle of Anglicanism in Melanesia and remains predominantly Anglican to this day, even boasting its own bishop, who oversees the Diocese of Banks and Torres, the smallest in the entire Anglican Communion.

---

9   *Mama* is the usual term of address for Anglican priests. It is an abbreviation of the Mota term for father's brother, *mamagai*.

On Mota, however, not everyone celebrated. In the village of Tanorosa, Patteson Roy, a former deacon and headmaster, and once an MP and government minister, had pinned his last glimmer of political hope on the presidential election, only to realise that this window of opportunity was now firmly shut. For the past four decades, Patteson has been an influential figure on the island. He is the only Motese to visit Europe, having spent six months at a seminary in Scotland. He has also served as headmaster of the local Mota school and as principal of Arep, the only secondary school in Torba. After Patteson successfully ran as an independent candidate in the 2002 parliamentary elections, he became the first Mota MP. With a hung parliament, he went on to become an unlikely kingmaker, siding with the second Edward Natapei government and earning himself the ministerial portfolios of Ni-Vanuatu Business and then of Education for his support.

Patteson Roy's success went beyond the Motese's wildest dreams. And in the months that followed his election, around 30 Mota men and several complete households left for the capital of Vila.[10] These were either Patteson's entourage of loyal supporters expecting reward for their faithfulness by being offered positions, or adventure seekers eager to use the opportunity while they had friends and relatives with stable incomes that could provide for them if they failed to make ends meet—which they invariably did. Consequently, en route for my second fieldwork in December 2002, much to my surprise I discovered that almost 100 Motese were living in Vila. When I left Vanuatu five years earlier, the Mota diaspora in the capital city counted a mere 20, mainly young bachelors on short-term adventures and a few uxorilocally married men. The people I met in Vila this second time around expressed either a clear understanding that this was the beginning of a new era of golden prospects or that this was a once in a lifetime opportunity to be capitalised upon before it inevitably would be taken from them. The sentiments of the people on Mota were divided more or less along the same lines. To his many supporters, Patteson's election marked the beginning of proper '*divelopmen*', which, in their opinion, had been kept from them due to the nepotistic islandism of people further south. Now, the time had finally come for the Motese to benefit from pork barrel politics. Patteson's political opponents, on the other hand, insisted that the successful strategy of an independent

---

10   Without exaggerating the connotational impact, it is worth mentioning that in Mota, *vila* means 'lightning'—which in the Mota Hymn Book frequently features as a metonym for all the earthly dangers from which the Motese require the Lord's protection.

candidate backed by a majority of his fellow islanders would be a one-off. Once the more populous islands in Torba realised that their fission along party lines had cost them a seat, they would replicate the Mota tactics and easily regain lost terrain. As might be expected, his opponents did not have much faith in Patteson Roy's dedication to the welfare and development of their backward island. In order for Mota to rise, *kalkalō*, investments in school buildings, new teachers, transportation and other infrastructural developments were needed. Otherwise, the rest of Vanuatu would continue to move ahead while Mota fell even further behind, and those who aspired to lead a different life from that of their forebears would have few other options than to leave for Santo or Vila. They were convinced that Patteson and his group of newly minted and salaried civil servants would not provide more than the equivalents of beads and mirrors: meat, kava and tea for the Independence Day celebrations, and some iron roofing for the church in the villages where he had carried the vote.

Patteson did his best to prove the naysayers wrong. He and his political secretary Jeves set aside a significant share of their monthly salary for community purposes. Less than a year after he assumed office, we received a radio message announcing that a new 16-foot community boat with two outboard engines would arrive the next day, to replace the leaking aluminium dinghy that had been donated by the French colonial government at the dawn of independence almost 25 years earlier. Even Peter, the local National United Party leader, grudgingly acknowledged that they had done well. The boat and other minor projects were signs of the longer-term changes that constituted Motese notions of *divelopmen*, the very changes that he had been adamant would never be forthcoming during Patteson's tenure. But Peter was nonetheless convinced that the boat would soon succumb to mismanagement and lack of caution negotiating the treacherous Mota reefs. He also made sure that no NUP supporters showed up for the boat's inauguration ceremony. By circumventing the long-established fault lines between the political parties, Patteson's election had destabilised the structure of allies and opponents. His extraordinary good fortune in holding the balance of parliamentary power could be tolerated, but faking gratitude at a public display of an opponent's political success was simply beyond the pale. Also, in Vanuatu, the political tide turns quickly. Peter knew that his time would come.

Eventually, he and the other sceptics were proven right. The boat was not carved out for such rough landings, and after a mere two years, it was beyond repair. So when Patteson Roy lost his seat in the 2006 election to an independent candidate from a more populous island, again as Peter had predicted, he returned to find the boat permanently resting on the reef. His intentions had been for the best, but this could not outweigh the ineptitude of some of his supporters. So apart from hurricane lanterns to all villages and a couple of new church roofs, his many initiatives to improve the conditions of his fellow islanders had failed. Time had now come to improve his personal lot. The severance pay he had received after losing his seat was substantial by most standards. By Mota terms it was a fortune, which he used to buy stocks and open a store in his village of Tanorosa. But managing a sound business while juggling the requests that followed a bigman's sense of noblesse oblige soon outstripped his resources. The demands of his political supporters were particularly difficult to meet. Since he had tried to distribute his allowance and other gifts in ways that showed no particular political bias, those who had supported him felt they had more legitimate claims to his relative wealth now that his tenure was over and he had returned significantly better off than when he left. After all, his gains had come through their agency. Even a deft political player like Patteson found no way around these expectations. Also, he had invested all his hopes in a successful rerun in the 2010 elections, and he realised that he would not stand a chance without his supporters. So he dished out.

Deprived, yet hopeful

When I met Patteson again in 2012, I could not help feeling sorry for him. The suit-wearing minister who had seen me off at the Bauerfield airport in 2003 was now a pauper in rags. He had built no less than six houses on his land, but several of these were dilapidated and the rest lay in varying states of disrepair. On the door to his store was a note saying that he no longer allowed credit, while pleading for those who owed money to settle their debt. I learnt from others that he no longer had goods to sell since he did not have money to restock. None of his children lived on the island, so he could not rely on them for support in gardening and copra production. Ruth, his wife, had resumed her position as a nurse at the Mota dispensary after their return from Vila, but her income did not go very far. In short, Patteson had become the epitome of the Mota *masara*, 'a man without means'. This became all the more painful as he struggled to keep up appearances of his earlier dignified existence, and his failed attempts only exposed him to ridicule by his political opponents.

Shortly after his return, the Mota Chiefs' Council had chosen him as the island's head chief, *mwōe maranaga*, and president of the council. But he had not called a meeting in a long time, allegedly because he had embezzled the 42,000 vatu sent by Torba Province to pay for the construction of a meeting house, or *gamal*, where they could teach children *kastom* stories. People believed that he failed to call new meetings to prevent the topic of the lost money from being raised. The consequence was a communal stalemate on the island, with very few decisions being made beyond the village level.

However, when I talked to him about his prospects, Patteson was remarkably upbeat. He told me that all he had to do now was wait for one thing: the appointment of a new head of state. And this would inevitably be him. When I cautiously asked why this was so, he provided two reasons. First, that the office of the president of the Republic of Vanuatu rotated between the provinces, and it was now Torba's turn. Second, in Torba there were only two candidates, himself and one other, who was ineligible due to his criminal record. Consequently, when news of the impending presidential election came through, his fortunes would change yet again. '*Sowlue, i nau we tōga nerei gap*', 'so, you see, I am simply waiting'. The result of the presidential election would turn out to be an agonising end to Patteson Roy's last shred of hope. But, after all, he did return to Mota. The fate of some who failed to do so is even less enviable.

Stranded futures

After Patteson lost his seat and left for home in 2006, a number of his staff and voluntary entourage stayed on, hoping for another opportunity and knowing that life on a drought-plagued island had little to offer. By 2012, the tables had turned. Mota had enjoyed a succession of more than ample rainy seasons and rich harvests, while virtually every Motese in Vila had endured long pecuniary dry spells. Among them was Bill, who when I first arrived on Mota in 1996 soon became one of my closest friends and helpers. His generous enthusiasm had always been an encouragement in the midst of fieldwork turmoil. His awe when listening to stories from the world outside Vanuatu and his seemingly naïve curiosity on virtually any topic imaginable were heartening to a fresh arrival struggling to come to terms with a new and unknown existence: 'I know something that is worth knowing, it's not just the other way around'. I soon realised that his inquisitiveness fuelled a remarkably analytic mind. He had followed Patteson Roy to Vila in 2002 to work at the reception desk in one of the government ministries and had later been joined by his wife Veronica and their children. When I met him again in 2012, he had not held a single job in several years, and the family relied on Veronica's meagre income from picking eggs in a chicken farm. Even though he still did his best to present an upbeat version of life, he readily admitted that the outlook was grim. His only hope now was to save 7,000 vatu, approximately US$70, to pay for a passport. This would make him eligible for an apple-picking scheme in New Zealand, by which ni-Vanuatu would spend some months working in orchards and usually return with a decent surplus. Even though most of the local recruiters preferred men from their home islands, with a passport at least he would stand a chance. Bill gave only one reason for wanting to go to New Zealand: that the earnings would cover the return fare to Mota for the whole family. He had news from his brother Selwyn, who had moved back to Mota a few years ago after having worked almost 20 years for a diving company in Vila, that parts of their matrilineal land had been encroached upon and that use rights to other parts of their land had been challenged.

Veronica's lineage, to which their children belonged, faced the same problems. RōLea and Sogov, her mother and father, had come to Vila to look after their grandchildren when Veronica and Bill were still regularly employed. After their income declined, Veronica and Bill found shelter in a small house next to the chicken farm, while RōLea and Sogov moved to a shack in the opposite direction 10 kilometres outside Vila, where they had leased some land for cultivation. First they had sold their produce in the Vila market, but now they would prepare the food themselves and sell it as 'wasemaot', hors d'oeuvres-like treats to counter the foul taste of kava, in a kava bar in downtown Vila. The elderly couple would usually walk the 10 kilometres to and from town, since the Vila minibus drivers rarely took the trouble of going to such remote places, at least not without demanding the full taxi fare. We discussed the rumours of the challenges to their land rights as well as the outright land grabs. Veronica's brother, Welgan, had remained on Mota in order to protect their rights but his mild manner made him an accommodating counterpart to the much more assertive claimants. RōLea had instructed her more temperamental children not to talk back, even though their opponent's claims were outlandish. One of their opponents, RōLea's brother's son, was the regional head of a political party and would in that capacity pay irregular visits to Vila. RōLea and several other members of their family were always there to greet him at the airport. They never mentioned the land issues but welcomed him in a manner befitting a dear family member—in the hope that he might take example from their magnanimous conduct and change his ways, RōLea said laconically. But she was deeply concerned about the future of her children, and the lack of opportunity to go back to Mota and present her case on their behalf weighed heavily on her mind.

Bill followed me to the airport to see me off. Comparing his life when I first met him with his situation 16 years after was a disheartening exercise. He was involuntarily idle and chronically penniless, with no immediate prospects apart from the highly uncertain apple-picking scheme, knowing that his lineage land was gradually being seized by others, which would make it even harder to return home. This was even before adding the recent hike in violent crimes and sorcery in Vila to the equation, which in effect imposed an after-dark curfew on all members of his household. The factors that initially made him leave Mota for Vila were by now almost completely reversed. Mota was a land of at least some opportunity, in addition to having the virtue of being Home. Vila had become the site of their shortcomings as well as a site for fear.

Most Motese in urban settings share Bill's experience. The sense of terror that followed Mark's death further corroborated the perceived precariousness of life among the Motese diaspora. To the Motese on other islands, Mota's recent agricultural prosperity, combined with the limited access to wage labour and sorcery-induced bursts of moral panic and social turmoil, meant that most of the factors behind their decision to leave the island had now turned in Mota's favour. It was no longer just a safe haven where everybody knows your name. It had become a place of opportunity, at least by comparison to their current lot. The choice to leave for home seemed more appealing than ever before—and the inability to do so ever more taxing.

Concluding remarks: Beyond the point of no return

As I write these words, the climate change talks in Paris are moving to a close, while Vanuatu is undergoing the effects of the most severe El Niño-induced droughts in decades, aggravating the damages of Cyclone Pam, another weather phenomenon of virtually unprecedented intensity. Most scientific climate projections suggest that in the future, such extremes will be the new normal. On Mota, which I will visit again in a few weeks' time, no water has been available since September, even though they are well into the usually wet summer season, whereas during my 2012 visit, in the dry months of June and July, it rained every single day. To a horticultural subsistence economy, such disturbances to the weather patterns seriously affect the traditional calendar for planting and growth, challenging the virtues of relative stability and predictability that island life, after all, has had to offer, which somewhat evened out the outsider's view that Mota lacked in *divelopmen* and sophistication of modern living. To the older generation, such disparaging assessments were tokens of pride rather than cause for offence, since they confirmed their self-image that Mota is the stronghold of Banks Islands tradition. But during my first two fieldworks, the educated and the younger generation felt slightly embarrassed by their neighbours' assessment of life on Mota as backward. However, during my last visit in 2012, their view had aligned with that of the elderly. It was now a widely held opinion that neither education nor migration had brought much increase in opportunities or improved quality of living. Life on the island had indeed proven to be the better way. The deprived returnees are emblematic of the disenchantment with the promises of *divelopmen*. Even the high-flying Patteson, who had returned as a man of means, ended up a pauper. Occasionally, his political rivals might gleefully express, 'He thought himself above us, but now he's back cutting copra'. But to most, this was yet another confirmation of an ever more established fact: That to people from Mota, the world outside the island had little to offer. By turning the very symbols of outsiders' scorn into a matter of pride, the embarrassment the younger generations previously felt has been transformed into a factor behind cultural resilience.

On the one hand, this upbeat attitude is an asset, since it bolsters cultural and economic self-sufficiency. And in 2012, it was heartening to see Mota being considered a place of opportunity and prospects. But given the changing demographic and climatic conditions, it is doubtful whether this turn towards isolationism will be viable in the long run. In order to secure sustainability and a measure of predictability, options must remain open. Put bluntly, diversification is part of the extended carrying capacity of the island. The possibility to live elsewhere for shorter or longer periods of time, because of education, employment, or sheer adventurousness, has throughout our 150 years of historic records formed a part of Mota ecology. The consequences of the current drought will remind the Motese that life on the island is volatile, while all the factors that made people fear an urban existence and long for home remain in place. To the Motese, the future seems to offer precarious livings, both on and off the island.

References

Armstrong, ES 1900, *The history of the Melanesian Mission,* Isbister and Company, London.

Bratrud, T 2011, 'Finding ways: Community and its challenges on Ahamb, Vanuatu', Unpublished MA thesis, Department of Social Anthropology, University of Oslo, Norway.

Eriksen, A 2008, *Gender, Christianity and change in Vanuatu.* Ashgate, Aldershot.

Firth, R 1970, *Rank and religion in Tikopia*, Beacon Press, Boston.

Forsyth, M & Eves, R (eds) 2015, *Talking it through: Responses to sorcery and witchcraft beliefs and practices in Melanesia*, ANU Press, Canberra. doi.org/10.26530/OAPEN_569113

Graeber, D 2015, 'Radical alterity is just another way of saying "reality"', *HAU: Journal of Ethnographic Theory*, vol. 5, no. 2, pp. 1–41. doi.org/10.14318/hau5.2.003

Hess, S 2009, *Person and place*, Berghahn, New York and Oxford.

How, FD 1899, *Bishop John Selwyn*, Isbister, London.

Knauft, B 2002, *Exchanging the past*, University of Chicago Press, Chicago.

Kolshus, T 2008, 'Adopting change. Relational flexibility as vice and virtue on Mota, Vanuatu', *Pacific Studies*, vol. 31, no. 3/4, pp. 58–86.

Kolshus, T 2013, 'Codrington, Keesing, and Central Melanesian *mana*: two historic trajectories of Polynesian cultural dissemination', *Oceania*, vol. 83, no. 3, pp. 316–327. doi.org/10.1002/ocea.5027

Kolshus, T 2014, 'A house upon Pacific sand', in E Hviding & C Berg (eds), *The ethnographic experiment. A.M. Hocart and W.H.R. Rivers in Island Melanesia, 1908*, Berghahn, New York and Oxford, pp. 155–178.

Kolshus, T & Hovdhaugen, E 2010, 'Reassessing the death of Bishop John Coleridge Patteson', *Journal of Pacific History*, vol. 45, no. 3, pp. 331–356. doi.org/10.1080/00223344.2010.530813

Martin, JL 2015, *Thinking through theory*, WW Norton & Company, New York and London.

Mitchell, J 2011, '"Operation Restore Public Hope": youth and the magic of modernity in Vanuatu', *Oceania*, vol. 81, no. 1, pp. 36–50. doi.org/10.1002/j.1834-4461.2011.tb00092.x

Rio, K 2007, *The power of perspective*, Berghahn, New York and Oxford.

Rio, K 2011, 'Policing the Holy Nation', *Oceania*, vol. 81, no.1, pp. 51–71. doi.org/10.1002/j.1834-4461.2011.tb00093.x

Rio, K 2014, 'A shared intentional space of witch-hunt and sacrifice', *Ethnos*, vol. 79, no. 3, pp. 320–341. doi.org/10.1080/00141844.20 13.778308

Rio, K & Eriksen, A 2013, 'Missionaries, healing and sorcery in Melanesia', *History and Anthropology*, vol. 24 , no. 3, pp. 398–418. doi.org/10.108 0/02757206.2013.789434

Rousseau, B 2015, 'Finding the diamond: Prosperity, secrecy, and labour in Vanuatu', *Oceania*, vol. 85, no. 1, pp. 24–37. doi.org/10.1002/ ocea.5071

Sayer, A 2000, *Realism and social science*, Sage, London. doi.org/ 10.4135/9781446218730

Taylor, JP 2015, 'Sorcery and the moral economy of agency: an ethnographic account', *Oceania*, vol. 85, no, 1, pp. 38–50. doi.org/ 10.1002/ocea.5072

Tonkinson, R 1981, 'Church and *kastom* in Southeast Ambrym', in M Allen (ed.), *Vanuatu. Politics, economics and ritual in Island Melanesia*, Academic Press, Sydney, pp. 237–268.

Zeitlyn, D & Just, R 2014, *Excursions in realist anthropology*, Cambridge Scholars Publishing, Newcastle.

9

Migration and homemaking practices among the Amis of Taiwan

Shu-Ling Yeh

Abstract

The research observes how Amis migrants reconstruct their homelands as the source of feelings of stability and identity under pressure from the wider politico-economic and sociocultural context of Taiwan. Amis homemaking practices in their homelands play important roles in migrants' self-understanding, for practices anchored in the place of origin provide a sense of security to move in the world. The maintenance and reproduction of this place of origin, and ongoing exchanges within extended family and village networks, also express the Amis's consciousness of their increasing links with the wider world. This study begins by considering the 'native' place of migrants, focusing on how the Amis people construct and imagine their home community through translocal processes. These observations provide initial insights into how social networks and cultural practices in the native place mediate changes arising from national development and the capitalist economic system. It discusses how migrants maintain and make visible their ongoing commitment to homelands through material displays of wealth, in houses, cars, pig feasts, etc. By contrast, people who remain in the villages use the collective context of prayer and church to communicate with the migrant members.

Introduction

When compared with the feeling of stability that comes from living in a fixed place, the process of constantly moving is typically imagined as something unstable. People that have left homelands are often seen as both leaving behind the important spaces and networks that define identity and as struggling to adapt to life in a new place (Gupta and Ferguson 1992; Malkki 1992). However, with the development of increasingly effective transportation and information networks, the movement of people, capita, and information is faster and more convenient for many migrants. Travelling back and forth between one's 'native' place, and new place of residence, is a frequent and familiar experience for many people in the 21st century. For those from remote villages in Taiwan, moving away from homelands is an important mechanism both for securing a means of livelihood and for furthering personal educational development. This chapter focuses on the Amis people, an aboriginal people whose traditional territories are located in the eastern part of Taiwan. Migrations by Austronesian-speaking aborigines[1] in Taiwan are often described in terms of drifting aimlessly or becoming displaced (Li 1978; Lin 1981). Such easy descriptions, however, tend to overlook the continuous effort those migrants put into contributing to their hometowns, as well as creating homes in new places. As explored here, adding extensions to houses in remote areas using remittances from migrants, and rebuilding a village church, are just two examples of how, faced with the twin pressures of negotiating changes in wider Taiwanese society and the constraints of state policy, the Amis people[2] have strived for a sense of stability in both their native homelands and the unfamiliar destinations to which they have migrated.

---

1   There are 16 officially recognised aboriginal groups on the island, making up less than 2 per cent of the total population. Linguistically, Taiwan aboriginal peoples all belong to the Austronesian language family, widely dispersed throughout Southeast Asia, the islands of the Pacific Ocean, and Madagascar. According to recent linguistic and archaeological research, Taiwan is the possible homeland of the Austronesians (Bellwood 1991, 1997; Blust 1999; Pawley 1999). This hypothesis is the most important support for Taiwan's position of being part of the Pacific World.

2   The Amis are the largest aboriginal Austronesian-speaking group in Taiwan with a population of 200,023. It has also been suggested that the language of the Amis is the closest Taiwanese language historically to Malayo-Polynesian (Reid 1982). Thus information regarding the character of Amis migration should have relevance for anthropological discussions regarding the character of Pacific migration. For centuries, Amis communities have been concentrated in Hualien and Taitung counties along Taiwan's east coast. In the 1960s, the Amis began to migrate to urban areas in search of work or education. Nowadays, more than half of the Amis population are living in urban areas.

Previous research has mostly used push and pull theory to explain the movements of Aboriginal people in Taiwan to urban areas. The foci of this research includes motivations for migration; occupational distribution, types of employment and the socioeconomic status of Aboriginal people in urban areas; living arrangements and socio-psychological adaptation; relationships between different ethnic groups; and social support networks and return flows to home villages (cf. Tsai and Huang 2008; Liu 2009). Although these studies have accumulated important observations on the movement of Aboriginal people, most use macro-level quantitative research methodologies. There is a lack of micro-level qualitative work surveying links between county and city, political and economic systems, social psychology, and cultural traditions. Anthropology as a discipline has already moved beyond push and pull theory and discourses on a single path to modernisation, and now focuses on the complex and diverse phenomena involved in the migration process. When migrants cross geographical boundaries, they establish and maintain multiple dynamic and fluid social relationships. A dense exchange network created and developed by the Amis migrants with their homelands will be explored in this chapter.

There are many factors involved in the movement of the Amis people between rural and urban areas, including the political and economic structure of the wider society, personal reasons for (and forms of) migration, an individual's stage of life at the time of migration, gender and generational differences, identity politics and inherited and newly created forms of culture during the migration process (cf. Brettell 2007; Lee and Francis 2009). In addition, the concept of social remittances has also focused research attention on the flow of ideas, practices, identities and social capital between the native place and migration destination (Levitt 1998, 2001). The research presented here observes how Amis migrants reconstruct their homelands as the source of feelings of stability and identity under pressure from the wider politico-economic and sociocultural context of Taiwan. Amis homemaking practices in their homelands play important roles in migrants' self-understanding, for practices anchored in the place of origin provide a sense of security to move in the world (Hage 2004; McKay 2010). The maintenance and reproduction of this place of origin, and ongoing exchanges within extended family and village networks, also express the Amis's consciousness of their increasing links with the wider world.

This study begins by considering the 'native' place of migrants, focusing on how the Amis people construct and imagine their home community through translocal processes. These observations provide initial insights into how social networks and cultural practices in the native place mediate changes arising from national development and the capitalist economic system (Fox and Sather 1996; Jolly and Mosko 1994; Mosko 1999, 2001). I observe how resources and support are mobilised, how remittances are distributed and spent, and how migrants are helped to settle down in and adapt within migrant contexts. These observations are then applied to an investigation of how resources and experiences from the contexts of migration influence community development in the native place and the economic and social ecology of places that supply migrants. In addition, I draw upon the accumulated anthropological research on Amis culture and society (Chen 1987, 1989; Hsu 1991; Huang 1991, 2005a, 2005b; Liu et al. 1965; Suenari 1983; Yuan 1969), and in particular analysis of family and kinship networks, cultural practices and values (Yeh 2009a, 2009b, 2012, 2013, 2014) to provide a more nuanced understanding of Amis migration, balancing political and economic variables with personal and cultural variables (Johnson and Werbner 2010).

Overall, this study attempts a preliminary account of how the Amis of Cidatayay[3] have created a community of fate that spans both urban and rural settings. It does so by observing how group members who remain in Cidatayay and those who migrate maintain closely intertwined exchange networks. It points to the synthesis of the translocal cultural order, rather than the antithesis of rural and urban (cf. Appadurai 1996; Huang 2006, 2008; Lubkemann 2007; Rapport and Dawson 1998; Sahlins 1999). In particular, the study uses fieldwork data on social practices in Cidatayay, including around the construction of a church in the village and memorial activities, to investigate how group members who remain in their native village and those who migrate elsewhere for work or study collectively build and maintain a feeling of shared identity and belonging. It discusses how migrants maintain and make visible their ongoing commitment to homelands through material displays of wealth, in houses, cars, pig

---

3   I conducted fieldwork at Cidatayay and its nearby Amis villages during September 2000 – January 2001 and July 2005 – September 2006. Cidatayay village is located at the foot of the coastal mountain range, facing the Pacific shoreline. It is a compact settlement composed of 72 matrifocal households integrated into a single community largely as a result of the central male initiation organisation. Nowadays, almost four-fifths of the village members migrate to urban areas for work or study. It takes about seven hours to drive from Taipei to Cidatayay.

feasts, etc. By contrast, people who remain in the villages use the collective context of prayer and church to communicate with the migrant members. In the context of movement and change, the study discusses homemaking practices of the Amis and how the Amis construct and imagine feelings of stability and belonging away from their homeland.

The native place as the source of feelings of stability and identity

According to my observations in Cidatayay, community members who had migrated away from the village for work were not necessarily alienated from friends and family who had remained behind. Absentee community members continued to be involved in complex networks of exchange and maintained frequent contact with their village when away from home. In particular, if any community member was in trouble while working outside the village, the news was always immediately relayed back home. On hearing the news, friends and relatives made a public address announcement requesting members of the church[4] to gather at the house of the person involved. These gatherings enabled community members to understand how the incident occurred and to offer prayers for the victim. In one instance, a young person from the community working in Northern Taiwan suffered a serious accident riding his motorbike while under the influence of alcohol. As he was undergoing emergency treatment, members of the church back in the village received news of the accident and immediately paid a visit to his elderly mother who was living alone (the youth's father had already passed away). The mother was obviously extremely distressed and worried about her son's accident. The gathered church members prayed for around half an hour under the guidance of lay ministry. Following the prayers, most of church members stayed behind with the mother.

Besides using hymn and prayer to call for God's protection and to calm the anxieties of the victim's family, church members also offered comfort by accompanying and talking to family members. However, the Amis people do not normally dwell for long on the solemnity or sadness of the

---

4   Since the Catholic Church began sending missionaries to Cidatayay village in the 1950s, more than 90 per cent of its population is now recognised by the Church as Catholic. However, Cidatayay villagers still hold the annual harvest ceremony and many pig sacrifices to continue their exchange relationship with their ancestors, despite nominal conversion to Catholicism.

occasion. After the prayers were over, the mother offered rice wine, drinks and betel nuts to those who had come to pray for her son and to keep her company. Together with other elderly women from the community, the mother smoked tobacco and chatted, gradually relieving her anxiety. In Amis villages, visits like this could often last for days. Furthermore, other community members who were also working in Northern Taiwan visited the accident victim and gave assistance, while frequently reporting back home to friends and relatives on his recovery.

A similar case occurred in the nearby Ta'man village. One day after dinner, church members gathered in a courtyard for prayer following a public-address announcement. An older member of the community, who was working in Taipei and had purchased a property in Northern Taiwan, had had a vehicle accident. However, while recovering at the hospital, he cut his wrists and throat with a fruit knife. As the injury to his throat was especially serious, he was placed in the respiratory care unit of the hospital. The injured man's elder brother, who was still living in the village, gave a detailed account of his younger brother's condition to church members who came to pray, telling them that depression had caused his brother to engage in self-harm. He said he hoped that everyone's prayers would help his brother overcome his predicament. When the prayers finished, church members talked about the younger brother and his life outside the village. The elder brother, who had previously worked as a lay minister, reminded his fellow church members: 'Every person and every family faces difficulties, do not take things too hard. We need to pray more and help each other.'

Prayers for the safety and welfare of the migrant members took place during regular Sunday mass, family worship and other ceremonies marking religious festivals including the harvest festival, the Month of Mary and Christmas Day. News from those working outside the village was often conveyed in such public prayer sessions. Aside from regular prayer and expressions of concern, food produced back in the homeland was one of the best ways to maintain links with family and friends who had moved away. It often happened that a member of the community would return home for a few days. When it was time to leave, a dozen or more women would gather in the family courtyard to see him or her off. At the same time, the women would give the departing community member pickled vegetables and meats they had prepared to deliver to their sons and daughters working in the north. The love of each mother meant that cars heading north from the village were always packed full, and mothers could continue to produce food and nourish their children living far away. Aside from asking fellow group members who were travelling north to carry food, the President Transnet Corp express delivery service now provided an important conduit for sending goods and expressions of concern to family members living away from home.

For community members who had moved away, the home village remained an important source of identity and security. The feeling of protection that the home village offered could be seen in the ceremony blessing a newly purchased car, which many community members carried out in the village. When compared to rituals involving people or houses, the car-blessing ritual was relatively simple. Normally carried out by lay ministry, who led the congregation in hymn and prayer beside the newly purchased car, the car was then sprinkled with holy water and either a crucifix or holy icon was hung inside the vehicle. When the ritual was complete, the owner would provide food and drink to thank the faithful for their prayers. The home village not only offered solace and assistance when one of its own had an accident or faced an unforeseen event, it also gave community members the impetus to work hard to accumulate material wealth in order to share or to show off their achievements. During the harvest festival in July and Lunar New Year in February, community members gathered at their home village. Those living outside the village chose this time to carry out their car blessing ritual, because more of the faithful would be gathered to strengthen the prayer, and more community members would recognise their hard work and be envious of their success.

The ritual blessing of a new car was one way to show off achievements and to enhance one's reputation in the home village. Another was house improvement. In less than 50 years, houses in Cidatayay had changed rapidly from mainly thatched huts to houses with tiled roofs, to single-storey concrete houses, and finally to two- or three-storey concrete houses. These changes reflected the growing linkages between village residents and wider Taiwanese society, in particular increasing economic ties. When residents talked of the transformation of their houses, there was a strong connection with the history of community members moving away for work. The income from males working at sea in the 1960s enabled most village families to rebuild their homes using more sturdy concrete. Subsequently, work on construction projects using formwork frames in the west and central areas of Taiwan and even as far away as the Arab countries from the 1970s enabled families to add extra floors to or rebuild their houses in the village. The community member who established the new trend in rebuilding homes was often referred to in the recollections of village residents. Individuals who successfully directed outside resources into the construction of sturdy and comfortable houses in the village were commended on many different occasions, inspiring other members of the community to follow their example.

To a certain extent, community members used the upgrading of the houses to show off their economic success gained in working outside the village. However, it is also clear from the recollections of residents that the construction of homes with two or more storeys was closely related to dense local exchange networks. Although houses were no longer built with the help of the paternal-fraternal organisation[5] or friends and relatives as in the past, the process by which each family in the village rebuilt their home showed how community members linked the process of physically altering the family house with the sharing of food among group members. Community members stated that in the past, the stages of demolishing the old property, pouring the concrete and completing the new house would each be celebrated by slaughtering a pig, which would be shared with everyone in the community. Homeowners stated that if they did not slaughter a pig and organise a feast,[6] they would not feel at ease. Many of the two or more storey buildings in the village reflected the capability and desire of community members living away from home to help develop their native village. In addition, the successful operation of the Daoming Credit Union,[7] which was established in the village in 1968, was an important mechanism for directing cash accumulated from work outside the village back to the village. On the one hand, credit union staff constantly advised people on the importance of saving. At the same time, they encouraged the

---

5   The paternal-fraternal organisation is a male initiation organisation of each Amis village. This unique organisation of the Amis village not only structures the relations of its members on the idiom of family relationships, but plays an indispensable role in the production and reproduction of the entire Amis village community. It is through the overarching paternal-fraternal system that the numerous matrifocal houses in any given Amis village are integrated into an encompassing kinship-based society. See Yeh (2012) for more information on the overall structure of the Amis paternal-fraternal organisation and how the classificatory father-son and elder-younger-brother relations between and within the initiation sets are explicitly represented by the concepts and practices of the Amis.

6   See Yeh (2013) for more information about the meaning of pig sacrifice in the era of mobility.

7   In 1967, Father Seeiner Meinao Dominik selected two outstanding members of the congregation to attend mutual-aid society training in Taichung. Subsequently, these two individuals led the development of the Catholic Mutual Aid Society, encouraging church members to develop the habit of saving to prepare for unexpected contingencies. The society also offers emergency loans, allowing members to avoid exploitation by high interest loans. The Daoming Credit Union Mutual Aid Society was formally established in March 1968 in the Ta'man Village and currently has more than 1,300 members covering aboriginal communities at Carapongay, Ta'man, Cidatayay and Pasongan.

habit of saving money by organising competitions between families and villages to see who could save the most money.[8] On the other hand, in order to grow their business, the staff also encouraged members to borrow money to build houses, resulting in the construction of a large number of houses with two or more storeys in the area.

Although the successful construction of a house, made possible by the hard work of community members away from the village, was marked by the ritual slaughter of pigs and a lively inauguration, for most days of the year the house felt deserted. With many family members away from home for work, only the elderly grandparents and young grandchildren were left in the large house. The majority of those living away from the village return home for the harvest festival and Lunar New Year, as well as for events such as weddings and funerals and ceremonies to mark the completion of a house. When those living away from the village returned home, village residents were particularly active in attending activities and banquets organised by the paternal-fraternal organisation and the local community development association, attending wedding ceremonies hosted by other families, or having parties with the initiation set brothers or relatives from the same kin group. It was very rare for such gatherings to be limited to only members of a single household. It could be said the local people made as much as possible of returnees' visits to eat, sing and dance together either in the village public square or in the domestic household courtyard. The lively household at these times contrasted sharply with the more sombre atmosphere on normal working days. In the past, when working on formwork, carpenters, friends and relatives from the same village would contract work as a group, living together at the work site. After work, they would eat and drink together. By sticking with and looking after each other, the workers could adapt to life away from home. People from the village remained nostalgic about those days. However, after a rule was introduced preventing workers from living on the work site, people spread out into rented accommodation in many different places. If they gathered together in someone's home, they worried about disturbing the neighbours. The loneliness of urban life made them treasure the happy times when they could return to the village and see family and friends again.

---

8   In order to achieve target savings rates, leaders divide into zones of responsibility, encouraging society members to save a certain amount every month—for example, saving NT$1,500 a month wins a prize while saving NT$50,000 in a year wins a high-savings prize. At each meeting of the credit union, successful savers are publicly commended for their efforts, teaching community members the value of the credit union and encouraging saving.

For the local people, the family home was not only a space where family members live. The family house was also a place where ancestral spirits would come back to visit (cf. Fox 1993).[9] Therefore, many community members living outside the village mentioned the need to return for the harvest festival in order to open the door of the family house and worship the ancestors. Ensuring that the ancestral spirits summoned back by the paternal-fraternal organisation through song and dance had a house to return to was the responsibility of their descendants. Even though the locals had accepted the Catholic faith for many years, their belief in the power of ancestors to influence people's fate remained unchanged. For instance, in the case of attempted suicide mentioned above, many community members explained his difficulties by the fact that he had made fewer visits back to the village to worship his ancestors over recent years. Therefore, as his life was still in danger, his family and relatives from the village called on church members to gather at his family house for group prayer. It was hoped that this gathering could enliven the house and help this suffering relative escape danger. At present, due to the demands of work, community members were less likely to return home to observe the Stations of the Cross before Easter, the Month of Mary and other Catholic religious festivals. However, they normally asked friends and family in the village to help them open the door of their family house and even decorate a manger for Christmas, allowing for church members praying door-to-door to enter the house and perform a ceremony.

Before Easter, church members who had stayed behind in the village carried a large cross from house to house to observe the Stations of the Cross. During the Month of Mary, the faithful carried a statue of Mary from the church to each home in the village reciting the Hail Mary prayer, and on Christmas Eve they went carolling from house to house. The crowd departed from the church located in the centre of the village, visiting the homes of each of the faithful in order. Finally, they returned to the centre of the village for a banquet and celebrations. This kind of process invoked the close relationship between family and the village community and the nature of the family itself. Local residents attached great importance to this collective power centred on the community, as each family would require its assistance at some point or another to pray for the peace and wellbeing of home and family. The group worked together to pool the

---

9   Houses are given great prominence throughout the Austronesian-speaking world. As a physical entity, as a cultural category and as a repository of ancestral objects, the house has the capacity to provide social continuity. See Fox (1993) for more information about Austronesian houses.

community's resources, which were then spread among each family and member of the community. This type of community action was not the result of the arrival of Catholicism in the community. Ethnographic records from the past and the continued practice of traditional harvest ceremonies showed that the community pooled its resources, which were then distributed to families and individuals (Liu et al. 1965). For example, after summoning the spirits and the ancestors to participate in the harvest festival, the paternal-fraternal organisation visited the house and accepted the hospitality of each member of the organisation. Locals regarded these visits as a way to share strength and good fortune, blessing family members and the family home with good health for the coming year.

This central pooling of resources valued the collective strength of the community, and was regarded as a vital method and practice for the strengthening of individuals and families. Both those who remained behind in the village and those who had moved away for work actively contributed to the construction of their community. This could be further understood by describing the rebuilding of the village parish church and events to celebrate its 10th anniversary. Furthermore, these processes revealed the structure of social life in the contemporary Cidatayay community. As Sahlins (1999: xix) suggests, the to-and-fro of goods, ideas and people on the move in the folk–urban continuum illustrates:

> the structural complementarity of the indigenous homeland and the metropolitan 'homes abroad,' their interdependence as sources of cultural value and means of social reproduction. Symbolically focused on the homeland, whence its members derive their identity and their destiny, the translocal community is strategically dependent on its urban outliers for material wherewithal.

The rebuilding of the church and the 10th anniversary celebrations

According to locals, Catholicism arrived in Cidatayay around 1956. In the early years, Catholic mass and missionary activities were held in a simple thatched hut built on the edge of the village. Within a few years, the missionary work had met with some success, and the space was no longer adequate for the growing congregation. In 1962, a Swiss priest from the Yiwan parish, Father Seeiner Meinao Dominik raised the funds to purchase cement and other building materials, while members of the church in Cidatayay moved gravel from the beach to the old site of the men's house in the centre of the village. A modern single-storey church was constructed on the site, reflecting the church's ambition to replace the men's house as the central gathering place in the village. However, after construction of the church was completed, the paternal-fraternal organisation immediately began building a new men's house on empty land next to the church, which they then rebuilt with concrete in 1983. These developments indicated that the growth of the church in the village faced limits, particularly given the difficulties organising male church members. After the large migration of men away from the village for work after the 1960s, this issue became even more apparent. The problems organising male church members were reflected in the fact that the development of church groups had been almost entirely dominated by women. Around 1974 the Church began issuing the Romanised Amis Bible which was studied by mostly female students in the church or homes of lay missionaries. Women absorbed the romanisation of their language and studied the Church's methods of prayer and communication. As a result, they subsequently took on important roles on many religious occasions, for instance prayer meetings for the sick or deceased.

The church constructed in 1962 was made possible by the funds provided by the local parish priest and the labour of church members. According to church members, after 30 years exposure to the elements, the concrete had begun to peel, exposing the steel frame of the building. Church members were concerned about the safety of holding mass in the building and expressed their desire to rebuild the church to the local priest. However, the Hualien diocese and Yiwan parish, to which the church belonged, did not have the funds available to rebuild the church. As a result, the congregation at Cidatayay decided to rebuild the church by themselves. Recounting the building of today's two-storey church, all church members agreed that this could not have been achieved without the mobilisation of the paternal-fraternal organisation and everyone's concerted efforts. In July 1994, as the migrant workers returned to the village to celebrate the harvest festival, church members held a meeting on the rebuilding project. At the meeting, it was agreed that every church member would donate NT$12,000[10] to the reconstruction fund. The meeting also elected the members of the *lasingpin* initiation set for the preparatory committee, based on their oratory and other skills, to oversee planning and fundraising

---

10   At the time of my research AU$1 = NT$25.

for the challenging project. The committee worked through the paternal-fraternal organisation, recruiting the fathers of the youth (*mama no kapah*) and '*laklin*' members (known collectively as youth leaders) of that organisation to join them in visiting Cidatayay church members at their workplaces across the island to raise money for the reconstruction of the church.

Figure 1: The Cidatayay Catholic Church
Source: Photograph by author.

Members of the *lasingpin* initiation set stated that although they were in theory engaged in fundraising, their work was more like collecting a levy, or as they joked, collecting protection money. This process was similar to the July harvest festival or the carnival on the second day of the Lunar New Year when youth leaders also went from house to house levying activity funds (Yeh 2009b: 19). Many local public activities were not funded by free donation; all members of the group had to contribute to the effort. In fact, this method established the relationship between the whole and the part; each member was an indispensable part of the group, and the force of the group was essential for the wellbeing of each of its members. The levying of fees acted as a frequent reminder to members of their responsibilities to the group. The successful completion of the new church involved the work of many people. A total of 40 or 50 people, including members of the preparatory committee and youth leaders, sometimes joined by their wives and children, visited workplaces and the homes of church members. Collectively, the group persuaded community members of the need to reconstruct the church. Such gatherings outside the village reminded migrant workers of their duties to the community and significance of community relations. Everyone's hard work helped raise more than NT$5 million within six months. In February 1995, with ample cash in the reconstruction fund, work on the new church began. The church was completed a year later.

The two-storey church was a proud symbol of the spirit of togetherness of Cidatayay believers, and source of identity funded jointly by village residents and those who moved away for work. In particular, many of those working away from the village not only gave the NT$12,000 sum agreed at the meeting, but also provided a tabernacle, statue of the Virgin Mary, lighting equipment, keyboard, electric fans and other objects for the church. Cidatayay residents frequently recounted to me that after construction and fitting out the church, more than NT$1 million in surplus funds was deposited at the Daoming Credit Union Mutual Aid Society. Subsequently, some of these funds were used for related maintenance costs and for the construction of a Mother Mary altar and two public hearths at the north side of the church. The church and Mother Mary altar were not just the pride of the village, they also revealed the power of their social relationships, acting as a space to develop collective ties and affinities through group prayer and eating. In particular, they offered a stable sense of belonging for those working away from the village. Many important ceremonies marking major life changes, including weddings and funerals, were conducted in this space. In addition, these buildings were a source of envy for congregations from other churches, who often held up the paternal-fraternal organisation in Cidatayay as an example of how to successfully raise money. Just as the new car blessing ceremonies, rebuilding of family houses, and money saved in the Mutual Aid Society promoted mutual competition in the village, the reconstruction of the village church promoted competition between churches in the parish. The competition was more pronounced because each church was almost completely based around traditional village units.

In 2006, the paternal-fraternal organisation and church representatives held a meeting where it was decided that the 10th anniversary of the completion of the church would be held with the carnival on the second day of the Lunar New Year. The members of the *lasingpin* initiation set and youth leaders were entrusted with making preparations for the celebrations. At the Lunar New Year, most residents working or studying away from the village had a vacation period which allowed them to return to the village to rest and reunite with friends and family. Cidatayay's convention on local self-government clearly stipulated that a carnival was to be held on this day and forbade individual families from holding weddings and other family celebrations. Anyone found in violation of this regulation could be fined NT$20,000. This demonstrated the authority of the paternal-fraternal organisation as well as its responsibility for bringing residents together. The organisation worked hard to bring together the labour and material resources of the village to put on a carnival for residents of the village, and for those scattered across the island, to renew their ties and identities through the sharing of food and laughter.

Preparations and activities for the 2006 carnival and the church's 10th anniversary were primarily arranged by the paternal-fraternal organisation, with church representatives taking a supporting role. The entire process again demonstrated the leadership capabilities of *lasingpin* members and their ability to bring people together. To demonstrate the unity and vitality of the Cidatayay community to those inside and outside the village, they first used funds in the Mutual Aid Society to order jackets printed with a message to mark the anniversary of the Cidatayay Catholic Church. All church members were asked to wear these jackets for mass and the subsequent lunchtime banquet and celebrations. Wearing the same outfit was a way of showing off group identity and ties, and was a well-known practice among the Amis people. Aside from the common outfit worn by all members of the community, small groups within the community, including the initiation sets, church groups and officials from the community development association, wore uniforms representative of their different groups in certain situations to show their collective power and unity. In the song and dance competitions organised by the paternal-fraternal organisation and community development association, one of the standards for judging was often whether the team outfits matched. Teams were thus encouraged to buy a uniform and individuals working away from the village often helped group members back in the village purchase more fashionable clothes.

Activities to celebrate the 10th anniversary of the Cidatayay Church began with a morning mass. Mass was celebrated by Father Rev. Valerian Chen DHL from the Taitung area, and members of the congregation also invited Father Christopher Kelbert from the Da'nan Catholic Church in Taoyuan to jointly celebrate the mass. Many community members working outside the village had received regular assistance from Father

Kelbert, and his prayers ensured that their work was carried out safely and smoothly. Mass on that day was mostly attended by the middle-aged and elderly, and the male youth were busy setting up activities under the direction of the youth leaders. The community elders took responsibility for less mobile religious activities such as prayer, while the youth threw their efforts into helping organise activities. This division of labour based on age was reflected in many group activities in Amis communities. However, on this important day, some of the young females hoped for a more lively mass. They asked to play the guitar and lead the singing of hymns, which never occurred at mass at other times in the year, but was allowed because of the special nature of the occasion. The head of the group emphasised that they had first actively sought the support of the elders. This was important in Amis society because respect for seniority and the division of labour between young and old meant it was very rare for a group of young women to lead the singing of hymns. The experience and learning of youth outside the village presented an alternative to existing age- and gender-based divisions of labour.

Figure 2: Cidatayay believers dressed in the same jackets attending the Mass for the 10th anniversary of their local church

Source: Photograph by author.

After the completion of mass, residents gathered in the village square to participate in festivities organised by the youth leaders, including a ball-kicking game. Prizes were awarded and residents took part in order, which showed that in contemporary Cidatayay, the paternal-fraternal organisation acted as the main centre for community life, the complex network of social relations, and the passing on of social and cultural values. As they were taking part in the activity in turn, the atmosphere was one of joy and laughter. The women prepared plastic bags to gather together the soy sauce, dishwashing liquid, rice wine and other prizes won by family members. To raise funds for the carnival, youth leaders collected NT$300 from each household in the community and NT$500 from each male working outside the village. The funds were spent on prizes for group party games and food and drink for the banquet. This regular pattern of gathering together and sharing revealed the effectiveness of the paternal-fraternal organisation in mobilising and bringing together residents. In addition, using everyday items as prizes showed the awareness of youth leaders toward basic household needs. Every year, the youth leaders recorded the payment of fees by each male working away from the village on a large red poster. As the group made their way to the village square to join in the activities, the poster was placed in a highly visible location. Village residents stopped and looked as they passed the poster to discuss the lives of those working outside the village and at the same time showed concern for those individuals who had not paid their fees or lost contact with home. The tightly written names and amounts in black ink on red paper summarised the close relationships of exchange between those working away and their home village, evoking feelings of mutual expectation and concern, and reinforcing their responsibility to the village and the importance of remittances for the development of Cidatayay.

In past years, feasting in the village square at the carnival had centred on a pig feast organised by the paternal-fraternal organisation, which also distributed work at the feast, as well as the sharing of the pork and seating arrangements for the meal. In 2006, because the diocese bishop, priests and representatives of neighbouring churches were invited to the celebration, the lunchtime banquet was held in Han Chinese style. Although a Han Chinese head chef was invited to prepare the banquet, the youth of Cidatayay under the direction of the youth leaders still laid out the chairs and tables, distributed the rice wine and drinks to each table, and worked together to complete preparations for the feast, allowing outside guests and the local congregation to quickly find their seats and start enjoying their meal. I previously mentioned that large and small Amis villages in the area often compared themselves and competed with each other. To ensure the reputation of Cidatayay, community leaders and elders regularly reminded the youth of the spirit of hard work and service, and the importance of showing the order and unity of the community in front of guests.

The rice wine and drinks at the feast were purchased by the *lasingpin* initiation set from the three general stores in the village. They informed me that they were careful to distribute purchases evenly between the three stores and not favour one over another. This policy was helpful for the internal leadership and management of the paternal-fraternal organisation. Although community members who lived outside the village could buy goods cheaper outside the village stores, they also believed in the need to support these stores to allow them to continue in business. These stores were not only convenient for village residents, but also provided a meeting place for information exchange. Whenever a migrant worker returned home, as soon as he stepped off the bus he would be given a warm welcome by village residents sitting and chatting outside the general store, asked for change from the bus to buy drinks and snacks, and invited to share the latest news with friends and relatives. This practice, known by locals as *ocoli*, allowed for more frequent and diverse exchange of information between town and country, between those who had stayed and those that had moved away.

During the celebrations village residents, regardless of whether they remained in the village or had moved away, split into groups based on age or gender for song and dance performances, both traditional and modern. Those living outside the village, and especially the youth, performed the most current popular song and dance routines to demonstrate their vitality to the elders. The uninhibited performances of the young people filled the village square with joyous festivity that made the elders laugh. Aside from financial remittances back home, this was one of the most important ways of giving and showing respect to the older generation, and expressing gratitude for their prayers and protection.

The coordination of the outfits and song and dance routines in front of friends and family in the village demonstrated the strength of their relationship and understanding between members of the individual initiation sets, and was therefore extensively discussed and rehearsed before the event. Migrant members gathered near where they lived to plan and practice the performance, revealing the extension of village networks way beyond the boundaries of the village itself. These networks centred on the exchange of information, mutual companionship and care, and even competition allow community members to work together outside the village. By trying to work together or live near each other, relationships from homeland could be maintained in the new place. The celebrations marking the 10th anniversary of the Cidatayay Church, from the initial preparations to the mass, games, banquet and performances held on the day, showed the pride of the people of Cidatayay at the successful efforts of the entire community to rebuild its church and maintain the togetherness and vitality of the community. The celebrations on that day continued until around three to four o'clock in the afternoon. As the residents finished the celebrations by dancing together hand-in-hand in a circle, they also formed the wish to hold a 20th anniversary celebration for the church in another 10 years.

Conclusion

This paper has demonstrated how community members who remained behind in the village and those that migrated away constructed and imagined their home village as they interacted directly within wider Taiwanese society. It has also examined how a sense of stability and a centre for identity was created during the process of movement and change. In particular, the paper has illustrated by way of specific ethnographic examples the dynamic exchanges within and across the translocal community, by moving beyond the static binary divisions between home village/city, traditional/modern, and periphery/core that had characterised much previous research. Many exchanges and homemaking practices between the Amis residents in and outside the village, and their joint efforts to develop their community, meant that the migration of the Amis could no longer simply be described in terms of dependency theory or labour movements from the global periphery to global core, but instead reflect how a space for existence was created through relationship networks, cultural customs and the exchange of information and resources. In particular, for many community members who had moved away from the village, the care and blessings of family and friends who remained at home was an important source of feelings of stability and security. In addition, the relationships of exchange and competition centred on the development of the home village were an important motivation to work hard outside the village.

Of course, the relationship between the migration of the Amis and their construction and imagination of homeland exists on a number of complex levels. My initial observations of the home village do not compare in detail the migration conditions and experiences across different periods in time, the differences in the sense of stability and creation of space for existence between males and females as well as different generations, or different strategies for expanding space for existence in urban areas and maintaining links with the home village. In the future, it will be necessary to reveal more about the personal migration experiences of the Amis, as well as how they produce a sense of stability and space for existence during the process of migration. This will help us understand how, with the passage of time and the complex interaction of the world inside and outside the community, migrants use relationship networks and cultural wisdom to creatively bring together the traditional and modern and actively deal with ever-changing contemporary life. In this way, a people that are frequently regarded as having 'no history' by mainstream society can recount their own life patterns and history of movement. This will also provide quantitative surveys and political and economic analyses on migrations by Taiwanese aboriginals with a valuable reference on culture, relationship networks and actors.

Acknowledgements

I am deeply grateful to the people of Cidatayay and Ta'man villages, who have continued to allow me to participate in their lives and to learn their knowledge. The research and writing of this article were financially supported by the Ministry of Science and Technology (Taiwan) under the Grants NSC-103-2420-H-143-001-2R and MOST-106-2410-H-143 -009-. I would like to thank Professor Helen Lee and Dr John Taylor for organising the session of Mobilities of Return in the annual meetings of the Association for Social Anthropology in Oceania and for editing the volume. I have greatly benefited from the comments and criticisms of many colleagues who have read previous drafts of this and related papers including Mark Mosko, James Fox, Ying-Kuei Huang, Wen-Te

Chen, Shiun-Wey Huang, Shu-Yuan Yang, the participants of the ASAO meetings, and anonymous reviewers. Any and all shortcomings contained herein are my own.

References

Appadurai, A 1996, *Modernity at large: cultural dimensions of globalisation*, University of Minnesota Press, Minneapolis.

Bellwood, P 1991, 'The Austronesian dispersal and the origin of languages', *Scientific American*, vol. 265, no. 1, pp. 88–93. doi.org/10.1038/scientificamerican0791-88

Bellwood, P 1997, 'Taiwan and the prehistory of the Austronesian-speaking peoples', *Review of Archaeology*, vol. 18, no. 2, pp. 39–48.

Blust, R 1999, 'Subgrouping, circularity and extinction: some issues in Austronesian comparative linguistics', in E Zeitoun & PJ-K Li (eds), *Selected papers from the 8th International Conference on Austronesian Linguistics*, Institute of Linguistics (Preparatory Office), Academia Sinica, Taipei, pp. 31–94.

Brettell, C 2007, 'Theorizing migration in anthropology: the social construction of network, identities, communities, and globalscapes', in C Brettell & J Hollifield (eds), *Migration theory: talking across disciplines*, Routledge, New York, pp. 113–159.

Chen, W-T 1987, 'Reconsideration of the Amis kinship system', *Bulletin of the Institute of Ethnology Academia Sinica*, no. 61, pp. 41–80.

Chen, W-T 1989, 'The study of age-set systems and its theoretical implications: a Taiwanese case', *Bulletin of the Institute of Ethnology Academia Sinica*, no. 68, pp. 105–144.

Fox, J 1993, 'Comparative perspectives on Austronesian houses: an introductory essay', in J Fox (ed.), *Inside Austronesian houses: perspectives on domestic designs for living*, Department of Anthropology, Research School of Pacific Studies, The Australian National University, Canberra, pp. 1–28.

Fox, J & Sather, C 1996, *Origins, ancestry and alliance: explorations in Austronesian ethnography*, Department of Anthropology, Research School of Pacific and Asian Studies, The Australian National University, Canberra.

Gupta, A & Ferguson, J 1992, 'Beyond "culture": space, identity and the politics of difference', *Cultural Anthropology*, vol. 7, no. 1, pp. 6–23. doi.org/10.1525/can.1992.7.1.02a00020

Hage, G 2004, 'Migration, hope and the making of subjectivity in transnational capitalism', *International Journal of Critical Psychology*, vol. 12, pp. 107–121.

Hsu, M-T 1991, *Culture, self, and adaptation: the psychological anthropology of two Malayo-Polynesian groups in Taiwan*, Institute of Ethnology, Academia Sinica, Taipei.

Huang, S-W 1991, *The investigation of the Amis society and culture in East Coast National Scenic Area*, The Administration of East Coast National Scenic Area, Taitung.

Huang, S-W 2005a, *Images of others, regional variations and history among the Amis*, Institute of Ethnology, Academia Sinica, Taipei.

Huang, S-W 2005b, *State, village leaders and sociocultural change: a case study of the Amis in Iwan during the Japanese colonial period*, SMC Publishing Inc, Taipei.

Huang, Y-K 2006, *Visions of anthropology*, Socio Publishing Co, Taipei.

Huang, Y-K 2008, 'Local societies under the neoliberalism', *Chinese Review of Anthropology*, vol. 8, pp. 108–125.

Johnson, M & Werbner, P 2010, 'Introduction: diasporic encounters, sacred journeys: ritual, normativity and the religious imagination among international Asian migrant women', *The Asia Pacific Journal of Anthropology*, vol. 11, no. 3–4, pp. 205–218. doi.org/10.1080/144 42213.2010.517510

Jolly, M & Mosko, M 1994, 'Prologue to Transformations of Hierarchy: Structure, History and Horizon in the Austronesian World', *History and Anthropology*, vol. 7, no. 1–4, pp. 1–18. doi.org/10.1080/02757 206.1994.9960839

Lee, H & Francis, ST 2009, *Migration and transnationalism: Pacific perspectives*, ANU E Press, Canberra.

Levitt, P 1998, 'Social remittances: migration-driven local-level forms of cultural diffusion', *International Migration Review*, vol. 32, pp. 926–948. doi.org/10.2307/2547666

Levitt, P 2001, *The transnational villagers*, University of California Press, Berkeley, CA.

Li, Y-Y 1978, 'The adaptation of Taiwan Aborigines in the urban contexts', in *Studies and Essays in Commemoration of the Golden Jubilee of Academia Sinica*, Academia Sinica, Taipei, pp. 717–739.

Lin, J-P 1981, 'The urban Aborigines in the northern area of Taiwan', *China Tribune*, vol. 12, no. 7, pp. 21–28.

Liu, C-C 2009, 'Migration of Taiwan Aborigines: Clime-up or Stumble in Life Course?', PhD thesis, National Chengchi University.

Liu, P-H, Chiu C-C, Shih L & Chen C-C 1965, *Social structure of the Siu-Ku-Luan Ami*, Institute of Ethnology, Academia Sinica, Taipei.

Lubkemann, SC 2007, 'Kinship and globalization', *Anthropological Quarterly*, vol. 80, no. 2 (Special Issue).

Malkki, LH 1992, 'National Geographic: the rooting of peoples and the territorialization of national identity among scholars and refugees', *Cultural Anthropology*, vol. 7, no. 1, pp. 24–44. doi.org/10.1525/can.1992.7.1.02a00030

McKay, D 2010, 'A transnational pig: reconstituting kinship among Filipinos in Hong Kong', *The Asia Pacific Journal of Anthropology*, vol. 11, no. 3–4, pp. 330–344. doi.org/10.1080/14442213.2010.513400

Mosko, M 1999, 'Magical money: commoditisation and the linkage of *maketsi* ("market") and *kangakanga* ("custom") in contemporary North Mekeo', in D Akin & J Robbins (eds), *Money and modernity: state and local currencies in Melanesia*, University of Pittsburgh Press, Pittsburgh, pp. 41–61.

Mosko, M 2001, 'Syncretic people: sociality, agency and personhood in recent charismatic ritual practices among North Mekeo (PNG)', *The Australian Journal of Anthropology*, vol. 12, no. 3, pp. 259–274. doi.org/10.1111/j.1835-9310.2001.tb00076.x

Pawley, A 1999, 'Chasing rainbows: implications for subgrouping and reconstruction', in E Zeitoun & J-K Li (eds), *Selected papers from the 8th International Conference on Austronesian Linguistics*, Institute of Linguistics (Preparatory office), Academia Sinica, Taipei, pp. 95–138.

Rapport, N & Dawson, A 1998, *Migrants of identity: perceptions of home in a world of movement*, Berg, Oxford.

Reid, A 1982, 'The demise of Proto-Philippines', in A Halim, L Carrington & S Wurm (eds), *Papers from the Third International Conference on Austronesian Linguistics*, vol. 2, Pacific Linguistics, Canberra, pp. 201–216.

Sahlins, M 1999, 'What is anthropological enlightenment? Some lessons of the twentieth century', *Annual Review of Anthropology*, vol. 28, no.1, pp. i–xxii. doi.org/10.1146/annurev.anthro.28.1.0

Suenari, M 1983, *Social organisation and its change in the Amis of Taiwan*, Tokyo University Press, Tokyo.

Tsai, FCL & Huang, S-W 2008, 'Socio-cultural continuities and transitions of Amis urban life: a preliminary analysis and future aspects from literatures', in P Guo, C-H Huang & M-R Lin (eds.), *Essays in Honour of Professor Pin-Hsiung Liu*, Institute of Ethnology, Academia Sinica, Taipei, pp. 273–306.

Yeh, S-L 2009a, 'The encompassing kinship system of the Austronesian-speaking Amis of Taiwan: continuity and change', PhD thesis, Department of Anthropology, The Australian National University.

Yeh, S-L 2009b, 'Rethinking the age-set organisation of the Austronesian-speaking Amis', *Journal of Eastern Taiwan Studies*, vol. 13, pp. 3–28.

Yeh, S-L 2012, 'The process of kinship in the paternal/fraternal house of the Austronesian-speaking Amis of Taiwan', *Oceania*, vol. 82, no. 2, pp. 186–204. doi.org/10.1002/j.1834-4461.2012.tb00128.x

Yeh, S-L 2013, 'Pig sacrifices, mobility and the ritual recreation of community among the Amis of Taiwan', *The Asia Pacific Journal of Anthropology*, vol. 14, no. 1, pp. 41–56. doi.org/10.1080/1444221 3.2012.747557

Yeh, S-L 2014, 'Contemporary community life of the Austronesian-speaking Amis of Taiwan', *Journal of Austronesian Studies*, vol. 5, no. 1, pp. 1–30.

Yuan, C-R 1969, *The Makutaai Ami of Eastern Taiwan-an ethnographic report*, Institute of Ethnology, Academia Sinica, Taipei.

Contributors

Rachana Agarwal
Department of Anthropology, Brandeis University, Waltham, Mass., USA.

Leslie Butt
Department of Anthropology, and Centre for Asia-Pacific Initiatives, University of Victoria, British Columbia, Canada.

Alan Howard
Department of Anthropology, University of Hawaii, Honolulu, USA.

Wolfgang Kempf
Institute of Cultural and Social Anthropology, University of Goettingen, Goettingen, Germany.

Thorgeir Kolshus
Department of Social Anthropology, University of Oslo, Norway.

Helen Lee
Department of Social Inquiry, La Trobe University, Melbourne, Australia.

Kirsten McGavin
School of Social Science, University of Queensland, Brisbane, Australia.

Jenny Munro
Lecturer in Anthropology, School of Social Sciences, University of Queensland, Brisbane, Australia.

Gerdha Numbery
Department of Anthropology, Cenderawasih University, Jayapura, Papua, Indonesia.

Jan Rensel
Department of Anthropology, University of Hawaii, Honolulu, USA.

John Taylor
Department of Social Inquiry, La Trobe University, Melbourne, Australia.

Shu-Ling Yeh
Department of Public and Cultural Affairs, National Taitung University, Taiwan.